PARKWAYS OF THE CANADIAN ROCKIES

Bow Lake

by Brian Patton

SUMMERTHOUGHT
BANFF, CANADA

ACKNOWLEDGEMENTS

In addition to those people recognized in the first edition of this book, I would like to thank the many members of the Parks Canada interpretive service and visitor services department who provided suggestions, corrections, and information on future roadside developments and alterations.

A special thanks to L. A. Taylor who took time to read much of the manuscript and provided important information on the Icefields Parkway chapter. And to Geoff Holroyd of the Canadian Wildlife Service who read and commented on much of the text and provided 90% of the ornithological material which has been added to this revision. Any blunders which remain are strictly the author's responsibility.

A thank you to Craig Richards, photo technician at the Whyte Foundation, for processing the author's black and white film.

And yet again, my appreciation to my wife Louise who provided even more patience, illustrations, and encouragement than in the first edition of this book.

ILLUSTRATION AND PHOTO CREDITS

All pencil and pen-and-ink illustrations are by Louise Patton.

All colour and contemporary black and white photographs used in this edition were taken by the author with the exception of the grizzly bear illustration on page 24 which was taken by Canmore wildlife photographer Hälle Flygare. Historical photographs are courtesy of the following:

Archives of the Canadian Rockies, Banff — pages 4, 31, 32, 33, 35, 43, 51, 55, 67, 77, 79, 81, 89, 93, 95, 107, 109, 112, 138, 143, 144.

Glenbow-Alberta Institute, Calgary — page 73.

Public Archives of Canada, Ottawa — pages 29, 30, 52.

Provincial Archives of British Columbia, Victoria — pages 41, 135.

My deepest appreciation to all of the above institutions and their staff for their assistance.

ISBN 0-919934-12-9

Copyright © Summerthought, Ltd., 1982

First printing, 1975
Revised edition, 1982

Summerthought Ltd.
P.O. Box 1420
Banff, Alberta T0L 0C0

Printed and bound in Canada
by Friesen Printers, Altona

To my parents,
who first brought me to these mountains.

Mount Athabasca.

CPR locomotive at Field, July, 1894.

Archives of the Canadian Rockies

Preface

Any guidebook becomes dated with the passing of time, and this volume is no exception. In the seven year period since the first edition of *Parkways of the Canadian Rockies* was published campgrounds and picnic areas have been removed, highways have been upgraded and relocated, new interpretive viewpoints have been developed, and more background material on the natural history of the parks has surfaced. It has been a period of great growth and development in Canada's mountain parks, affected in no small part by the rapid growth of the nearby urban centres of Calgary and Edmonton. In addition to the physical changes which have occurred during these years, Canada has converted to a whole new system of weights and measures — a conversion which has an unsettling effect on a book filled with distances and elevations.

So, having taken all of these factors into consideration, the time certainly seems right for a new edition of *Parkways of the Canadian Rockies*. Over the past two years highways have been remeasured in kilometres, physical changes have been noted, and new interpretive material has been inserted where it seems useful. But over and above the obvious revisions, the book has been totally redesigned in the hope that it might be more functional for the park visitor. The physical dimensions of the book have been increased which allows for better display of photographs. With this increase in page size, there is now room to include maps in the left-hand margin of each two-page spread giving visitors a graphic, running perspective of the country they are travelling through.

Since North America is still a continent in the midst of metric conversion, and since many automobiles still possess odometers which read in miles, distances in the road description margins are provided in both kilometres (bold face type) and miles (light face italic type).

Other measurements of distance and elevation used in the text are also "bilingual", elevations being provided in metres and feet, such as Castle Mountain (2766 m/9,076 ft). While some may criticize this space-gobbling tactic, it is my purpose to give readers a sense of the size and the grandeur of the Canadian Rockies, and if a visitor is unfamiliar with metric terms, as many North Americans still are, this affect will be lost.

I hope that the changes made in this book will be useful and welcome, and that *Parkways of the Canadian Rockies* will help to make your stay in the mountain parks more educational and enjoyable.

Brian Patton
Banff, 1982

Contents

Introduction   7

Geology   9

Climate and Life Zones   11

Common Trees   13

Wildflowers   15

Wildlife   25

Mammals   25

Birds   28

Historical Highlights   29

Trans Canada Highway   34

Banff and Vicinity   50

Bow Valley Parkway   68

Lake Louise and Vicinity   77

Banff Windermere Parkway   81

Icefields Parkway   90

93-Alternate Highway   120

Yellowhead Highway   132

Jasper and Vicinity   142

Maligne Lake Road   146

Index   150

The Weeping Wall rises above the Icefields Parkway and the North Saskatchewan River.

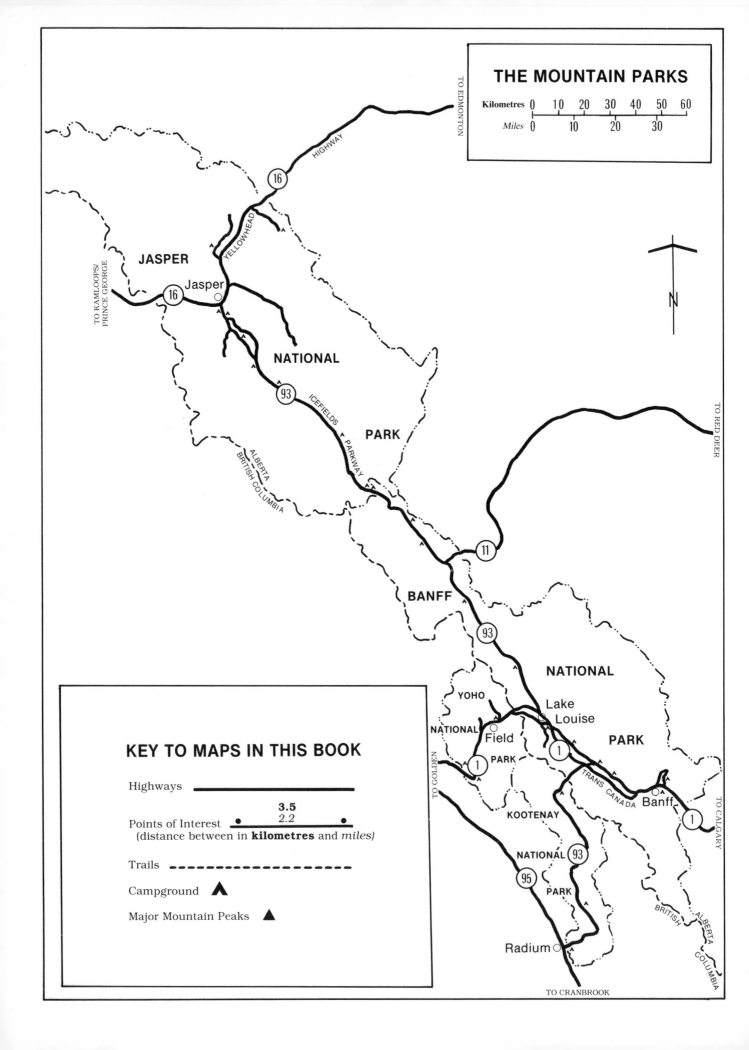

THE MOUNTAIN PARKS

Kilometres 0 10 20 30 40 50 60
Miles 0 10 20 30

TO EDMONTON

HIGHWAY

16

YELLOWHEAD

JASPER

16 Jasper

TO KAMLOOPS/
PRINCE GEORGE

NATIONAL

93 ICEFIELDS

PARKWAY

ALBERTA
BRITISH COLUMBIA

PARK

TO RED DEER

N

11

BANFF

93

NATIONAL

YOHO

Lake
Louise

NATIONAL Field

PARK

1

PARK

TO GOLDEN

TRANS CANADA

Banff

1

TO CALGARY

KOOTENAY

NATIONAL 93

95 PARK

BRITISH
COLUMBIA
ALBERTA

Radium

TO CRANBROOK

KEY TO MAPS IN THIS BOOK

Highways ─────────────

                              3.5
                               2.2
Points of Interest •─────────•
(distance between in **kilometres** and *miles*)

Trails ▪▪▪▪▪▪▪▪▪▪▪▪▪▪▪▪

Campground ▲

Major Mountain Peaks ▲

Introduction

HOW TO USE THIS BOOK. For years we have tended to think of the four contiguous mountain parks of Banff, Jasper, Yoho and Kootenay as separate entities. But, despite natural features which seem to give each of these parks its own unique character, the boundaries drawn between them are strictly artificial, concocted by the mind of man primarily for the purpose of administration. In reality, as you enter the mountain parks, you are visiting one huge 20,280 square kilometre (7,800 square mile) national park — one of the largest areas of mountain parkland in the world.

Mount Athabasca.

Parkways of the Canadian Rockies treats this vast area as a single park, referring to the separate parks only as regions or districts within the whole, and using the park names merely as a means of helping to orient the visitor. The chapters follow the main roadways through the parks, which, like the flora, fauna, and geological formations, run oblivious of man-made boundaries.

In designing the book, I have concentrated on describing features visible from the numerous roadside viewpoints, picnic areas, and campgrounds, secure in the belief that a national park cannot be fully appreciated from a moving vehicle. It is hoped the book will encourage the visitor to get out of his car, camper, motor-home or whatever, and try to learn just what this exceptional region is all about.

The first section of the book briefly outlines the natural and human history of the region. By reading through this section, you might better understand some of the roadside descriptions found later in the book. Some terms used in both the natural history introduction and the roadside descriptions may seem obscure and overly technical, but I have purposely tried to avoid "writing down" to the reader. Most of these terms are repeated and features re-explained wherever good examples appear on a given tour, so that by the time the traveller leaves the parks, he should have a pretty good idea of what certain features look like and how they were created.

Since many of the roads in the mountain parks can be travelled starting from either end, distances have been included in the margins for both directions. For example, if you are westbound on the Trans-Canada Highway, you can read through that chapter in the normal front-to-back fashion, following the distances in the left hand margin; if you are eastbound, you must turn to the end of the chapter and work backwards, following the distances in the right hand margin. The distances printed in **bold type** are in kilometres and those in *italic type* are in miles.

A word of caution about distances: it is probably not advisable to try to follow a long highway on your car odometer. Unless you have a trip odometer that can be set at zero at the start of the tour, you would do better to just make a quick calculation of distance between points of interest as you go (the distance between points of interest is shown on the accompanying maps). Anyway, there are discrepancies among car odometers, and trying to match distances with the book over a long trip would undoubtedly be a frustrating task.

Shorter chapters on prime areas of interest are scattered throughout the book. In these chapters, natural and human history are treated in more detail, and many pleasant drives, bicycle outings, and nature hikes are described.

And, just one last friendly word of advice: take your time as you travel through the mountain parks. Stop as often as possible and look around. Study the features described and try to understand the processes involved in their creation. Try to envision the Indians and early white men who first explored these valleys, imagining their wonder and awe in this silent and magnificent land. It has taken nearly a billion years to create the scenery you see here today. To even begin to appreciate the incredibly long evolution of this mountain range takes more than just a cursory glance through a car window at a fleeting landscape.

A SPECIAL PLACE. Canada's national parks are provided as museums of nature to be preserved for this and future generations. In a sense, the roadways within the mountain parks are a compromise to this ideal. They provide easy access to large numbers of people, yet with the greater influx each year, the job of preserving these wonders in their natural state becomes increasingly difficult.

Because of the potential for creating irreversible damage, it behooves every park visitor to travel as lightly upon the landscape as possible and to leave the parks just as they were found. This is not a difficult task, requiring merely a basic courtesy and adherence to a few simple rules:

Animals should never be fed, no matter how great the temptation. Few people realize the harm that can be done through this seemingly innocent practise. National parks are not zoos, and there will be no zookeeper to care for sick animals after you leave.

Wildflowers must never be picked. Some flowers are so fragile as to be disturbed even by a nearby footfall. Others, if picked, will never grow again. The true beauty of a flower is within its natural setting.

Keep hatchets and axes away from trees. Never use a living tree for firewood or a spruce-bough bed.

Rocks and fossils are the creation of millions of years of geological activity. They are an irreplaceable heritage which should never be disturbed.

Never discard trash in the park. To toss litter out of a car window or onto the ground in a national park is the ultimate act of disrespect. Always use a trash receptacle or a litter bag in your car.

Fires may only be set within fireplaces and are seldom permitted in picnic areas. Many backcountry campsites have no provision for wood fires, and camp stoves are a necessity. And always be careful with matches and cigarettes.

HIKING. One of the best ways in which to see the parks is by abandoning the busy roadways for the relative peace and serenity of the trail. Containing nearly 3200 kilometres (2,000 miles) of trails, the mountain parks provide one of the best hiking areas in North America. Trails vary from short, half-hour nature walks to extended wilderness treks of a week or longer. Topographical maps and trail pamphlets are available at park information centres, as are up-to-date trail condition reports. Hiking and mountaineering guidebooks can be purchased at private book outlets in both Banff and Jasper.

Athabasca Glacier

Backpackers must obtain camping permits from park information centres prior to any overnight trips. Campers, off-trail travellers, and mountaineers may also register with the warden service if they wish.

BOATING. Canoeing and rowing are popular pastimes on many park lakes and rivers. The best rivers for canoeing and kayaking are the Bow in Banff Park, the Kootenay in Kootenay Park, and the Athabasca in Jasper Park. Most other rivers are too small and turbulent for navigation.

With the exception of Lake Minnewanka in Banff Park, and Pyramid and Medicine Lakes in Jasper, boats with motors are not permitted on the rivers and lakes of the mountain parks.

FISHING. Many lakes and streams within the parks have been stocked with a variety of trout. Species include Rocky Mountain whitefish, rainbow, cutthroat, brown, eastern brook, Dolly Varden, and lake trout. Park fishing licences, regulations concerning seasons and information on best streams and lakes may be obtained from park information centres.

PARK INTERPRETIVE SERVICE. Throughout the summer season, the Park Interpretive Service conducts a full schedule of activities designed to acquaint the visitor with the natural and human history of the parks. Trail hikes conducted by park naturalists are held throughout the week, and interpretive slide talks and movies are provided in the evenings at most of the larger campgrounds. Interpretive brochures, pamphlets, and displays as well as information concerning park naturalist activities are available at information centres in downtown Banff (Banff Avenue), Lake Louise, and Saskatchewan River Crossing in Banff Park; Marble Canyon and Kootenay West Gate in Kootenay Park; downtown Field, the Yoho Valley Road entrance, and Yoho West Gate in Yoho Park; the Columbia Icefield and downtown Jasper (Connaught Drive) in Jasper Park.

The Bow River and Castle Mountain.

Geology

It has been over 600 million years since the oldest rock in this section of the Rocky Mountains was formed — a span of time beyond human comprehension. In the rock layers of these mountains, stacked one on top of the other, the geological past has been recorded in a steady, almost monotonous progression of sandstone, limestone, and shale. The story of the Canadian Rockies is not one of thundering volcanoes and glowing lava flows, but rather a very quiet tale of still, tepid seas, imperceptible movements in the earth's crust, and the inexorable grind of glacier ice.

THE BUILDING BLOCKS OF A MOUNTAIN RANGE. In the late Precambrian era, the world was a very different place than it is today. Six hundred million years ago, the ancestral continent of North America probably hovered quite close to the equator, and its western coastline followed near the western margin of today's Great Plains: a flat, arid, lifeless land, its western shore bordered a shallow ocean which covered a continental shelf.

The desert land mass eroded slowly, and its rivers poured sediment into the coastal ocean. As layers of sand, silt, clay and lime mud accumulated to a thickness of many thousands of metres on a gradually subsiding sea floor, the sedimentary material began to coalesce into rock: sand became

Mount Louis, a dogtooth shaped mountain created when layers of limestone are uplifted and tilted nearly vertical.

sandstone and quartzite; silt and clay deposits were transformed into siltstone, shale and argillite; and lime mud precipitate turned to limestone.

Throughout the Paleozoic era, a period of some 400 million years following the Precambrian, there was little change in the pattern of affairs on this obscure desert coastline. At times there would be disruptions — volcanic islands would appear several hundred miles off the western shore, or the sea floor would emerge temporarily above the ocean waters — but mostly, the relationship of the slowly eroding continent and its shallow undersea shelf remained unaltered.

Despite the apparent stability, life was evolving in the sea. During the Precambrian era, organisms were very primitive — cabbage-shaped colonies of algae clung to the ocean floor, seaworm-like creatures slithered beneath the surface of the mud and silt, and a variety of small, soft-bodied invertebrates floated in the still waters. Two hundred million years into the Paleozoic, life forms were more varied and abundant: animals with bi-valved shells called brachiopods emerged and proliferated; extensive reefs of coral grew readily in the hospitably warm waters; and early crustaceans called trilobites swam near the ocean foor. By the end of the era, the fish had made their appearance in the ocean, and the first primitive plants had crept tentatively onto a landscape that remained arid and inhospitable. And each living thing that died in the ocean added its body to the ever-increasing thickness of sedimentary rock on the continental shelf.

THE CREATION OF THE MOUNTAINS. Starting around 200 million years ago, the basic stability which existed along the western margin of the continent for so many millions of years was disrupted. Over a span of 50 million years most of western Canada was lifted above the surface of the ocean; the horizontal beds were uplifted and deformed by forces applied along the margin of the continental shelf. In the area of present-day British Columbia, mountain ranges were formed and eroded away, molten rock intruded the sedimentary beds laid down during the Paleozoic and Precambrian, and by the end of the 170 million year era, there was little left of the original material which had been deposited on the floor of the ancient coastal sea.

Yet, in the region of today's Alberta-British Columbia border, beds of sedimentary rock remained relatively unaltered throughout the Mesozoic. Uplifted above the surface of the ocean, the land was low, swampy, and covered with vegetation. But, despite the withdrawal of the sea, sedimentary rock continued to form in the region, as silt and gravel-laden streams drained the ranges to the west. Some of the marshy vegetation was buried beneath the layers of silt, creating the coal seams common within the Front Ranges of the mountains today. The well-washed gravels from the western ranges also coalesced, forming a pebbly rock called conglomerate.

Approximately 70 million years ago, the forces of mountain building reached the last of the essentially undisturbed sedimentary beds — an accumulation over 10,000 metres (30,000 feet) thick — and the Rocky Mountains were formed. As pressure was applied from the west, general uplift occurred throughout the region, and beds of limestone, shale, and sandstone were bent and fractured. Layers of rock were folded so tightly in some sectors they bent back on top of themselves, beds shattered in long parallel faults, and narrow slices of mountains were shoved up in an easterly direction along the fault surfaces. Meanwhile, the forces of weathering continued their work, as wind and water created rounded peaks and narrow V-shaped gullies and valleys.

Brachiopod fossil.

THE SCULPTING OF THE RANGE. The final chapter in the creation of the Rocky Mountains was the sculpting of the range by glaciers — a comparatively recent event of the last two million years. As the climate of the Northern Hemisphere cooled by just a few degrees and great ice sheets began to descend over the face of North America, glaciers began to form in the Rocky Mountains and descend the valleys, grinding toward the prairies where they would often join together with the great continental ice sheet.

The major tongues of ice within the range created large U-shaped valleys, while lesser glaciers gouged into the sides of mountains creating deep, bowl-shaped depressons called cirques. Often the cutting action of the major glaciers would truncate the high valleys carved by the alpine glaciers, leaving them "hanging" on the side of the larger valleys. Sometimes glaciers would attack a mountain from three or more sides to create a sharp pinnacle or spike called a horn.

As glaciers advanced and retreated during the four major ice ages, the drainage patterns of valleys were altered many times. Great ridges of rock and gravel debris called moraines were deposited by the retreating glaciers, diverting rivers and damming lakes. Silt and gravel piled up in the valley bottoms, deposited by glacial meltwaters.

We can judge by evidence left from the most recent of these glacial advances that ice filled the main valleys, such as the Bow, up to a level of 2400 metres (8,000 ft) above the sea. The minimum thickness of these great valley glaciers was between 500 and 800 metres (1600 and 2600 feet). During these glaciations, only the highest mountains would have lifted their summits above the grinding ice.

Since the end of the last major ice advance, just over 9,000 years ago, minor sculpting of the range has been carried on by alpine glaciers and the forces of weathering.

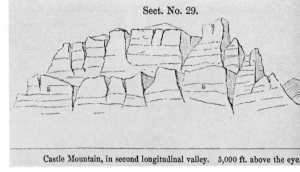

Sect. No. 29.

Castle Mountain, in second longitudinal valley.   5,000 ft. above the eye.

Castle Mountain, as sketched by Dr. James Hector in 1858, displays a classic example of the castellate mountain structure which occurs when massive layers of limestone interspersed with shale remain nearly horizontal.

Climate and Life Zones

If you started hiking in one of the lowest mountain valleys and climbed directly to the summit of the nearest high peak, one of the things you would notice along the way is the dramatic change in forest and plant cover. In the space of 8 kilometres or less you would have climbed through a variety of plant communities roughly equivalent to those found on a 1600 kilometre (1,000 mile) trek from the Canadian prairies to the high arctic.

CLIMATE. As might be expected, climate plays a major role in determining the vegetative cover, and in mountainous terrain, altitude is one of the factors which most affects temperature and, hence, climate. Generally, a loss of 1.7°C (3°F) may be expected with every 300 metres (1,000 ft) of elevation gained. The town of Jasper at an elevation of 1058 metres (3,472 ft) above sea level has a mean annual temperature of 2.8°C (37.1°F) while Banff, at 1383 metres (4,538 ft) records an annual mean of 2.3°C (36.2°F); Lake Louise at 1534 metres (5,032 ft) has a rather chilly mean of 0°C (32°F).

Latitude has a dramatic effect upon mountain climate. For example, the further south you travel in the Rocky Mountains, the higher is the limit of tree growth. In the Canadian mountain parks, timberline occurs at around

2200 metres (7,200 ft) above sea level, while in the state of Colorado trees grow to a level near 3500 metres (11,500 ft). It is also curious that Banff, at an elevation of 1383 metres (4,538 ft) above sea level, has a climate nearly identical to that of West Yellowstone, Montana at 2032 metres (6,667 ft) and Leadville, Colorado at 3106 metres (10,190 ft).

Distance from the Great Divide as well as altitude seem to affect the amounts of precipitation received along the eastern slope. For example, mean annual precipitation is 330 mm (13 in.) at Jasper townsite, 480 mm (19 in.) at Banff, 560 mm (22 in.) at Castle Junction, and 790 mm (31 in.) at Lake Louise. Winter snowfalls show a similar relationship. The mean annual snowfall for Banff is around 200 cm (80 in.), while at the Mount Norquay ski area, just 300 metres (1,000 ft) above the town, it is closer to 250 cm (100 in.). Jasper records an annual snowfall of around 140 cm (54 in.), Lake Louise 495 cm (195 in.), and the Sunshine Village ski area 760 cm (300 in.).

Most of the area within the mountain parks is affected by weather systems sweeping across the cordillera from the Pacific, as well as by those descending over the prairies from the arctic. The western cordilleran air masses bring the maritime-like conditions often experienced in the western half of the range, while the eastern boreal fronts bring the temperature extremes and low precipitation common to the Front Ranges.

Microclimatic variations also help to dictate the distribution and nature of plant cover in the mountains: exposure of the slope to sun and prevailing winds, temperature inversions which lock cool air in the valley bottoms, and chinooks along the eastern slopes all affect growth in certain localities.

LIFE ZONES. For years biologists have attempted to identify and classify the various life zones which occur in the mountains of the North American west. It has not been an easy task. While certain species of trees and plants tend to group together in a particular type of environment and at a certain altitude, there is much overlapping and many exceptions to the rule. Especially when it is realized that altitude is not alone in determining vegetative patterns, but that factors such as slope exposure, soil type, prevailing winds, and kind and amounts of precipitation play a role as well.

The most common means of distinguishing life zones is through variations in forest cover. Using this as the criterion, botanists have identified three primary zones in the mountain parks.

The highest life zone is actually the treeless alpine tundra generally found above the 2200 metre (7,200 ft) level. Resembling the rolling tundra of the arctic in its lower reaches, the alpine zone supports a plant cover of shrub willow, grasses, sedges, heaths and forbs. Growing season in this high terrain seldom exceeds 60 days and desiccating winds gust at speeds averaging three times greater than in the valleys below.

After passing down through a narrow band of stunted spruce and fir referred to as the Krummholz (meaning "crooked wood"), the subalpine zone is entered. The climax species of this forest are spruce and alpine fir. Also found scattered along the upper reaches of the zone are stands of alpine larch and whitebark pine.

The low elevation forest, which is referred to as the montane zone, is the most limited of the three life zones. Roughly speaking, the montane occurs below 1460 metres (4,800 ft), though it can climb to near 1520 metres (5,000 ft) on south-facing slopes. Growth is open with forest interspersed with grassland. Key forest species include white spruce, Douglas fir, limber pine, and aspen poplar. Ground cover includes low growing junipers and kinnikinnick.

Cover along the dry, lower reaches of the Athabasca Valley in Jasper Park resembles the montane, but many botanists believe it to be more closely related to the prairie grasslands. The montane is vaguely defined on the western slope of the Rockies as well, some areas seeming to bear a greater resemblance to the interior Douglas fir forest of British Columbia.

In both the montane and subalpine forests, lodgepole pine proliferates as a fire succession species, its cones so adapted as to open after the passing of a forest fire. Wherever extensive stands of lodgepole pine occur in the parks, it may be assumed a major fire has taken place. Eventually, the more tolerant species of spruce and alpine fir will grow up beneath the lodgepole canopy and replace it.

As the visitor travels through the parks and endeavours to identify the various life zones, he would do well to remember that no single species or community of plants and animals is an island unto itself. Boundary lines and zone classifications do not exist in nature, only in the mind of man. All are connected to the whole. The loss of even one tiny flower has unknown repercussions elsewhere within the ecosystem.

And, while we are present in this scene, even though we may seem to be only visitors and passive observers, we are a part of this ecosystem. Our presence is noticed.

The upper reaches of the subalpine forest as it begins to thin out into the treeless alpine tundra.

Common Trees

SPRUCE. Two species are common to this region — western white spruce *(Picea glauca)* and Engelmann spruce *(Picea engelmannii).* Western white spruce is generally found at lower elevations, Engelmann spruce at higher, but the two hybridize throughout the range so identification is difficult. A climax tree of the subalpine forest, spruce is the most common species found in the Rocky Mountains. Square, stiff needles about 2 centimetres (¾ in.) long and very prickly to the touch (in contrast to soft fir and Douglas fir needles). Cones are about 5 centimetres (2 in.) long with smooth-margined, close-fitting scales; pendulous on the branch.

ALPINE FIR. *Abies lasiocarpa.* The other climax species of the subalpine forest. Smooth, grey, resin-blistered bark which provides the pungent odor typical of this forest type. Needles are soft and flat, about 3 centimetres (1 in.) long. Erect cones grow only in the upper reaches of the tree; scales are shed from around the spike-like cone axis so that an intact cone seldom reaches the ground.

LODGEPOLE PINE. *Pinus contorta.* A fire-succession species found in both the montane and subalpine. Needles grow in pairs and are about 5 to 7 centimetres (2 to 3 in.) long. Cones about 2.5 to 5 centimetres (1 to 2 in.) long, sometimes with sharp, curved prickles; cones usually remain closed when shed from the tree, opening when heated by a passing fire. All pure, even-aged stands of lodgepole pine in the mountain parks were generated by forest fires. Eventually lodgepole is replaced by the climax species of spruce and alpine fir.

A small western white spruce begins the climb to sunlight beneath the dense canopy of a lodgepole pine forest. Given time and no forest fires, spruce will eventually replace the lodgepole as the dominant forest species.

Dense, even-aged stands of lodgepole pine are always a sign of a past forest fire.

DOUGLAS FIR. *Pseudotsuga menziesii.* Typical of dry, open, south-facing slopes in the montane zone. A thick, deeply furrowed bark when mature, which makes the species fire-resistant. Needles are flat, soft, about 2.5 centimetres (1 in.) long. Cones are similar to spruce (pendulous) but have distinct pitchfork-like bracts protruding from beneath the scales.

LIMBER PINE. *Pinus flexilis.* Similar in description to the whitebark pine of the subalpine zone, except that it is found on dry, open slopes at much lower elevations. Like the whitebark, it is a five-needled pine (needles clustered on the branches in bundles of five), but cones are longer at 8 to 20 centimetres (3 to 8 in.).

WHITEBARK PINE. *Pinus albicaulis.* Found near timberline. Often stunted and twisted in form. Needles grow in groups of five and are about 5 to 8 centimetres (2 to 3 in.) long. Similar in appearance to limber pine, but the cones are smaller.

ALPINE LARCH. *Larix lyallii.* Found in the upper reaches of the subalpine zone. Tree form is often twisted and gnarled; branches appear black and lacy. Needles are pale green in summer, very soft and fine, about 3 centimetres (1 in.) long and spirally arranged; turn yellow-gold in September and are shed. Northern limit of the species near Hector Lake in Banff Park.

ASPEN POPLAR. *Populus tremuloides.* The most common deciduous tree in the parks. Most identifiable by the waxy, white bark and nearly circular leaves which are about 3 to 4 centimetres (1½ in.) in diameter. Leaves are dark green on top, pale beneath and have a short, sharp tip; flutter rapidly in a breeze due to flattened stalk, giving the tree the name trembling aspen. Grows on open slopes and is a fire-succession species. Reproduces vegetatively through root suckers, creating clones which are genetically identical.

COTTONWOOD POPLARS. Two species are found in the mountain parks — balsam poplar *(Populus balsamifera)* and black cottonwood *(Populus trichocarpa).* Two very similar species which often interbreed making identification even more difficult. Easily differentiated from aspen poplar, however, by longer, triangular shaped leaves which average 7 to 12 centimetres (3 to 5 in.) in length. Both species are more limited in range than aspen, growing primarily on moist sites near major streams or rivers. The name cottonwood comes from the light, fluffy seed which is released in early summer and which often fills the air with tiny tufts of white cotton.

Other species which grow in the mountain parks, but which are limited to only a few locales include black spruce *(Picea mariana)*, western larch *(Larix occidentalis)*, tamarack *(Larix laricina)*, western red cedar *(Thuja plicata)*, Rocky Mountain juniper *(Juniperus scopulorum)*, and white birch *(Betula papyrifera)*.

Wildflowers

Illustrations for the following common wildflowers can be found on pages 17 to 21.

1. **ALPINE ANEMONE.** *Anemone drummondii*. Buttercup family. 10 to 20 cm (4 to 8 in.) high. A small, white-flowered anemone which is common in the higher meadows of the subalpine and alpine zones. Blooms in June and July.

2. **BUNCHBERRY.** *Cornus canadensis*. Dogwood family. 8 to 16 cm (3 to 6 in.) high. One of the smallest members of the dogwood family with the obvious dogwood-style white flower. A common ground cover on shady forest floors where it comes into bloom in June and July.

3. **CONTORTED LOUSEWORT.** *Pedicularis contorta*. Fig-wort family. 20 to 30 cm (8 to 12 in.) high. A flower of sheltered alpine meadows and timberline fringes. Numerous white, shell-shaped flowers grow on each stalk. Flowering season is from mid-July to late August.

4. **COTTON GRASS.** *Eriophorum* sp. Sedge family. 25 to 60 cm (10 to 25 in.) high. One of the most obvious of mountain flowers since it grows in wet, boggy places where it is easily recognized by its white, fluffy seed head. Most often seen in soggy alpine meadows and along high, marshy streams in July and August.

5. **FRINGED GRASS-OF-PARNASSUS.** *Parnassia fimbriata*. Saxifrage family. 13 to 30 cm (5 to 12 in.) high. A familiar flower of the cool, shady forests. Flowers are solitary and white atop a leafless stem; leaves are clustered around the base of the stems. Blooms in July and August.

6. **GLOBE FLOWER.** *Trollius albiflorus*. Buttercup family. 13 to 25 cm (5 to 10 in.) high. Most frequently found in wet, marshy areas of the subalpine zone. One of the earliest flowers to bloom following the melting of the snow.

7. **MARSH MARIGOLD.** *Caltha leptosepala*. Buttercup family. 15 to 30 cm (6 to 12 in.) high. Blooms shortly after the melting of snow, thriving in boggy, wet hollows both above and below timberline.

8. **ONE-FLOWERED WINTERGREEN.** *Moneses uniflora*. Wintergreen family. 5 to 12 cm (2 to 5 in.) high. One of the most beautiful flowers of the shaded forest floor, possessing a single, nodding white flower shaped like a small star. Also known as single delight, it blooms from mid-June through late July.

9. **OX-EYE DAISY.** *Chrysanthemum leucanthemum*. Daisy family. 30 to 60 cm (12 to 24 in.) high. This is an introduced species which has not spread far beyond roadsides and low elevation meadows. Blooms throughout the summer and is most abundant along the Banff-Windermere Parkway.

10. **SPARROW'S EGG LADY SLIPPER.** *Cypripedium passerinum*. Orchid family. 15 to 30 cm (6 to 12 in.) high. A beautiful, white orchid which grows in cool, boggy forests. Blooms in June.

11. **SPOTTED SAXIFRAGE.** *Saxifrage bronchialis*. Saxifrage family. 10 to 15 cm (4 to 6 in.) high. A low, mat-like plant with five-petalled white flowers spotted with tiny red dots. Blooms on open, rocky terrain throughout the subalpine zone in June and July.

12. **SWEET-FLOWERED ANDROSACE.** *Androsace chamaejasme*. Primrose family. 3 to 10 cm (1 to 4 in.) high. Tiny, fragrant white flowers which grow in open areas of the montane and subalpine zones throughout the summer.

13. **WHITE MOUNTAIN AVENS.** *Dryas hookeriana*. Rose family. 5 to 12 cm (2 to 5 in.) high. A low, mat-like plant with white flowers that grows on dry and rocky ground from timberline up into the alpine zone. Blooms from June through August.

14. **WHITE CAMAS.** *Zygadenus elegans*. Lily family. 30 to 60 cm (12 to 24 in.) high. Grows in open meadows from the montane up into the subalpine zone. Flowers are greenish-white and shaped like a six-pointed star, growing on a tall, typical lily plant. Bulbs are poisonous giving the plant the nickname death camas. Blooms throughout July and August.

15. **WHITE MOUNTAIN HEATHER.** *Cassiope tetragona*. Heath family. 10 to 30 cm (4 to 12 in.) high. A common ground cover of the alpine zone, often found growing with yellow or red mountain heather. The tiny, white bell-like flowers appear in the early weeks of the summer.

16. **ALPINE BUTTERCUP.** *Ranunculus eschscholtzii*. Buttercup family. 5 to 12 cm (2 to 5 in.) high. A low-growing flower of the alpine zone which is most always found in wet bogs. The waxy yellow cup-like flower blooms through July and August.

17. **AVALANCHE LILY.** *Erythronium grandiflorum*. Lily family. 15 to 35 cm (6 to 15 in.) high. Grows in moist subalpine and alpine meadows, blooming in early summer along the edge of retreating snowbanks. Also known as the glacier lily, snow lily, and dogtooth violet.

18. **GAILLARDIA.** *Gaillardia aristata*. Daisy family. 20 to 50 cm (8 to 20 in.) high. A brilliant, yellow flower that carpets the open slopes of the lower valleys during the latter half of the summer. Also known as brown-eyed susan.

19. **GOLDEN FLEABANE.** *Erigeron aureus*. Daisy family. 2 to 12 cm (1 to 5 in.) high. One of the prettiest and most easily identified fleabanes thanks to its diminutive size and brilliant yellow flower. It blooms in the upper reaches of the subalpine in July and August.

20. **HEART-LEAVED ARNICA.** *Arnica cordifolia*. Daisy family. 25 to 60 cm (10 to 24 in.) high. A showy yellow flower found in semi-open areas of the subalpine forest. Distinguished from other arnicas by its heart-shaped leaves. Blooms throughout the summer.

21. **YELLOW COLUMBINE.** *Aquilegia flavescens*. Buttercup family. 30 to 60 cm (12 to 24 in.) high. Most commonly found in sunlit patches of the subalpine forest as well as on rough, rocky slopes. Blooms in early summer.

22. **YELLOW MOUNTAIN AVENS.** *Dryas drummondii*. Rose family. 10 to 30 cm (4 to 12 in.) high. A dense, mat-like plant which grows on rocky river flats and open meadows in the lower valleys. A small, nodding yellow flower in June and early July that turns to a wispy, white seed head after midsummer.

23. **YELLOW VIOLET.** *Viola orbiculata*. Violet family. 5 to 8 cm (2 to 3 in.) high. A tiny but beautiful flower growing in moist, shaded subalpine woods. Blooms into midsummer.

24. **SHRUBBY CINQUEFOIL.** *Potentilla fruticosa*. Rose family. 30 to 90 cm (12 to 36 in.) high. A woody shrub found on open slopes and meadows which bears bright yellow, five-petalled flowers. Often proliferates where grazing mammals are common.

25. **STONECROP.** *Sedum stenopetalum*. Orpine family. 7 to 15 cm (3 to 6 in.) high. Bright yellow, star-shaped flowers cluster above succulent stems and leaves on this tiny plant. As with domestic varieties, it is a flower of the rock garden, growing in dry, stony terrain at lower elevations where it blooms in late spring and early summer.

26. **BROAD-LEAVED WILLOW HERB.** *Epilobium latifolium*. Evening Primrose family. 15 to 45 cm (6 to 18 in.) high. Also known as mountain fireweed, this is a shorter relative to the common fireweed. However, its pink-purple flowers are larger and more brilliant. Found on stony river flats where it blooms in July and August.

27. **CALYPSO.** *Calypso bulbosa*. Orchid family. 8 to 15 cm (3 to 7 in.) high. A common flower of the shaded forest floor, and most often found beneath the canopy of a lodgepole pine forest. Also known as fairy slipper and Venus' slipper. Blooms early and through midsummer.

28. **FIREWEED.** *Epilobium angustifolium*. Evening Primrose family. 60 to 150 cm (24 to 60 in.) high. The tallest and best-known flower in the mountain parks. Grows along roadsides and in forest burns — wherever the landscape has been disturbed. Blooms from early June to September.

29. **INDIAN PAINTBRUSH.** *Castilleja miniata*. Figwort family. 25 to 50 cm (10 to 20 in.) high. Grows in profusion from the low valleys of the montane zone to the treeless alpine tundra, and appears in a variety of colours ranging from deep red through pink to pale yellow to white. Blooms throughout the summer.

30. **MOSS CAMPION.** *Silene acaulis*. Pink family. 1 to 4 cm (1 to 2 in.) high. The pincushion plant with tiny pink flowers grows in low, moss-like patches on the tundra and scree slopes of the alpine zone. Growth of the "cushion" is very slow, and it may not produce flowers until its tenth year. Sends down a moisture-seeking taproot for as much as a metre or more below the surface of the tundra.

31. **MOUNTAIN SORREL.** *Oxyria digyna*. Buckwheat family. 5 to 20 cm (2 to 8 in.) high. A moisture-seeking plant of the high elevations. Usually found on rocky terrain where it blooms in June and July.

32. **NODDING ONION.** *Allium cernuum*. Lily family. 12 to 50 cm (5 to 20 in.) high. A relative of the cultivated onions which close inspection with one's nose will confirm. The flower head is composed of a number of tiny, pink lilies. Found on dry slopes from the montane into the lower subalpine. Blooms throughout much of the summer.

33. **RED MOUNTAIN HEATHER.** *Phyllodoce empetriformis*. Heath family. 15 to 25 cm (6 to 10 in.) high. With white and yellow heather, this is the typical ground cover of the alpine meadows. An evergreen plant covered with dozens of tiny pink bells during the early summer.

34. **PINK PUSSY-TOES.** *Antennaria rosea*. Daisy family. 15 to 20 cm (6 to 8 in.) high. A flower which gets its name from its tightly clustered pink flowers which resemble the soft pad of a cat's paw. It is a plant of moist meadows and open slopes which blooms from June through August.

35. **SHOOTING STAR.** *Dodecatheon radicatum*. Primrose family. 10 to 30 cm (4 to 12 in.) high. Most commonly found growing in boggy meadows, though there is a similar species (Dodecatheon conjugens) which inhabits higher and somewhat drier terrain. Blooms in early summer.

36. **TWIN FLOWER.** *Linnaea borealis* var. *americana*. Honeysuckle family. 5 to 10 cm (2 to 4 in.) high. Perhaps the most delicate and beautiful inhabitant of the shaded forest floor. The tiny, twinned, pink flowers rise from stems which run across the ground. Blooms in early summer.

37. **WESTERN WOOD LILY.** *Lilium philadelphicum*. Lily family. 30 to 60 cm (12 to 24 in.) high. More often thought of as a prairie or foothill species, this large, showy flower is found in the dry, open areas of the montane zone. Colour can change from near red to brilliant orange during the midsummer blooming season.

38. **WILD ROSE.** *Rosa acicularis*. Rose family. 30 to 90 cm (12 to 36 in.) high. The flower of the Province of Alberta is not nearly as common in the mountains as it is on the prairies. Most often found along roadsides in the lowest valleys where it blooms from June until August.

39. **WIND FLOWER.** *Anemone multifada*. Buttercup family. 8 to 40 cm (3 to 15 in.) high. A single, small flower atop a slender stem. Colour is most commonly white or deep red. An early bloomer on the grassy slopes of the montane.

40. **ASTER.** *Aster* sp. Daisy family. 25 to 60 cm (10 to 24 in.) high. One of the latest flowering species, usually coming into bloom in late summer and September. There are several aster species which grow in the mountain parks, and they are difficult to identify from one another as they are from the similar fleabanes which flower earlier in the summer.

41. **BLUE CLEMATIS.** *Clematis columbiana*. Buttercup family. A woody vine that creeps across the floor of semi-open forests, often climbing over logs and into the branches of trees and shrubs. Flowers are large, approximately 10 centimetres (4 in.) across. Blooms in early summer at lower elevations.

42. **PHACELIA.** *Phacelia sericea*. Waterleaf family. 15 to 40 cm (6 to 15 in.) high. Also known as scorpion weed. Found in open situations and in rocky terrain usually in the upper half of the subalpine zone. The spikes are heavily flowered with violet-blue blooms. Comes into flower in midsummer.

43. **PRAIRIE ANEMONE.** *Anemone patens*. Buttercup family. 8 to 15 cm (3 to 6 in.) high. Covered with fine, silky hairs, it is the first flower to bloom at lower elevations in the spring. Also known as the Pasque flower, since it sometimes blooms by Easter.

44. **ALPINE FORGET-ME-NOT.** *Myosotis alpestris*. Borage family. 10 to 20 cm (4 to 8 in.) high. This tiny blue flower is the beauty of the tundra, blooming in the short alpine growing season of midsummer.

45. **COMMON BLUEBELL.** *Campanula rotundifolia*. Bluebell family. 15 to 45 cm (6 to 18 in.) high. Blooms throughout the summer, usually at lower elevations and in open, sunny surroundings, though it is also found under shaded conditions and at levels up to the alpine tundra. Also known as the common harebell.

1. Alpine Anemone

2. Bunchberry

3. Contorted Lousewort

4. Cotton Grass

5. Fringed Grass-of-Parnassus

6. Globe Flower

7. Marsh Marigold

8. One-Flowered Wintergreen

9. Ox-Eye Daisy

10. Sparrow's Egg Lady Slipper

11. Spotted Saxifrage

12. Sweet-Flowered Androsace

13. White Mountain Avens

14. White Camas

15. White Mountain Heather

16. Alpine Buttercup

17. Avalanche Lily

18. Gaillardia

19. Golden Fleabane

20. Heart-Leaved Arnica

21. Yellow Columbine

22. Yellow Mountain Avens

23. Yellow Violet

24. Shrubby Cinquefoil

25. Stonecrop

26. Broad-Leaved Willow Herb

27. Calypso

28. Fireweed

29. Indian Paintbrush

30. Moss Campion

31. Mountain Sorrel

32. Nodding Onion

33. Red Mountain Heather

34. Pink Pussy-Toes

35. Shooting Star

36. Twin Flower

37. Western Wood Lily

38. Wild Rose

39. Wind Flower

40. Aster

41. Blue Clematis

42. Phacelia

43. Prairie Anemone

44. Alpine Forget-Me-Not

45. Common Bluebell

Golden-mantled ground squirrel

Hoary marmot

Columbian ground squirrel

Pika

Red squirrel

Least chipmunk

The two largest members of the deer family found in the mountain parks - the elk (top) and the moose (bottom).

Black bear

Halle Flygare

Grizzly bear

Mountain goat

Bighorn sheep

Mule deer

Coyote

Wildlife

THE MAMMALS. Most mammals in the parks are quite mobile, moving freely from one life zone to another particularly with the seasons. Yet, like trees and flowers, animals have preferences and tend to range in the areas which provide them with the best food supply, protection from their enemies, and shelter from the elements.

Following are some of the most commonly observed mammals in the parks and some easily accessible areas where they may be seen. (Photographs on pages 22 to 24 .)

PIKA. *Ochotona princeps.* 15 to 20 centimetres (6 to 8 in.) long. A small grey to buff-coloured bundle of fur that lives in the rockslides of the subalpine and alpine slopes. Though from the same order as the rabbits and hares, pikas have small round ears and the tail is not visible. Does not hibernate, remaining active throughout the winter and living off the piles of "hay" (dried grasses and forbes) stored within their rockslide burrows. Look for pikas in rockslide areas near Bow Summit and Sunwapta Pass on the Icefields Parkway, or in similar terrain on any timberline or alpine trails.

LEAST CHIPMUNK. *Eutamias minimus.* 9 to 11 centimetres (3½ to 4½ in.) long exclusive of tail. The common chipmunk of the mountain parks, it is also the smallest. Stripes extend from the end of the nose to the base of the tail. Runs with tail erect. Found in both the montane and subalpine forests, often living in logs or near rockslides. It is common in all areas of the mountain parks, but most often seen at heavily visited points of interest such as the Sulphur Mountain summit ridge at Banff and Maligne Canyon near Jasper. Hibernates.

COLUMBIAN GROUND SQUIRREL. *Spermophilus columbianus.* 25 to 30 centimetres (10 to 12 in.) long exclusive of tail. The most common ground squirrel in the parks. Coat is mainly mottled grey. Lives in colonies and in underground burrows, usually in open grassland or meadows from the montane zone to above the timberline. Often seen sitting erect near a burrow, giving a shrill chirp of warning. Hibernates in winter, and colonies in the lower valleys disappear underground as early as mid-August. Can be seen most anywhere in the mountain parks where extensive, open meadows occur, but the largest colonies tend to congregate near picnic areas such as Upper Bankhead on Banff's Lake Minnewanka Drive, Wapta Lake in Yoho Park, and roadside stops east of Jasper on the Yellowhead Highway.

GOLDEN-MANTLED GROUND SQUIRREL. *Spermophilus lateralis.* 15 to 20 centimetres (6 to 8 in.) long exclusive of tail. Often mistaken for a large chipmunk; unlike the chipmunk, the golden-mantled ground squirrel's body stripes do not extend onto its face, and it is much larger in size. Most often found on semi-open ridges and rockslides from the montane forest to near timberline, and frequents much the same areas of the mountain parks as the least chipmunk. Hibernates.

RED SQUIRREL. *Tamiasciurus hudsonicus.* 17 to 20 centimetres (7 to 8 in.) long exclusive of tail. The common tree squirrel of the mountain parks. Reddish colouration and noted for a sassy temperament, staccato chattering and scolding. Most common in the spruce-pine forest of the lower subalpine forest. Red squirrels are responsible for the large piles of cone scales left on the forest floor which are known as "midden heaps"; these mounds actually conceal cone caches used for winter food. Red squirrels are active throughout most of the year.

HOARY MARMOT. *Marmota caligata.* 45 to 50 centimetres (18 to 20 in.) long exclusive of tail — 4 to 9 kilos (10 to 20 lbs). Related to the eastern woodchuck, marmots live in rockslides and rocky meadows at or above timberline. Feeds on meadow plants. Often seen sunning on large boulders. Hoary marmots are also known as the whistlers or whistling marmots because of their long, shrill whistle of warning. A shy animal which is not easily seen from any park roadway, but many short day hikes, such as those around Lake Louise, will take the visitor into marmot country. Hibernates.

BEAVER. *Castor canadensis.* 65 to 75 centimetres (26 to 30 in.) long exclusive of tail — 14 to 25 kilos (30 to 55 lbs). The largest rodent in the parks, the beaver is a dweller of the low elevation ponds and marshy streams. Usually locates near stands of aspen and shrub willow, building lodges and dams. Noted for long front teeth which are used for gnawing down trees. Its flat tail is used for swimming and often for slapping the water in warning. The best beaver-watching area of the mountain parks is the 2nd Vermilion Lake and the backwaters along the Sundance Canyon Road near Banff.

MUSKRAT. *Ondatra zibethicus.* 25 to 35 centimetres (10 to 14 in.) long exclusive of tail. Resembles a small beaver except for the distinctive tail which is narrow and flattened on the sides. An inhabitant of low altitude ponds and streams. Spends most of its time swimming about among the shoreline cattails and rushes which it uses for lodge building. Also dens in streamside banks. Is found in the montane zones of the mountain parks, but best sighting areas are Vermilion Lakes and Johnson Lake near Banff, and the many low elevation lakes near Jasper such as Wabasso.

PORCUPINE. *Erethizon dorsatum.* 40 to 50 centimetres (16 to 20 in.) long exclusive of tail — 4 to 10 kilos (10 to 25 lbs). A slow, lumbering inhabitant of all levels of the subalpine forest, and unmistakable in its protective coat of long, sharp quills. Feeds on twigs and the inner bark of trees, and is often responsible for widespread damage due to its habit of girdling trees. Contrary to popular belief, a porcupine does not "throw" its quills; quills are barbed and release easily when touched by a foreign object, however. Porcupines will often crawl into trees for protection. They are nocturnal, so are seldom seen in the parks. Most often encountered in the daytime on forested trails, and may be a bit more numerous in Jasper Park than anywhere else.

COYOTE. *Canis latrans.* 10 to 15 kilos (25 to 35 lbs). The coyote is quite prolific in some sections of the mountain parks, and with its unusually healthy coat in this range, it is often mistaken by visitors for a wolf. (Wolves are not numerous in the parks and seldom seen near roadways.) Stands about the height of a medium-size dog, with a pointed nose and bushy tail. Patrols the meadows and forests of the montane and lower subalpine zones where it feeds on ground squirrels, voles, and mice. Noted for its eerie, wavering howls at night, when one or two individuals can sound like a large pack. Most frequently seen in the montane grasslands near Banff and Jasper (wherever ground squirrels are numerous).

BLACK BEAR. *Ursus americanus.* 90 to 225 kilos (200 to 500 lbs). Ranges in coloration from black through cinnamon to blonde. It is the smallest of the North American bears, and is distinguished from the grizzly bear by its more pointed face and lack of a shoulder hump. Tends to range lower than the grizzly as well, keeping to the main valleys of the montane and lower subalpine forests. Agile tree climbers despite their size. Omnivorous. Dormant in winter. Most often seen along the Banff-Windermere Parkway and the Icefields Parkway.

GRIZZLY BEAR. *Ursus horribilis*. 135 to 360 kilos (300 to 800 lbs). Grizzlies are usually dark brown, though they can range from blonde to nearly black; hairs are often tipped with grey. Are usually much larger than black bears, possessing a flat, broad face and a well defined hump over the shoulders. They possess poor eyesight but an excellent sense of smell. Range from the lowest valleys up into the alpine meadows. Semi-dormant in winter, usually not spending as much time in the den as black bears and more prone to taking midwinter strolls. Seldom seen by park visitors, though more frequently in the backcountry than along the highways. Most frequent roadside sightings are along the Trans-Canada Highway near Lake Louise and around Johnston Canyon west of Banff (but too infrequent to even seriously consider).

BIGHORN SHEEP. *Ovis canadensis*. 70 to 135 kilos (150 to 300 lbs). Distinguishable from the mountain goat by its brownish colored coat, white rump patch, and, in the male, massive curled horns. Tends to range on open slopes, from the montane to the alpine, though it is an extremely sure-footed animal on sheer, rock faces. Older males tend to stick together in "bachelor" flocks for much of the summer, joining the females again in autumn for the rut. A flock ranges along the Trans-Canada Highway just west of the Banff townsite overpass, and individuals are nearly always seen there. Other good areas include the lower Sinclair Canyon in Kootenay Park and the Athabasca Valley east of Jasper townsite.

MOUNTAIN GOAT. *Oreamnos americanus*. 45 to 135 kilos (100 to 300 lbs). Coats are pure white, and both males and females possess smooth, pointed black horns. Habitat is almost exclusively high, inaccessible cliffs and ledges, except where animals venture down to natural mineral licks. Probably the most sure footed of the North American mammals, tending to spend more time on precipitous cliffs than even bighorn sheep. Not frequently or easily seen, but the best chance is the Mount Wardle mineral lick near Hector Gorge on the Banff-Windermere Parkway. Another mineral lick beside the Icefields Parkway 37 kilometres (23 miles) south of Jasper townsite also attracts a local herd from time to time.

ELK. *Cervus canadensis*. 275 to 450 kilos (600 to 1000 lbs). Distinguished by its reddish-brown coat and pale rump patch. Much larger than the mule deer. Herds tend to inhabit the lower valleys through much of the year, though they will move up into the high country in midsummer. Males sport huge racks of antlers which they shed very late in the winter or in early spring. The rutting season begins in September when the valleys are alive with the hoarse bugling of the bulls. Elk are also known as wapiti. Most numerous in the autumn along the Trans-Canada Highway east from Banff, along the Banff-Windermere Parkway in the McLeod Meadows area, and near the Whistlers Campground section of the Athabasca Valley near Jasper.

MULE DEER. *Odocoileus hemionus*. 55 to 180 kilos (125 to 400 lbs). A much stockier animal than the white-tailed deer. Coloration varies over the year from reddish-brown to grey. Tends to stay in the lower valleys and along the open slopes of the montane zone. Receives its name from its large, mule-like ears. Males grow antlers annually, losing them in midwinter. Not as prone to precipitous flight as white-tailed deer, often stopping for an inquisitive glance at an intruder — a fatal flaw outside the park during the hunting season. Feeds mainly on shrubs and twigs. Can be seen on the montane grasslands of the Bow, Athabasca, and Kootenay Valleys in spring and fall, and are quite common on Tunnel Mountain at Banff and Old Fort Point near Jasper.

MOOSE. *Alces alces.* 360 to 500 kilos (800 to 1100 lbs). The largest of the North American deer, moose are ungainly looking animals with a large drooping snout and a dewlap hanging from the throat. Males possess broad, palmate antlers which are shed in early winter. Seem to prefer major valleys and lower elevations, and particularly swamp and river-bottom environments, but due to the short supply of this kind of terrain in the Rocky Mountains, they tend to spend more time browsing on willow branches than elsewhere in its North American range. Most frequently seen along the Icefields Parkway from Bow Summit to Sunwapta Pass.

Birds

Nearly 300 species of birds have been recorded within the boundaries of the mountain parks. A few are permanent residents, many visit only seasonally to mate and nest, while others merely pass through on annual migrations. Perhaps, even more than the mammals, birds are sensitive to their environment, tending to frequent those niches within the mountain ecosystem which most suit their needs.

Gray jay

In the lower valleys where aquatic environments abound in the backwaters of major rivers and the small, glacially formed kettles, a variety of waterfowl may be found. Migratory waterfowl are most often seen from early April to late May and, again, during September and October. Many ducks, grebes, swans, and geese use the lakes as rest stops on migratory routes. Mallards, harlequin ducks, Barrow's goldeneye, common mergansers, green-winged teal, pintails, and red-necked grebes are among the nesting species. The only permanent resident of note among the waterfowl is the mallard, though common and Barrow's goldeneye and common mergansers are present throughout much of the year. Other birds attracted to the lowland marshes and lakes include such expert fish-catchers as the osprey and bald eagle, while the cheery song of the redwinged blackbird is often heard ringing from the shoreline cattails.

Clark's nutcracker

The birds which most visitors come in contact with and notice are the scavengers of the Corvidae family — the jays, magpies, and crows. The gray jay is one of the most common of mountain birds; also known as the Canada jay, whiskey jack, or camp robber, it is considered by many to be the symbol of the mountain forest. The Clark's nutcracker resembles the gray jay in many respects, but for its longer beak, distinct black wings, and somewhat more raucous manner. Ravens are year round residents of the mountains and much larger than their look-alike cousins, the summer visiting crows. The black-billed magpie is probably the most flamboyantly beautiful bird in the parks, with a distinctive streaming tail which is longer than its body.

Raven

Species which favour the open, montane environment include mountain and black-capped chickadees, mountain bluebirds, flickers, dark-eyed juncos, and pine siskins. The higher and more dense canopy of the subalpine forest is favoured by boreal chickadees, hermit and varied thrushes, winter wrens, ruby-crowned kinglets, and crossbills. Along the banks of fast moving streams, belted kingfishers, swallows, and the occasional dipper may be seen.

The woodpecker clan is well represented in areas where trees are dead or dying, such as burns and mature, river bottom forests. Most commonly seen are the northern three-toed woodpecker, the hairy woodpecker, the downy woodpecker, and, the giant of the family, the pileated woodpecker. The alpine tundra is the home of the white-tailed ptarmigan, grey-crowned rosy finch, horned lark, water pipit, and golden eagle.

During the late spring and summer the best hours for birding are in the early morning between five and ten o'clock (dawn comes early in this latitude!). Enthusiastic birdwatchers should pick up the species checklist available at park information centres.

Black-billed magpie

Historical Highlights

1754 Hudson's Bay Company employee Anthony Henday sights the Rocky Mountains from near present-day Red Deer, Alberta.

1800 The first known crossing of the main ranges of the Rocky Mountains is made by two North West Company voyageurs named Le Blanc and La Gassi, probably via Howse Pass.

1800 Duncan McGillivray, a trader with the North West Company, is believed to have penetrated the mountains as far as Brazeau Lake in his search for a route across the Rockies.

1807 David Thompson, a trader and surveyor for the North West Company, crosses the Rockies by way of Howse Pass and establishes the first fur trade post in the Columbia Valley

1810 Joseph Howse, a trader with the Hudson's Bay Company, crosses the path which would one day bear his name and competes for furs with the Nor'westers in the Rocky Mountain Trench.

1811 Turned back by the Piegan Indians at the entrance to Howse Pass, David Thompson moves north and crosses the range by way of the Athabasca Pass in mid-winter.

1811 Henry's House is established near the present site of Jasper as a way station for fur trade brigades crossing the Athabasca Pass.

1812 Jasper's House is established by the North West Company on the Athabasca River not far from the present eastern boundary of Jasper Park.

1824 George Simpson, Governor of the Hudson's Bay Company, makes his first journey across the Great Divide by way of Athabasca Trail. Names the Committee's Punch Bowl — a small lake on the summit of Athabasca Pass.

1825 Thomas Drummond is the first trained naturalist to visit the Rockies, spending a year making collections in the vicinity of Jasper's House.

Voyageurs snowshoeing to the summit of Athabasca Pass, as painted by Henry James Warre in 1846.

Public Archives of Canada

1827 David Douglas, another British botanist, crosses Athabasca Pass and ascends Mount Brown, mistakenly judging it and a neighbouring peak to be 16,000 feet above sea level. When he returns to England, the false elevation is attached to the maps of the day.

1841 The first settlers to cross the Rockies are a group of Red River Metis on their way to the Oregon Territory. Led by James Sinclair, they cross White Man Pass and descend Sinclair Canyon.

1841 Hudson's Bay Governor George Simpson crosses the pass in present-day Banff Park which bears his name.

1845 A pair of British spies, Lieutenants Henry James Warre and Mervin Vavasour, cross White Man Pass while on a mission to the Oregon Territory. Warre, an accomplished artist, provides the earliest known paintings of the Canadian Rockies.

1846 Canadian artist Paul Kane travels over the Athabasca Trail, painting and sketching mountain scenery and natives along the way.

1847 A Wesleyan missionary named Rev. Robert Rundle holds services for the Stoney Indians on the shores of Lake Minnewanka.

Dr. James Hector (right) with John Palliser, leader of the Palliser Expedition of 1857-60.

1858 The Palliser Expedition explores the western prairies and mountains. The expedition geologist, Dr. James Hector, explores much of the country contained within the present mountain parks, naming many features along the way. Hector is the first white man known to have crossed the Vermilion and Kicking Horse Passes.

1859 A wealthy English sportsman, James Carnegie, the Earl of Southesk, makes a hunting trip to the eastern valleys of today's Jasper Park. Also travels south into the Banff vicinity via Pipestone Pass and the Bow River.

1862 Yellowhead Pass is used by gold seekers bound for the Cariboo country in central British Columbia.

1871 With the promise of a trans-continental railway, a party under British Columbia surveyor Walter Moberly is dispatched to run a preliminary survey through Howse Pass.

1872 Sandford Fleming, Engineer-in-Chief for the Canadian Pacific Railway surveys, chooses a route through the Yellowhead Pass for the trans-continental line. Fleming visits the pass personally in the autumn.

1872 Charles Horetzky, another Dominion surveyor, visits the Athabasca Valley briefly, taking the first photographs within the present mountain park environs.

1875   Maligne Lake is discovered by the railway surveyor Henry Macleod. After a long, hard journey, he names it Sore-foot Lake.

1881   Major A. B. Rogers, an American surveyor hired by the Canadian Pacific Railway, begins preliminary survey work in the Bow Valley and Kicking Horse Pass.

1882   Lake Louise is discovered by CPR packer Tom Wilson.

1883   The tracks of the Canadian Pacific Railway enter the mountains via the Bow Valley, reaching a point near Lake Louise by late autumn.

1883   Silver City booms to life at the foot of Castle Mountain with the arrival of the rails in the Bow Valley.

1883   Dr. George M. Dawson, a Dominion geologist, travels many of the last unexplored valleys of the Rockies south of the Kicking Horse Pass. Names many natural features in today's mountain parks, including Mount Assiniboine.

1884   The Canadian Pacific Railway tracks cross the Great Divide and descend the Kicking Horse Valley.

1885   A federal reserve of ten square miles is set aside surrounding the hot mineral springs at the base of Sulphur Mountain — the beginning of Canada's national park system.

1885   The last spike is driven for the Canadian Pacific Railway.

1886   Mount Stephen House at Field, British Columbia is the first Canadian Pacific Railway hotel constructed in the Rockies.

1886   The core of the future Yoho National Park is created with the establishment of a ten square mile federal reserve near the base of Mount Stephen.

1887   An area of some 260 square miles surrounding the Sulphur Mountain hot springs, the fledgling town of Banff, and Lake Minnewanka is set aside as the Rocky Mountains National Park.

1888   The Banff Springs Hotel is opened for business by the Canadian Pacific Railway.

1890   A small chalet is constructed on the shores of Lake Louise to accommodate guests.

The tent used by the first Superintendent of the Hot Springs Reserve, pitched at the foot of Cascade Mountain circa 1885 — the earliest days of Banff.
Archives of the Canadian Rockies

CPR locomotive at Mount Stephen House in Field, B.C., ca. 1888.
Archives of the Canadian Rockies

Alpine Club of Canada climbers inspect a crevasse, 1913.
Archives of the Canadian Rockies

1892   Toronto geologist A. P. Coleman, his brother L. Q. Coleman and L. G. Stewart, go in search of the 16,000 foot peaks recorded by David Douglas in 1827. The party fails to find Athabasca Pass, but explores much of presenty-day Jasper Park in the process, including Brazeau Lake, Poboktan Pass, Sunwapta River and Falls, and the magnificent Fortress Lake.

1893   The Coleman brothers, L. G. Stewart, and rancher Frank Sibbald reach Athabasca Pass. They discover that Douglas grossly overestimated the mountains' height.

1894   The exploration of the Lake Louise region is undertaken by a group of young Americans who call themselves the Yale-Lake Louise Club. They climb Mount Temple along the way — the first ascent of a mountain over 11,000 feet in the Canadian Rockies.

1896   The first alpinist to die in the Canadian Rockies is Philip Abbot, who falls while attempting a first ascent of Mount Lefroy near Lake Louise.

1898   The Columbia Icefield is discovered by two British mountaineers, J. Norman Collie and Hermann Woolley.

1899   The Canadian Pacific Railway brings Swiss guides to the Canadian west to lead tourists to the summits of local mountains.

1901   The Yoho Park Reserve is established, covering an area of some 828 square miles.

1901   Mount Assiniboine is climbed by the Rev. James Outram and the Swiss guides Christian Hasler and Christian Bohren.

1907   Jasper Park is established in anticipation of a trans-continental railway running up the Athabasca River and through the Yellowhead Pass.

1909   The Spiral Tunnels are constructed on the "Big Hill" west of the Kicking Horse Pass, reducing the grade on the CPR line from a maximum of 4.5 percent to 2.2 percent.

1911   The Grand Trunk Pacific Railway tracks pass up the Athabasca Valley and on toward the Yellowhead Pass. The town of Fitzhugh springs up along the tracks, to be renamed Jasper two years later.

1913   The first ascent of Mount Robson, the highest mountain in the Canadian Rockies, is made by two members of the Alpine Club of Canada led by Austrian guide Conrad Kain.

1915   Lac Beauvert near Jasper townsite is the site of the first tourist accommodation in Jasper Park when a tent camp is erected on its shores.

1915   The Canadian Northern Railway becomes the second line to run through Jasper Park, paralleling the Grand Trunk Pacific through Yellowhead Pass.

1915   Restrictions on the use of automobiles in Banff Park are lifted.

1920   Kootenay National Park is established.

1920   The Banff-Lake Louise Road is completed.

1921   The Jasper Park Lodge is constructed by the Canadian National Railway on the shores of Lac Beauvert.

1923   The Banff-Windermere Highway is completed.

1924   Fire destroys the Chateau Lake Louise.

1927   Fire destroys the north wing of the Banff Springs Hotel.

1930   The National Parks Act is passed by Parliament, establishing the boundaries of the mountain parks generally as they exist today and introducing the concepts of parks preservation under which our present parks system is managed.

1930   The first ski lodge in the parks is constructed in the mountains east of Lake Louise.

1931   Construction is commenced on the Banff-Jasper Highway.

1940   The Banff-Jasper Highway is completed and opened for travel.

Early touring cars beside the Vermilion Lakes near Banff, 1924.
Archives of the Canadian Rockies

The Lake Louise Chalet burning in 1924.
Archives of the Canadian Rockies

Trans Canada Highway

As the primary east-west highway through the Canadian Rockies, the Trans-Canada serves as an artery for both park visitation and transcontinental commerce, and it doesn't do either job very well. More than any other park road, this is a very dangerous highway for sight-seeing in a moving vehicle. The flow of traffic is very fast, and many cars and trucks are merely passing through the Rockies on their way to other destinations; their drivers have little interest in the scenery. If you plan to travel on the Trans-Canada Highway through Banff and Yoho Parks, make use of the many pull-offs and picnic areas along the way.

Approaching from the east, the highway enters Banff Park via the Bow Valley, follows that river past Banff and Lake Louise, ascends to the summit of the Kicking Horse Pass, and descends through the heart of Yoho National Park via the Kicking Horse Valley. The length of the journey from Banff East Gate to Yoho West gate is 128.2 kilometres (79.7 miles).

While the highway offers good views of most of the main peaks in the Bow Valley as well as access to several interesting trails, many visitors prefer to follow the more leisurely and scenic Bow Valley Parkway which parallels the Trans-Canada most of the way through Banff Park. (See Bow Valley Parkway, page 68 .)

The Trans-Canada Highway is the only road traversing Yoho Park. It provides excellent views of the narrow and rugged Kicking Horse Valley and its surrounding peaks, and all points of interest in the park can be reached by trails and roads which branch off the highway.

In addition to the problems of heavy traffic, park visitors should expect to encounter construction disruptions on the 13 kilometres (8 miles) of highway west of the Banff East Gate. A highway twinning project is underway on this section, and construction will eventually cut-off access to the Tunnel Mountain Road and Lake Minnewanka Road, 9.1 kilometres (5.7 miles) and 9.6 kilometres (6.0 miles) west of the Banff East Gate.

Eastbound travellers on the Trans-Canada tour should turn to page 49 and work backwards following distances in the right-hand margin.

0.0	**Banff National Park East Gate.**	**128.2** *79.7*

2.3
1.4 **Carrot Creek** is the first stream crossed by the Trans-Canada Highway inside the Banff Park East Gate. The gravel flats on either side of Carrot Creek are covered with poplar trees — the only abundant deciduous trees found in the Rockies. The poplars with the largest leaves, growing closest to the creek banks, are cottonwood poplars while the stands further from the stream are composed mainly of the smaller leafed aspen poplars.

125.9
78.3

Aspen usually colonize after a forest fire and reproduce vegetatively by sending out root suckers, thus, aspen stands are composed of clones, or related trees generated from a single, parent tree. In autumn, clusters of these interconnected trees turn gold together, sometimes while the rest of the stand is still lush and green.

The rugged, northeast face of Mount Rundle is a constant companion along the southwest side of the valley between the Banff East Gate and the Tunnel Mountain Road Junction. The mountain is actually a massif, or collection of mountain peaks, which stretches along the Bow Valley for over 16 kilometres (10 miles).

9.1
5.7 **Tunnel Mountain Road Junction.** The road intersecting with the Trans-Canada Highway from the west, climbs onto an old glacial outwash bench, passes by the Tunnel Mountain Campground, and terminates just over five kilometres (three miles) distant in Banff townsite. A scenic secondary route into Banff.

119.1
74.0

9.6
6.0 **Lake Minnewanka Road Junction.** An interesting 13.5 kilometre (8.5 mile) loop drive that passes by Johnson Lake, Two Jack Lake, Lake Minnewanka, and the historic mining town of Bankhead. Eventually returns to the Trans-Canada Highway at the Banff Traffic Circle, 3.5 kilometres (2.1 miles) west of this junction. (See Lake Minnewanka Drive, page 54 .)

118.6
73.7

At this present-day highway junction, there once stood a small coal mining town named Anthracite. The town came into being in 1886 shortly after the construction of the Canadian Pacific Railway and continued to operate until 1904 when the nearby town of Bankhead rose to prominence. One of the mine shafts entered the hillside near where the Lake Minnewanka Road climbs towards Johnson Lake today, and the old tailings piles still rise as grass-covered mounds beside the highway junction. The town of Anthracite stretched along the banks of the Cascade River pretty much where the Canadian Pacific Railway tracks run today, and the tiny, red railway shack beside the railway is very close to where the central business district stood.

The coal seams which were worked here are actually much younger than the rock with rises above the valley on either side, the older formations having been fractured then pushed up and over the younger coal-bearing shales during the uplift of the Rocky Mountains nearly 70 million years ago.

Between the Banff Traffic Circle and the Lake Minnewanka Road Junction, on the north side of the highway, you can see outcrops of

The mining town of Anthracite, circa 1888.

Archives of the Canadian Rockies

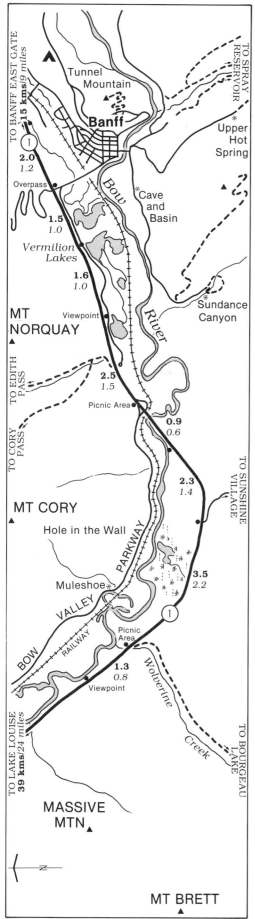

steeply tilted shale and sandstone beds. These beds are a part of the Kootenay Formation, the same group of rocks which contains the Anthracite coal seams. Geologists hypothesize that this region was once a flat-lying swamp area, rich in plant life. During the early stages of uplift and deformation in the western cordillera, silt-laden rivers from a mountain range to the west poured down into this marshland, the silt covering over much of the swamp vegetation. The vegetative material thus trapped eventually became coal, while the silt turned to the thin beds of shale we find here. All of this occurred somewhere between 170 and 80 million years ago.

13.1   **Banff Traffic Circle.** A confusing intersection for the unfamiliar. Keep   **115.1**
8.1   right and watch the signs carefully. The circle serves as the east exit to   *71.6*
Banff townsite as well as the west terminus of the Lake Minnewanka Loop Drive. (See Lake Minnewanka Loop Drive, page 54).

15.1   **Buffalo Paddock.** A herd of buffalo in the mountains may seem strange,   **113.1**
9.4   yet at one time, a species of wood buffalo roamed throughout the valleys   *70.3*
east of the Great Divide. Many of these animals were sighted and hunted by the early fur traders and surveyors in the Rocky Mountains, but by the late 19th Century, the animals had been hunted to extinction.

A fenced-in buffalo enclosure was established in this vicinity in 1898 when a small herd of plains bison were transferred to the park. (The area was actually known as the Animal Paddock in those days as it also contained such diverse species as elk, moose, Angora goats, Persian sheep, timber wolves, cougar, red foxes, antelope, and raccoon.) The buffalo herd grew to 107 members by 1909 when it was realized that such a large population could not survive in such a limited area, and the herd was thinned down to a more manageable size. In the autumn of 1980, the last nine plains bison were removed from the paddock, and in January, 1981, five wood bison were introduced from Wood Buffalo National Park, making the buffalo population in the paddock more true to the species which once roamed these mountain valleys.

A narrow roadway makes a circuit through the enclosure, and the best chance of seeing the wood buffalo close to the road seems to be in the morning or at dusk, for they often retreat into the trees at midday.

The paddock area also serves as an excellent, close-up viewpoint for the spectacular south face of Cascade Mountain — at 2998 metres (9,836 ft), the highest mountain in the immediate Banff vicinity. The mountain is typical of many in this section of the park, being composed of three well-defined formations — the massive, limestone cliffs of the Palliser Formation along the base of the mountain; the gentler broken-shale slopes of the Banff Formation midway to the summit; and the limestone cliffs on the Rundle Group in the peak. These rocks were deposited as sediment on the floor of a shallow inland sea between 330 and 400 million years ago.

17.1   **Banff Overpass.** This interchange serves as the west exit for Banff   **111.1**
10.6   townsite, and the turn-off for the Mount Norquay Ski Area. (See Mount   *69.1*
Norquay Drive, page 53 .)

18.6   **Vermilion Lakes Viewpoint.** As the Trans-Canada Highway traverses   **109.6**
11.6   along the base of Mount Norquay, it passes through the range of a flock of   *68.1*
Rocky Mountain bighorn sheep. Both rams and ewes are often seen along this section of highway, and the motorist should be forewarned of the ensuing traffic jams. (Stopping along this section of highway except at designated parking areas is illegal.)

In summer, the ewes and lambs tend to stay in flocks by themselves while the rams roam together in "bachelor" flocks. But, with the rutting season in late November and early December, the sexes are back together and usually remain so through the severe winter months. Sheep are extremely agile on sheer rock faces, aided by a soft, spongy pad under the hoof which gives the animals added traction. This uncanny climbing ability is often exhibited on the vertical rock-cuts along this section of the highway.

20.2 **Vermilion Lakes Viewpoint.** This pull-off is an excellent vantage point **108.0**
12.6 for the major mountains surrounding Banff as well as the many interest- *67.1*
ing features on the floor of the Bow Valley. (See Vermilion Lakes Drive, page 52   for a description of the natural history of the lakes.)

The Vermilion Lakes and Mount Rundle from a viewpoint on the Trans-Canada Highway.

Down-valley to the east is the Fairholme Range; the low, rounded mountain around which the town is built is Tunnel Mountain, 1692 metres (5,550 ft); the distinctive peak towering above both the townsite and Tunnel Mountain (and looking something like a tilted, writing desk) is Mount Rundle, 2949 metres (9,675 ft); the long, forested ridge to the right of Rundle is Sulphur Mountain, 2451 metres (8,040 ft); to the right of Sulphur is the Sundance Range; and, finally, the cluster of rugged mountains looking down the Trans-Canada to the west is the Massive Range.

22.7 **Bow Valley Parkway Junction.** A good choice for westbound motorists **105.5**
14.1 who want to relax and sightsee on their way to Lake Louise. (See Bow *65.6*
Valley Parkway, page 68   .)

23.6 **River Side Picnic Area.** Located on the banks of the Bow River, this **104.6**
14.7 picnic area offers good close-ups of the marshy, river-bottom environ- *65.0*
ment as well as views of the towering Massive Range to the west.

25.9 **Sunshine Village Road.** Used as access to one of Banff's most popular **102.3**
16.1 ski areas in the winter, motorists can drive up this gravel road for 9 *63.6*
kilometres (5.5 miles) to the Bourgeau Parking Area. From there hikers can continue up the limited access service road for 6.5 kilometres (4 miles) to the alpine meadows surrounding Sunshine Village, or branch off on trails leading to Healy Pass and the Egypt Lake region.

28.9 **Bourgeau Lake Trail.** A trail extending 7.4 kilometres (4.6 miles) up **99.3**
18.0 the Wolverine Creek valley to a small, subalpine tarn. *61.7*

29.4 **Wolverine Creek Picnic Area.** This roadside stop is situated in a mature **98.8**
18.3 forest composed primarily of western white spruce with a few aspen *61.4*
poplars. Wolverine Creek flows by the picnic area, and from its banks, you can see the jagged summits of the Sawback Range marching away to the northwest.

30.7 **Sawback Range Viewpoint.** This viewpoint is actually a long, paved **97.5**
19.1 pull-off along a guard rail, but if offers the best views of the Sawback *60.6*
Range across the Bow River to the east.

The Sawback Range is composed of steeply-tilted layers of Mississippian and Upper Devonian rock which was formed nearly 350 million years ago. Essentially horizontal at the time of their formation, the rock layers

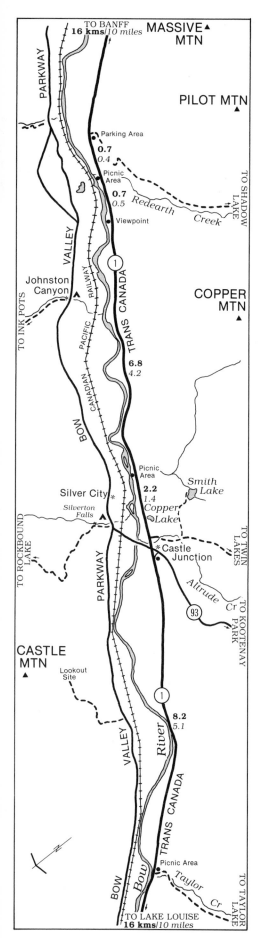

were tilted to their present high angle during the creation of the Rocky Mountains around 70 million years ago. Since that time, the forces of weathering have worked away at the nearly vertical strata to create these distinctive sawtooth-shaped mountain peaks.

Notice the cave just below the summit of Mount Cory (the major peak at the south end of the range). This 30 metre depression in the limestone cliffs is called the Hole-in-the-Wall and is believed to have been formed by meltwater from a huge valley glacier which once filled this valley from side to side and up to an elevation of 2400 metres (8,000 ft).

36.7   **Redearth Creek Parking Area.** This is a popular trail-head for hikes   **91.5**
22.8   and cross country ski tours leading to Shadow Lake and the Egypt Lake   *56.9*
region.

37.4   **Redearth Creek Picnic Area.** The Sawback Range is visible across the   **90.8**
23.2   valley, and Castle Mountain can be seen up-valley to the northwest.   *56.5*

38.1   **Castle Mountain Viewpoint and Mount Eisenhower Cairn.** This is   **90.1**
23.7   one of the best viewpoints for Castle Mountain, 2766 metres (9,076 ft).   *56.0*
The bulky, turreted peak is an excellent example of a layer-cake or castellate-type of mountain, i.e. the rock layers in the peak are essentially horizontal, and the action of weathering has created towers and battlements of rock which resemble those of a medieval castle. The similarity was not lost on Dr. James Hector of the Palliser Expedition who was the first white man to set eyes on the mountain in 1858 and subsequently named it Castle Mountain.

As you might notice from the plaque set into a large boulder at this roadside parking area, the mountain has not always been known as Castle. Following World War II, the people of Scotland decided to show their appreciation to the General of the Allied Forces Dwight D. Eisenhower by giving him a castle. Not to be outdone, then Prime Minister of Canada Mackenzie King declared that Canada would give the General an even larger castle and had the mountain renamed in his honour. Despite much local resentment to the change, the mountain was called Mount Eisenhower from 1945 until 1979 when the federal government decided that the original name should be reinstated. The first tower on the mountain retains the name of Eisenhower Peak, and tour bus drivers still jokingly refer to the treeless meadow below the tower as Eisenhower's Putting Green.

The Sawback Range is also quite visible from this viewpoint, its most spectacular summit being Mount Ishbel (2908 m/9,540 ft). Between Mount Ishbel and Castle Mountain a series of thrust faults (fractures in the rock) separates the younger rock of the Front Ranges from the older of the Main Ranges. The Front Ranges, of which Mount Ishbel and the Sawback Range are a part, compose more or less the eastern one-third of the Rockies and are carved from rock which is around 250 to 350 million years old; the Main Ranges, of which Castle Mountain and the peaks of the Great Divide are a part, are much older, having been carved from rock which was deposited as sediment in a shallow inland sea over 500 million years ago.

Other mountains visible from this excellent viewpoint are Pilot Mountain (2954 m/9,690 ft) looming above the highway to the south, and Mount Temple (3544 m/11,626 ft), the snow-capped peak predominant in the far distance to the northwest.

In late July and early August, the tall, showy wildflower called fireweed is often found growing along the steep bank which drops away from the viewpoint to the waters of the Bow River.

Castle Mountain.

44.9 **Copper Picnic Area.** A very pretty roadside stop by the Bow River. Take **83.3**
27.9 the time to slip down to the shore of the river for an excellent view of *51.8*
Castle Mountain.

46.2 **Copper Lake.** Located just off the southwest side of the highway, the **82.0**
28.7 lake was named for Copper Mountain (2795 m/9,170 ft), visible to the *51.0*
south. Several copper claims were worked on the slopes of the mountain
from 1883 into the early decades of the 20th Century.

46.7 **Altrude Creek Picnic Area.** This picnic area is situated in a forest **81.5**
29.0 composed mainly of lodgepole pine with a few spruce and poplar. Castle *50.7*
Mountain (2766 m/9,076 ft) rises majestically to the north. Altrude
Creek, which borders this stop, flows from the Great Divide on Vermilion Pass, just 10 kilometres (6 miles) distant to the west.

47.1 **Castle Junction.** The Banff-Windermere Parkway connects into the **81.1**
29.3 Trans-Canada from the south and west (see Banff-Windermere Parkway, *50.4*
page 81) while a short 800 metre spur road connects across the Bow
River to the Bow Valley Parkway (see Bow Valley Parkway, page 72).

The forest bordering the Trans-Canada Highway along most of the
route between Banff and Lake Louise is composed primarily of
lodgepole pine. As you pass along, notice the dense, even-aged nature of
these stands. Lodgepole pine is a fire succession species whose cones
only open *en masse* after being heated by a passing forest fire. In the
decades following the construction of the Canadian Pacific Railway,
much of the Bow Valley was burnt over by man-caused fires, and the
lodgepole forests are a result of these fires. If no further burning occurs,
the lodgepole pine will be unable to reproduce, and shade-tolerant spruce
and fir trees will eventually grow up beneath the present forest canopy to
take over as the climax forest species (species that are capable of
regenerating themselves).

55.3 **Taylor Creek Picnic Area.** On the east side of this roadside picnic area, **72.9**
34.4 the forest is composed of an almost pure stand of lodgepole pine, while a *45.3*
forest of spruce borders the west side. The lodgepole is the successor of a
forest fire, while the presence of large spruce trees indicates this section
of forest was spared the ravages of the fire (perhaps Taylor Creek acted as
the fire break which saved this stand.

If you walk out through the lodgepole forest, you will see small spruce
trees growing up beneath the dense lodgepole canopy. Barring another
fire, these shade tolerant spruce will one day replace the lodgepole as the
dominant forest tree.

Taylor Creek flows from Taylor Lake — a small tarn situated in a cirque
on the eastern slope of the Great Divide. A 6.3 kilometre (3.9 mile) trail
leads to Taylor Lake from the rear of the picnic area.

65.2 **Mount Temple Viewpoint.** Mount Temple (3544 m/11,626 ft), the **63.0**
40.6 highest mountain in the Lake Louise vicinity and the third highest in the *39.1*

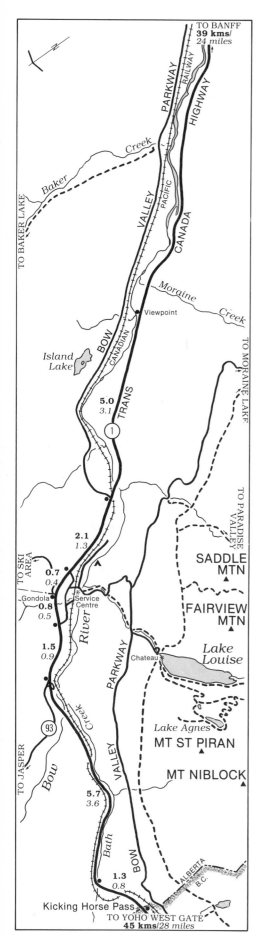

park, looms above to the west. Like many peaks in the Main Ranges of the Rockies, Mount Temple is composed of quartz sandstones and limestones of Precambrian and Cambrian age rock which are over 500 million years old. When this rock was being deposited as sediment in a shallow, inland sea, only the most primitive forms of life existed in the oceans and the land was totally lifeless.

Curiously enough, Mount Temple was not named because it resembles a temple, but rather for Sir Richard Temple, a British scientist who led an excursion to the Rockies in 1884.

Protection Mountain (2786 m/9,140 ft) is the long, relatively low wall of rock across the valley to the east.

69.7 *43.3*	**Bow River Bridge.**	**58.5** *36.4*

70.2 *43.7*	**Bow Valley Parkway Junction.** A slower, more relaxed and scenic road which parallels the Trans-Canada Highway on the east side of the Bow Valley nearly to Banff. (See Bow Valley Parkway, page 74 .)	**58.0** *36.0*

70.7 *44.0*	**Bow Valley Parkway Junction.** This is a short spur of the scenic parkway through the Bow Valley. It serves as the east exit to Lake Louise and the lower Lake Louise service centre, continuing on in a westerly direction to the Kicking Horse Pass and connecting with the Trans-Canada Highway again near Wapta Lake in British Columbia (see Bow Valley Parkway, page 74 , and Lake Louise Vicinity, page 77). This turn off also gives quick access to the Lake Louise Campground.	**57.5** *35.7*

72.3 *45.0*	**Lake Louise Service Centre Exit.** For westbound travellers this is the handiest exit for reaching the lower Lake Louise service centre. Connects in with roads going to the Lake Louise Campground and the lake itself. (See Lake Louise and Vicinity, page 77 .)	**55.9** *34.7*

73.0 *45.4*	**Whitehorn Sedan Lift and Lake Louise Ski Area Access Road.** By pulling off the highway here, the ski area access road can be used as a viewpoint for the major peaks of the Bow Range to the west.	**55.2** *34.3*

Mount Temple is at its most impressive from this point, capped by a small glacier and rising to 3544 metres (11,626 ft) above sea level; it is the highest mountain in the Lake Louise region. Equally impressive is the broad, ice-clad face of Mount Victoria (3464 m/11,365 ft) standing to the north of Mount Temple. Mount Victoria is the prominent mountain which serves as the backdrop for Lake Louise.

From this viewpoint, you can get some idea of what is meant by a "hanging valley." Distinct valleys can be seen both at the foot of Mount Temple's sheer north face and before Mount Victoria. Both of these were carved by alpine glaciers which advanced from the Great Divide. When a large valley glacier carved the Bow Valley, however, these smaller valleys were truncated and left "hanging" on the side of the main valley.

The Whitehorn Sedan Lift, just 400 metres off the highway from this junction, offers a three kilometre gondola ride to a terminal at the 2040 metre (6,700 ft) level on Whitehorn Mountain. From this vantage point, the entire Bow Range stretches out like a map across the western horizon. The road climbing up and around the hill to the southeast, travels to the parking area for the Lake Louise Ski Area 3 kilometres (2 miles) distant.

73.8   **Lake Louise Service Centre Exit.** For eastbound travellers this is the   **54.4**
45.9   handiest exit for reaching the lower Lake Louise service centre. Connects   *33.8*
in with roads going to the Lake Louise Campground and the lake itself.
(See Lake Louise and Vicinity, page 77 .)

75.3   **Icefields Parkway Junction.** One of the most scenic roads in the   **52.9**
46.8   mountain parks, leading northward along the eastern side of the Great   *32.9*
Divide for 230.3 kilometres (143.1 miles) to Jasper townsite. (See
Icefields Parkway, page 90 .)

At this junction, a distinctive outcrop of red-orange rock stands beside
the road. This slate-like rock is among the oldest to be found in the parks,
having been deposited as sediment on the floor of a shallow sea over 600
million years ago.

76.2   **Bow River Bridge.** At this point, the Bow River is only 32 kilometres   **52.0**
47.4   (20 miles) south of its source and is a much-reduced stream to that found   *32.3*
flowing through the townsite of Banff just 65 kilometres (40 miles)
down-valley.

77.0   **Mount St. Piran—Mount Niblock Viewpoint.** This viewpoint over-   **51.2**
47.9   looks the small, mountain stream of Bath Creek. Across the valley stands   *31.8*
the relatively low peak of Mount St. Piran (2649 m/8,691 ft) and the
much higher and more rugged Mount Niblock (2976 m/9,764 ft).

81.0   **Bath Creek Bridge.** This creek was named in 1881 when Major A. B.   **47.2**
50.4   Rogers, the cantankerous and colourful chief surveyor for the mountain   *29.3*
section of the Canadian Pacific Railway, took an unscheduled plunge
while trying to ford the stream on his horse. After the incident, his men
often commented on the murky, grey colour of the water (caused by the
rock flour washed down from the Bath Glacier) noting wryly that the
Major must be taking another bath.

Bath Glacier can just be seen on the broad slopes of Mount Daly (3152
m/10,342 ft) at the head of the valley to the northwest.

Major A. B. Rogers, chief surveyor for the CPR, who accidentally provided the name for Bath Creek.
Provincial Archives of B.C.

82.3   **The Great Divide.** Here, the Trans-Canada Highway crests the backbone   **45.9**
51.2   of the Rockies: all waters east of this point flow into the Saskatchewan   *28.5*
River system and eventually to Hudson's Bay, while those to the west
empty into the Columbia and the Pacific Ocean.

The pull-off at the pass is an excellent viewpoint for the rugged mountains at the northern end of the Bow Range — Mount Niblock (2976
m/9,764 ft) and Narao Peak (2913 m/9,557 ft). Rugged hanging valleys,
or cirques, have been cut between these peaks by the "plucking" action
of alpine glaciers (you can see a small remnant of one of these glaciers
near the head of the amphitheatre just below the summit of Mount
Niblock). The piles of gravel and rock debris near the mouths of these
valleys are called moraines and were deposited by retreating glaciers.

The Great Divide also serves as the boundary between Alberta and
British Columbia, Banff National Park and Yoho National Park.

82.9   **Kicking Horse Pass Viewpoint.** The crest of the Kicking Horse Pass lies   **45.3**
51.6   below the viewpoint at an elevation of 1625 metres (5,333 ft). The pass   *28.1*
was named by the geologist Dr. James Hector of the Palliser Expedition.

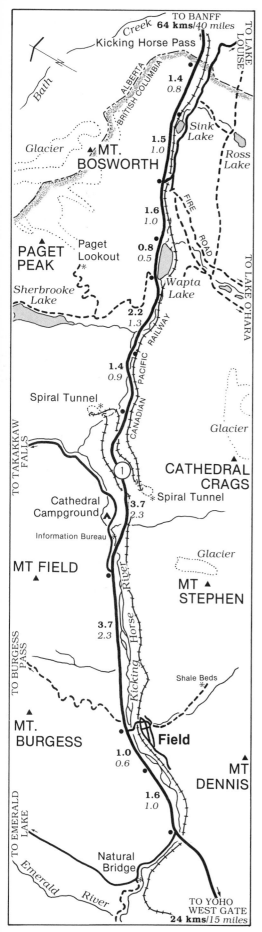

While exploring the pass in 1858, Hector was kicked by a packhorse and, while in an unconscious state, almost buried by his grieving Stoney Indian guides.

The right-of-way for the Canadian Pacific Railway was surveyed through this rugged gap in 1881, and three years later, the rails crested the height of land on their way west.

83.7   **Sink Lake Picnic Area.** Below the picnic area to the south lies Sink   **44.5**
52.0   Lake, so called because it has no visible outlet. Not unlike many such   *27.7*
lakes in the Rockies, its waters probably drain through channels underground.

85.2   **Bow Valley Parkway Junction.** This is the westerly terminus of a 64   **43.0**
53.0   kilometre (40 mile) scenic parkway which parallels the Trans-Canada   *26.7*
Highway to a point near Banff townsite. It is an exellent option for travellers desiring a more leisurely drive and ever-changing scenic vistas. (See Bow Valley Parkway, page 76 .)

86.8   **Wapta Lake Viewpoint.** In addition to Wapta Lake which lies on the   **41.4**
54.0   opposite side of the highway, there are views to Narao Peak and Cathedral   *25.7*
Mountain further to the west.

The forest here is in an advanced stage of recovery from a forest fire which swept this part of the valley many decades ago. The pine and poplar trees which entered the area following the fire, are now being replaced by spruce which have grown to an even greater height and are slowly forcing the fire succession species out.

An Historic Sites and Monuments Board of Canada plaque at this pull-off commemorates the passage of Dr. James Hector over the Kicking Horse Pass in 1858 and describes the choice of the pass as the route for the Canadian Pacific Railway in the 1880's.

87.2   **Wapta Lake and Wapta Lodge.** Across the lake to the south, the   **41.0**
54.2   forested valley of Cataract Brook leads off to the Lake O'Hara region   *25.5*
(inquire at lodge about <u>bus service</u> to this area). To the left of the valley stand the rugged peaks of the Bow Range — Narao Peak (2913 m/9,557 ft) in the foreground and the white, glacier-clad slope of Mount Victoria (3464 m/11,365 ft) beyond. To the right of the valley rises a collection of mountains which includes Vanguard Peak (2465 m/8,086 ft), Cathedral Mountain (3189 m/10,464 ft), and the Cathedral Crags (3073 m/10,081 ft).

Wapta Lake lies at 1586 metres (5,203 ft) above sea level and serves as the headwaters for the Kicking Horse River. Wapta is the Stoney Indian word for "river".

87.6   **Wapta Lake Picnic Area.** Like so many picnic areas located in moder-   **40.6**
54.5   ately open terrain, this is the site of a rather large colony of Columbian   *25.2*
ground squirrels. These buff coloured rodents can often be seen standing upright near the entrances to underground burrows, uttering sharp barks of warning when intruders come too near. Of course, a few weeks into summer and they become inveterate beggars. Views from the picnic area include Wapta Lake and the peaks of the Bow Range to the southeast.

A trail strikes off from the rear of the picnic area and climbs for 1.6 kilometres (1.0 mile) through the subalpine forest on the lower slopes of Paget Peak. At the 1.6 kilometre mark, the trail branches, the left-hand option reaching Sherbrooke Lake 1.3 kilometres (0.8 mile) further on, the right-hand climbing for 2.0 kilometres (1.2 miles) to Paget Lookout and an exciting panorama of the upper Kicking Horse Valley.

89.0   **Sherbrooke Creek.**   **39.2**
55.3   *24.4*

89.8   **"The Big Hill".** Here, at an old abandoned bridge over the Kicking   **38.4**
55.8   Horse River, trains used to begin their long descent down the steep grade   *23.9*
of "The Big Hill" to the town of Field. When the Canadian Pacific Railway was pushed westward from the summit of the Kicking Horse Pass in 1884, the tracks dropped straight down this canyon at a dizzy 4.5 percent grade. The first train that tried to descend the hill ran out of control, derailed and killed three men. In later years, when passenger trains came to the top of the hill, they would stop to test their brakes and sanding equipment, then proceed with the utmost caution. It took four engines to bring a train up the grade, creeping along at a meagre four or five miles an hour. Finally, in 1909, with the completion of two spiral tunnels halfway down the hill, the grade was reduced and the problem alleviated. Watch for the Spiral Tunnel exhibit 1.4 kilometres (0.9 mile) west of this roadside stop.

Locomotives labour up the Kicking Horse Valley in the early days of the CPR.

Archives of the Canadian Rockies

91.2   **Spiral Tunnel Viewpoint.** When the Canadian Pacific Railway was   **37.0**
56.7   completed down the Kicking Horse Valley in 1884, the tracks dropped   *23.0*
straight down from the summit of the Kicking Horse Pass to the town of Field at a grade which reached 4.5 percent in some sections. The steep grade resulted in many accidents, several deaths and high operating costs. In 1909, the grade was reduced through the construction of two spiral tunnels — one inside of Mount Ogden (visible below this viewpoint) and another inside the Cathedral Crags (the towering mountain to the south). The work took two years to complete using 1000 men and at a cost of $1,500,000. The tunnel cut through Mount Ogden is 887 metres (2,910 feet) long, while that looping around inside the Cathedral Crags is 975 metres (3,200 feet) long. As a railway timetable of the day described it: "The whole thing is a perfect maze, the railway doubling back upon itself twice, tunnelling under mountains and crossing the river twice in order to cut down the grade." The construction of the two tunnels reduced the grade to a manageable 2.2 percent. Where it had taken four locomotives to manhandle a train up the grade at five or so miles per hour before, two engines could now handle the job at a brisk 25 miles per hour.

This point-of-interest is also an excellent viewpoint for the Yoho Valley stretching away to the north. The peaks in the distance encircle the head of the valley and are located on the edge of the Wapta Icefield. The most prominent of these is the snow and glacier-clad pyramid of Yoho Peak (2760 m/9,056 ft).

94.9   **Yoho Valley Road Junction.** This 13 kilometre (8 mile)-long side road   **33.3**
59.0   stretches to some of the outstanding features found in Yoho Park, includ-   *20.7*
ing the Meeting-of-the-Waters of the Yoho and Kicking Horse Rivers and Takakkaw Falls — the highest waterfall in Canada.

Yoho Valley Road. Just 800 metres (0.5 mile) up the road, you come to the main information bureau for this part of the park. In addition to the

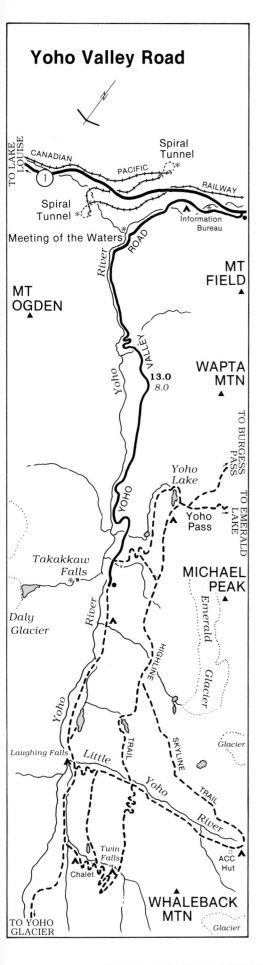

Yoho Valley Road

N

TO LAKE LOUISE

CANADIAN

PACIFIC

Spiral
Tunnel

RAILWAY

Spiral
Tunnel

Information
Bureau

Meeting of the Waters

River

ROAD

MT
OGDEN

MT
FIELD

Yoho

VALLEY

13.0
8.0

WAPTA
MTN

YOHO

Yoho
Lake

Yoho
Pass

TO BURGESS PASS

TO EMERALD LAKE

Takakkaw
Falls

Daly
Glacier

River

MICHAEL
PEAK

Emerald

Glacier

HIGHLINE

Yoho

Laughing Falls

TRAIL

Little

SKYLINE

Yoho

River

TRAIL

Glacier

Twin
Falls

Chalet

ACC
Hut

WHALEBACK
MTN

TO YOHO
GLACIER

Glacier

information and backcountry permits which are dispensed here, the parking area serves as an excellent viewpoint for this section of the Kicking Horse Valley.

This viewpoint is sandwiched between the cliffs of Mount Stephen on the south and Mount Field on the northwest. Looking to the lower slopes of Mount Field, at the foot of a sheer cliff, you can see a hole in the base of the wall beside a pile of black tailings. This is a shaft for the old Kicking Horse Mine. In 1884, during the construction of the Canadian Pacific Railway through the valley, lead-zinc ore was found in the talus at the foot of Mount Stephen. These finds resulted in the opening of the Kicking Horse Mine here on the slopes of Mount Field and the Monarch Mine high on the cliffs of Mount Stephen across the valley. Over a period of 60 years or so of intermittent operation, the mines yielded some 850,000 tons of ore. Grade on the ore was seven percent lead, ten percent zinc and 1.2 ounces of silver per ton. During the summer of 1952, operation of the mines became economically infeasible and they were closed down once and for all.

The sheer slopes of Mount Stephen are some of the most spectacular in the Canadian Rockies. The railway has cut a short tunnel through one of the cliffs at the base of the mountain, and on either side, snowsheds protect the tracks from winter avalanches.

At Kilometre 2.1 (Mile 1.3), a viewpoint looks across the valley to the Upper Spiral Tunnel in the slopes of the Cathedral Crags. The tunnel is one of two which circle back upon themselves to help reduce the grade of the Canadian Pacific Railway between Field and the Kicking Horse Pass.

Just 400 metres or so beyond the Spiral Tunnel Viewpoint, is an overlook for the "Meeting-of-the-Waters" — the junction of the Kicking Horse and Yoho Rivers. The rivers are veritable torrents, and the scene of their thundering together is quite awesome. Both rivers are fed from glaciers, yet the Kicking Horse is sparkling and clear while the Yoho is grey and silt-ridden. The answer to this riddle lies in a series of small lakes on the tributaries of the Kicking Horse which act as settling ponds for silty glacial outwash; the Yoho, on the other hand, is fed directly from the meltwater of glaciers which encircle the head of the valley less than 20 kilometres (12 miles) upstream.

One of the novelties of the trip up the Yoho Valley, is a pair of incredibly tight switchbacks that lift the road well above the floor of the valley in less than a kilometre. Travellers on tour buses get the biggest thrill from these tight turns, as their drivers are forced to back up until they bump the guard rails just inches from the sheer precipice in order to get their unwieldy vehicles around the 180 degree corners.

Beyond the switchbacks, the road travels through an area where avalanches have swept down from the upper slopes of Wapta Mountain, clearing trees from their paths and piling them on the valley floor like so many matchsticks.

Of course, the highlight of the Yoho Valley tour comes at the 13 kilometre (8 mile) mark where Takakkaw Falls thunders off a towering cliff of Cambrian limestone. Takakkaw Falls drops 380 metres (1,248 ft) to the valley floor, making it the highest waterfall in Canada and among the top dozen or so in the world. The falls are fed by the Daly Glacier — an arm of the Waputik Icefield which lies just out of sight beyond the top of the falls.

The road ends at the falls, and the trail bound for the uppermost reaches of the Yoho and Little Yoho Valley begins, leading to one of the outstanding hiking areas in the mountain parks.

A campground is located at Kilometre 1.1 (Mile 0.7), near the junction of the Yoho Valley road with the Trans-Canada Highway. Another walk-in campground is located 400 metres beyond the end of the road at Takakkaw Falls. Cathedral Mountain Chalets at Kilometre 1.0 offer accommodation, groceries and gasoline throughout the summer season.

Between the Field townsite junction and the Yoho Valley Road junction, the Trans-Canada Highway follows alongside the broad, gravel flats of the Kicking Horse River. Since the Kicking Horse is fed by the meltwaters of several nearby glaciers, it carries a great deal of gravel and silt in its water. When these fast-moving waters reach the gentler grade of the main valley bottom, their speed slows, their carrying capacity decreases, and much of this outwash material is deposited along these flats. Because silt and gravel are continually deposited here, the channels of the river are continually forced to shift and change, creating the braided stream pattern typical of all glacial outwash rivers.

98.2 **Burgess Pass Trail.** A parking area on the north side of the highway   **30.0**
61.1 serves as the trail head for the Burgess Pass hike. The trail leads to a high   *18.6*
col between Mounts Burgess and Field, 6.6 kilometres (4.1 miles) distant.

98.6 **Field Townsite Exit.** The townsite serves mainly as administration   **29.6**
61.3 headquarters for the park and a division point on the CPR line. Some   *18.4*
limited visitor services are available.

The village of Field is located at an elevation of 1242 metres (4,075 ft) above sea level — more than a vertical mile beneath the 3199 metre (10,495 ft) summit of Mount Stephen. The town was named for Cyrus W. Field, the promoter of the first trans-Atlantic cable, who journeyed to the Kicking Horse Valley shortly after the coming of the rails in 1884. A hotel, Mount Stephen House, was constructed near the railway station by the CPR in 1886, and it was the hub of tourist activity in the region until around 1918.

99.6 **Roadside Picnic Area.** This pleasant pull-off opposite the Kicking   **28.6**
61.9 Horse River offers an excellent panorama of this section of the valley, and   *17.8*
most particularly, the rugged slopes of Mount Stephen (3199 m/10,495 ft) looming above the village of Field.

Trilobite

Mount Stephen is typical of many peaks in the Main Ranges of the Rockies, being composed of shales, limestones and quartz sandstones that were deposited during the Cambrian period of the Paleozoic Era over 500 million years ago. At that point in geological history, life on the earth was limited to only a few primitive forms thriving in the oceans. In fact, geologists once thought life in these ancient oceans to be very limited indeed, until they discovered the fossil beds on the slopes of Mount Stephen and Mount Field. Some of the oldest and rarest fossils in the world have been uncovered on these slopes, most numerous being trilobites — crustacean-like animals common to the Cambrian seas.

Mount Stephen is named for George Stephen, the President of the Canadian Pacific Railway at the time of its construction through the Rockies.

101.2 **Emerald Lake Junction.** A 8.2 kilometre (5.1 mile)-long side road   **27.0**
62.9 leading northward to a striking blue-green lake at the foot of the President   *16.8*
Range.

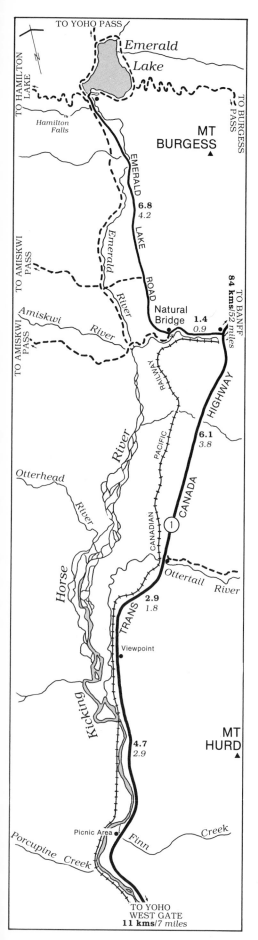

Tom Wilson, an early outfitter and guide in the Rockies, tells the story of how he tracked some pack horses out from the Kicking Horse Valley one summer's day in 1882:

"Through the bush, across small streams, then a little way up the mountain sides the tracks led me. After a time they returned to valley level alongside a creek that a few minutes later brought me to a beautiful sheet of water. I stood at the outlet of the mountain scenic gem known today as Emerald Lake."

This lucky discovery of Emerald Lake led to its becoming a major tourist attraction after the completion of the nearby Canadian Pacific Railway in 1885.

The lake's emerald colour is the result of silt-laden waters pouring into it from glaciers on the President Range. The fine, glacial flour remains suspended in the water, reflecting the green waves of the spectrum.

From the southern shore in front of the lodge, the peaks of the President Range rise across the water to the north, the most prominent Michael Peak at 2696 metres (8,844 ft) above sea level. By walking around to the west side of the lake on the shoreline trail to where an avalanche path has swept down to the lakeshore, a whole new perspective is gained, with the rugged summit of Mount Burgess (2583 m/8,473 ft) reflected in the blue-green waters.

A branch of the lakeshore trail near the north end of the lake leads to the broad alluvial fan which has washed out from the glaciers of the Emerald Basin to the northwest. While much silt makes its way into the waters of the lake, other silt and gravels have been deposited here in the form of a broad, fan-shaped flat, causing the inlet stream to break into several channels as it braids its way across the outwash plain to the lake.

Several trails lead out from the Emerald Lake vicinity, including branches from the lakeshore trail climbing to Yoho and Burgess Passes. A 5.5 kilometre (3.4 mile) trail makes a steep ascent from the west side of the parking area to a perfect hanging valley on the side of Emerald Peak containing Hamilton Lake.

Among several interesting features along the road to the lake, is the Natural Bridge on the Kicking Horse River at Kilometre 1.4 (Mile 0.9).

Emerald Lake Lodge provides accommodation and meals at the lake during the summer months.

| **101.4** | **Kicking Horse River Bridge.** | **26.8** |
| *63.0* | | *16.7* |

| **103.4** | **Highway Maintenance Camp.** | **24.8** |
| *64.3* | | *15.4* |

On the section of highway between the Ottertail River and the Highway Maintenance Camp, there are excellent views of the President Range — an island of high, glacier-clad mountains to the north (best seen by eastbound travellers). Several undesignated pull-offs can be used in viewing the range which lies between Emerald Lake and the Yoho Valley.

During the early part of this century, these mountains were a popular haunt of many world-renowned mountaineers, including Sir Edward Whymper — conqueror of the Matterhorn. Even today, they serve as a favourite recreation ground for hikers and ski mountaineers.

107.1 **Ottertail Valley Trail.** A gravel road cutting south from the highway **21.1**
66.6 serves as the beginning of a hiker's route up the Ottertail River. The trail *13.1*
stays low in this major valley all the way to the river's headwaters in
Kootenay Park.

107.3 **Ottertail River Bridge.** A small pull-off at the southwest end of the **20.9**
66.7 bridge provides a panoramic view of the President Range to the north. *13.0*
Looking to the slopes of Mount Hurd immediately to the south, you can
also see the blackened spars left in the wake of a fire which swept the
mountain in 1971.

110.2 **Kicking Horse Valley Viewpoint and Picnic Area.** This roadside pull- **18.0**
68.5 off overlooks the typical valley bottom habitat for a glacially-fed river. *11.2*
The floor of the valley is broad and flat, a result of the tons of gravel and
silt glacial outwash which have been spread across it. Forest cover is
spotty, consisting mainly of isolated stands of spruce and lots of low,
shrub willow; the ever-changing course of the river on these gravel-
choked flats has denied the stability necessary to develop a dense, mature
forest.

Above the river to the west, stands the forested ridge of Mount King,
streaked by the courses of winter avalanches.

The road-cut across the highway is composed primarily of Chancellor
Formation limestone. Several white veins of calcite run through the
formation, exhibiting many small compression folds. The general dip of
these bands, as well as that of the entire formation, is to the southwest.

114.9 **Finn Creek Picnic Area.** The picnic area is located on a flat by the shore **13.3**
71.4 of the Kicking Horse River, enclosed within a typical, low elevation *8.3*
forest of the western slope — western white spruce, lodgepole pine,
white birch and a few cottonwood poplars.

Looking like large bird nests, parasitic growths of dwarf mistletoe plague many spruce and pine trees in boggy sections of the valley.

White birch is not as commonly found east of the Great Divide as it is
here on the western slope. It is distinguished by its white bark which
seems to be forever peeling off in strips from around the trunk. Like
lodgepole pine and aspen, white birch relishes areas which have been
opened up by forest fire.

The most prominent mountain seen from the picnic area is Mount Hurd
(2827 m/9,275 ft) to the east; to the right of Mount Hurd, the summit of
Mount Vaux (3320 m/10,891 ft) peeks above a forested ridge.

116.3 **Kicking Horse River Viewpoint.** Mount Hunter is the long, forested **11.9**
72.3 ridge across the valley. Notice the gullies on the upper slopes of the *7.4*
mountain. In winter, snowslides originate near the summit of the ridge
and funnel down these gullies and into the forest below, sweeping trees
from their paths as they descend. These avalanche paths are visible in
summer as bright green, alder-covered swaths which look something like
ski runs cut through the forest.

117.9 **Glacier Striae Point-of-Interest.** Across the highway from this valley **10.3**
73.3 viewpoint are slabs of rock polished smooth by the passing of a large *6.4*
valley glacier during the last ice age. Rocks and gravel which were
imbedded in the "sole" of the glacier made small grooves and scratches
on the slab surface (notice how the scratches all line up in the same
direction, indicating the down-valley flow of the ice).

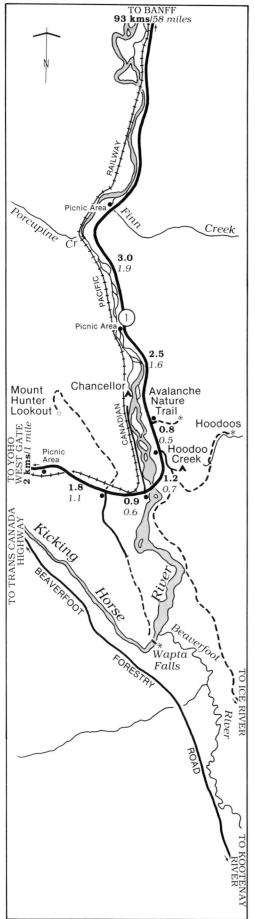

Further down-valley to the south are the relatively barren slopes of the Beaverfoot Range. These mountains lie beyond the boundaries of the national park and have been logged and burnt over by forest fires.

119.8 **Roadside Picnic Area.** A fire lookout tower is visible on the long ridge **8.4**
74.5 of Mount Hunter across the river to the west. On the opposite side of the *5.2*
valley, immediately to the east, rise the two craggy giants, Mount Vaux (3320 m/10,891 ft) and Chancellor Peak (3280 m/10,761 ft).

120.4 **Avalanche Nature Trail.** An excellent forest walk of a kilometre or so to **7.8**
74.9 the toe of a large avalanche slope and rock slide descending from the *4.8*
upper slopes of Mount Vaux (3320 m/10,891 ft).

Like so many areas along the Trans-Canada Highway, this was once swept by a forest fire. In the wake of this conflagration, lodgepole pine, aspen poplar, and white birch moved into the area — all species which depend upon fire to aid their reproduction and proliferation. But, since the fire, other species have begun to move in (particularly western white spruce), and one day these new trees will replace the fire succession species as the climax forest.

A few old Douglas fir trees may be found in this forest as well. These are the largest and oldest trees in the area, having survived the fire which swept this part of the valley over seventy years ago; their thick furrowed bark protected them from the killing heat and flame.

At the tip of the avalanche slope, you can look up to a narrow gully in the cliffs of Mount Vaux. Much rock debris has descended through this rift to the very edge of the forest. The rock slide now serves as an excellent path for snow avalanches, and many broken and fallen trees in the area bear witness to the most recent of these snowslides.

121.2 **Hoodoo Creek Campground.** A steep, 3.1 kilometre (1.9 mile) trail **7.0**
75.4 leads up from a parking area near the campground into the valley between *4.3*
Mount Vaux and Chancellor Peak to the Leanchoil Hoodoos. During the last ice age, much outwash (rock, gravel and silt) was deposited in the valleys by retreating glaciers. In the hoodoos area, this material has been partially cemented and, in many cases, protected from the forces of weathering beneath "cap-rocks". As a result, a hillside has been left with a ghostly army of clay, sand and gravel pillars topped with limestone hats.

Another short nature trail strikes off from the parking area near the campground, encircling an area of marsh and old beaver dams. Like most bog areas associated with past beaver activity, the surrounding forest is slowly encroaching in upon the swamp and will most likely reforest these flats in due time. The first warden cabin constructed in the park still stands along this trail. The cabin was built in 1904, shortly after the formation of Yoho Park, and its first permanent residents were Warden Jock Tocher and his wife in the early 1920's. The historic building is known both as the Tocher Cabin and the Deerlodge Cabin.

122.2 **Kicking Horse River Bridge.** **6.0**
76.0 *3.7*

122.4 **Chancellor Peak Campground.** The campground is located approx- **5.8**
76.1 imately 3 kilometres (2 miles) off the main highway via the old road on *3.6*

the west side of the river. The access road itself, particularly within the first 500 metres of the junction, makes a superb viewpoint for this section of the Kicking Horse Valley. Mount Vaux (3320 m/10,891 ft) and Chancellor Peak (3280 m/10,761 ft) tower majestically above the valley to the east, while Mount Ennis (3117 m/10,227 ft) stands at the head of the rugged amphitheatre between the two giants.

The Chancellor Peak Campground is situated in a typical river-bottom forest community of spruce, poplar and lodgepole pine. If you walk through this forest, you will probably see dense accumulations of material set within the branches of some of the trees, looking for all the world like huge bird nests. This is a parasite known as dwarf mistletoe, nicknamed witches'-broom. Mistletoe takes root in the branches through breaks or scars in the bark, drawing upon the tree for water and minerals. If the parasite continues to grow unchecked, it will eventually "starve" the tree to death through its demands for nourishment.

The Leanchoil Hoodoos.

123.3 **Wapta Falls and Mount Hunter Lookout Trails.** These two hikes of 2.4 **4.9**
76.7 kilometres (1.5 miles) and 3.5 kilometres (2.2 miles) respectively start *3.0*
on opposite sides of the highway. Wapta Falls, leading as it does to the largest waterfall in Yoho Park, is the more popular of the two trips.

To reach the actual trail head for the Wapta Falls hike, drive 1.6 kilometres (one mile) on the southbound Wapta Falls access road to the parking area for the trail. Wapta Falls is located at a bend in the Kicking Horse River where the water plunges over a broad cliff of impervious rock to form one of the most spectacular waterfalls in the park.

The Mount Hunter trail, which starts from the edge of the Trans-Canada Highway directly across from the Wapta Falls access road, climbs steadily along a gradually ascending ridge to an excellent panorama of the Kicking Horse Valley, Mount Vaux and Chancellor Peak, and the Beaverfoot River and Mountains.

125.1 **Roadside Picnic Area.** A forested picnic area located on a bend of the **3.1**
77.8 Trans-Canada Highway. *1.9*

Across the highway there is a major outcrop of very soft rock. The rock has many of the properties of talc. In fact, many local people refer to this rock as soapstone, though it cannot be carved due to the slaty cleavage which causes it to break easily along horizontal planes. It is believed this talc-like rock was originally limestone which, being along a major fault in the strata, was metamorphosed by heat and pressure into this softer material.

127.1 **Yoho Park Information Bureau.** **1.1**
79.0 *0.7*

127.9 **Warden Station.** **0.3**
79.5 *0.2*

128.2 **Yoho Park West Gate.** **0.0**
79.7

WESTBOUND	TRANS CANADA	EASTBOUND
Kilometres		**Kilometres**
Miles	HIGHWAY	*Miles*

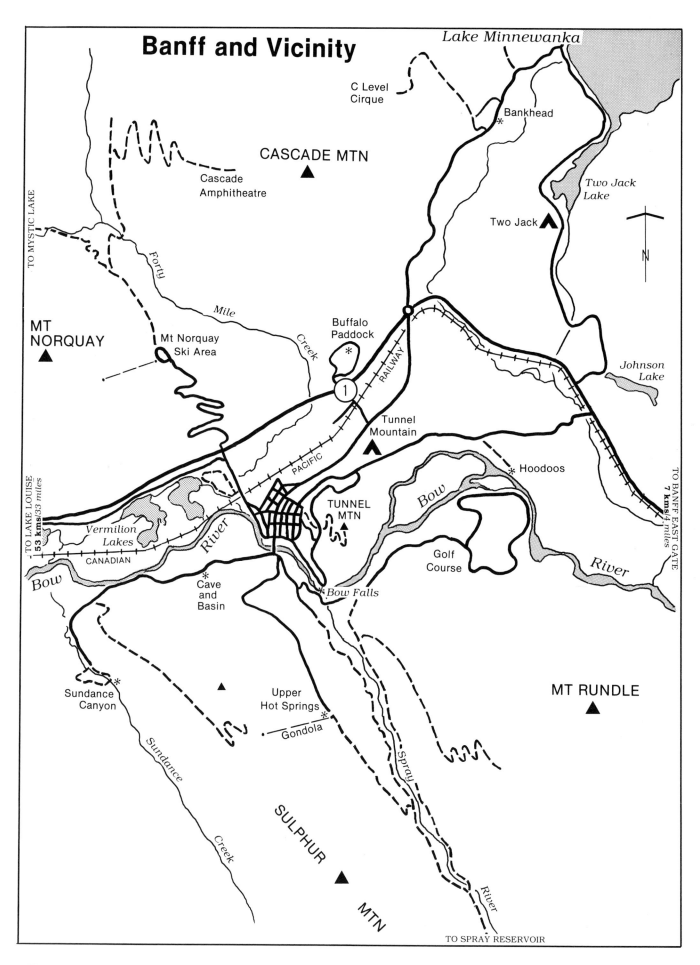

Banff and Vicinity

Lake Minnewanka

C Level
Cirque

Bankhead

Two Jack
Lake

CASCADE MTN ▲

Cascade
Amphitheatre

Two Jack ▲

*Johnson
Lake*

TO MYSTIC LAKE

Forty

Mile

MT
NORQUAY ▲

Mt Norquay
Ski Area

Creek

Buffalo
Paddock

RAILWAY

1

Tunnel
Mountain ▲

PACIFIC

Hoodoos

Bow

TO LAKE LOUISE
53 kms/33 miles

*Vermilion
Lakes*

CANADIAN

River

TUNNEL
MTN ▲

Bow

River

TO BANFF EAST GATE
7 kms/4 miles

Bow

Cave
and
Basin

Bow Falls

Golf
Course

Sundance
Canyon

▲

Upper
Hot Springs

Gondola

MT RUNDLE ▲

Sundance

Creek

SULPHUR

MTN ▲

Spray

River

TO SPRAY RESERVOIR

N

Banff and Vicinity

Banff is the oldest and largest of the townsites in the mountain parks, and it undoubtedly owes its existence to the discovery of hot mineral springs on the slopes of nearby Sulphur Mountain by two railway construction workers in 1883. Attempting to capitalize on the sulphur waters, the two workmen staked a claim to the springs and erected crude bathing facilities. In 1885, a government agent who visited the springs recommended these natural wonders be protected within a federal reserve. Believing the springs to be of "great sanitary advantage to the public", the Canadian government passed an Order-in-Council in November of 1885 creating a 10 acre preserve around the Cave and Basin Springs. Two years later, the area was expanded to some 260 square miles and designated as the Rocky Mountains National Park. Canada's first national park had been born.

As a means of promoting its newly constructed trans-continental line, the Canadian Pacific Railway set about building a number of luxury hotels in the mountain west. One of these was the Banff Springs Hotel, constructed on the south bank of the Bow River and opened for business in 1888. Other hotels and visitor services sprang up simultaneously on the north side of the river, and the town of Banff was on its way.

Named for Banffshire in Scotland, the birthplace of CPR President George Stephen, Banff soon became the major tourist centre for the Rocky Mountains, attracting wealthy visitors from around the world. Outfitters led pack trains on excursions into the mountains, and guides were imported from Switzerland by the CPR to lead clients to the summits of the many unclimbed peaks. In this way, much of the country beyond the town was first explored.

Through the early decades of this century travel to the park was primarily by train, a luxury reserved for the well-to-do. In fact, automobiles were prohibited in the park prior to 1915. But, with the construction of a roadway from Calgary in 1909, and the subsequent extension and improvement of roads within the park over the ensuing years, the automobile became an important means of access to Banff.

Today, Banff is a bustling town of some 4,000 year-round inhabitants, offering a long list of visitor services.

Roadways near Banff townsite. Banff townsite is fortunate in having one of the best networks of scenic roads available anywhere in the mountain parks. There is virtually no major feature in this section of the Bow Valley that cannot be viewed from one of these drives. While many visitors prefer to motor along these roads, stopping at the various pull-offs and viewpoints, the scenic drives are more ideally suited to bicycle excursions (bicycle rentals are available in the townsite). Roads are generally narrow and wind through the countryside, with the round-trip length of most tours averaging from five to 25 kilometres.

Downtown Banff as it appeared in 1888.
Archives of the Canadian Rockies

The Cave and Basin pool before the turn of the century.

Public Archives of Canada

Cave and Basin — Sundance Canyon Tour. 5.3 kilometres (3.3 miles) one-way. Starting from downtown Banff, cross the Bow River bridge and turn right onto Cave Avenue. The street leads out of town to the west, arriving at the Cave and Basin bathhouse in one mile.

The Cave and Basin Springs are the birthplace of Canada's national parks. It was around these hot mineral springs that a ten acre federal reserve was created in 1885, the core of today's Banff National Park. In the early days, bathers would descend into the Cave by means of a ladder through a hole in the cavern's ceiling, but since then a tunnel has been burrowed into the chamber so visitors might view this historic site. The maximum temperature of the Cave Spring is around 33°C (91°F) while the nearby Basin Spring is usually a degree or two warmer.

The Cave and Basin pool facilities are adjacent to this historic site and are being renovated by Parks Canada for the 1985 centennial of the Canadian parks system.

The road passes through the Cave and Basin parking area and descends to the banks of the Bow River, providing open views across the valley to the slopes of Mount Norquay (2522 m/8,275 ft), and the sharp, dogtooth summit of Mount Edith (2554 m/8,380 ft). Both mountains have been eroded from limestones and shales that are around 350 million years old.

The flooded forest on the opposite side of the road is the result of beaver activity. Beaver moved into the area in the mid-1970's, blocked the road culverts, and utilized the roadway as a dam. Watch for woodpeckers and swallows which make their homes in the flooded trees.

Further along on the right, one comes to more marshy areas, and a beautifully constructed beaver dam which contains a small pond. The pond is spring-fed, so it never freezes to the bottom. (It is unlikely that human engineers would have utilized nature so cleverly.) Watch for moose throughout these marshlands.

Enclosed within a forest of pine and spruce at the end of the road is the Sundance Canyon Picnic Area. A short two kilometre (1.3 mile) loop trail leads up along Sundance Creek from the rear of the picnic area and into the canyon, the first 400 metres or so of the trail running along a series of cascades and among huge boulders which have tumbled off the nearby cliffs. It is interesting to note that Sundance Canyon is located at the mouth of a large valley which once served as a major tributary to the Bow River, but thanks to the erosion of a gap at the southern end of the Sulphur Mountains ridge, the valley has been robbed of most of its runoff by the Spray River.

Vermilion Lakes Drive. 4.8 kilometres (3.0 miles) one-way. This road branches from the Mount Norquay Drive just south of the Trans-Canada Overpass (Banff's west exit), then runs quietly beneath that busy through-way for a leisurely trip along the Vermilion Lakes, a marshy overflow area for the Bow River.

At Kilometre 0.8 (Mile 0.5) the road arrives at the first Vermilion Lake. The lake is very shallow and fringed by grasses, rushes, sedges and swamp horsetail. Further back from the lake, on slightly drier ground, are the shrubs — willow, black currant, and bracted honeysuckle. Beyond these wetland shrubs comes the forest, mainly western white spruce with a few poplars. Here we have an excellent example of plant succession: as the lake slowly fills with silt and vegetative matter, the sedge-horsetail community will gradually encroach further and further into the lake, with the willow-shrub community close behind. Eventually, the lake and open area will totally disappear, reverting to the final stage of plant succession — a mature, climax spruce forest.

Actually, plant succession would have asserted itself long ago were it not for the activities of the local beaver. The first two Vermilion Lakes are little more than a giant beaver pond, and their water levels are controlled by a small dam which these industrious rodents have constructed on a nearby outflow creek. If the beaver were to abandon their dam, as has happened on occasion in the past, the lakes would become plant-choked sloughs.

In the middle of the First Vermilion Lake is an osprey nest. These fish-eating birds nest here annually, except for one season when a pair of Canada geese took over the nest and forced the ospreys to build elsewhere. Bald eagles have also used the Vermilion Lakes as a nesting ground in recent years.

Looking to the slope across the road from the lake, there is a very different type of forest cover. Here, the dry, south-facing exposure produces a typical open montane forest of Douglas fir, lodgepole pine, spruce and aspen. These slopes are also frequented by a herd of bighorn sheep which ranges along the lower reaches of Mount Norquay.

The second Vermilion Lake is less than a kilometre further along, and it displays much the same characteristics of plant succession as the first. Fish, too, are affected by the shallowness of these lakes. In winter, sunlight cannot penetrate the snow cover on the lakes, and the abundant aquatic plant life begins to die and decompose. As this process advances, the lakes become oxygen-starved and fish begin to die. The problem is at its worst during severe winters when the ice freezes nearly to the bottom of the lake, forcing the fish into a more confined space. Brook trout are the main inhabitants of the lakes, as rainbow trout seem more sensitive to the marginal oxygen situation.

Further along the second lake you will find the lodges and dams of a small beaver colony. Muskrat, too, are often seen swimming among the rushes along the shore.

The third and deepest Vermilion Lake is fed by a warm spring which passes under the road near the far end of the lake. The warm water keeps plants green in this corner of the lake year round, and a small patch of water is always open in winter making this a favourite fishing ground for slate-coloured birds called dippers.

The road ends at a small picnic area a short distance from the Trans-Canada Highway. Across the highway from this turn-around, is the trail to Edith and Cory Passes. A short distance up the Cory option gives an outstanding perspective of the Vermilion Lakes and the Bow Valley.

Dipper

Mount Norquay Drive. 5.8 kilometres (3.6 miles) one-way. This is one of the most scenic drives in the Banff vicinity, climbing to a viewpoint 300 metres (1,000 feet) above the valley floor.

To reach the Mount Norquay Road, follow the 'Highway 1 Westbound' signs out of town to the Trans-Canada interchange (Banff's west exit). Continue across the overpass and begin the steady, switchback ascent of Mount Norquay.

As with most south-facing slopes, this side of Mount Norquay is relatively dry and open, clothed by a forest of western white spruce, lodgepole pine, and aspen poplar with a few stands of Douglas fir. Mule deer are often seen along the roadway, as are bighorn sheep, both animals displaying a preference for the dry, open slopes where grasses are readily available as forage.

At a switchback 3.5 kilometres (2.2 miles) from the Trans-Canada overpass, there is an outcrop of steeply-tilted shale. The beds were formed from silt and mud deposited on the floor of a shallow ocean during the Triassic Period some 220 million years ago. By Canadian Rockies' standards, it is a relatively young formation.

Though there are several good viewpoints from the road looking out over the Bow Valley, the best is the last and highest one beside a broad, green meadow, 5.0 kilometres (3.1 miles) from the Trans-Canada Highway. From this overlook at 1675 metres (5,000 feet) above sea level, the major mountains and valleys to the south and east of Banff are all visible. Dominating the scene beyond the town is the gigantic, sloping summit of Mount Rundle (2949 m/9,675 ft) — a dipping-strata or "writing desk" type of mountain with beds of limestone and shale rising in a steady, even slope from the southwest to a sheer drop-off on the northeast face. Mount Rundle also displays the famous "sandwich" arrangement of rock formations so common in the Front Ranges surrounding Banff, with massive limestone cliffs in both its base and summit, and the gentler, eroded talus slopes of a shale formation sandwiched between.

Behind the Banff Springs Hotel, the U-shaped valley of the Spray River enters from the southeast; its shape is typical of all glacially-carved valleys. A major fault, or fracture, in the strata runs along the base of Sulphur Mountain beneath its northeast slope, and all of Banff's hot mineral springs surface near the strike of the fault.

The open meadow adjacent to the viewpoint is known locally as the "Green Spot." Like most slopes above the Bow Valley, this was swept by a forest fire sometime near the turn of the century. Around the fringes of the meadow, however, are huge Douglas fir trees which survived the conflagrations of the past, thanks primarily to their thick, fire-resistant bark. The meadow is populated by a rather large colony of Columbian ground squirrels.

Less than a kilometre above the viewpoint the road ends at the Mount Norquay Lodge and ski area. In summer, the area operates a gondola-chair lift to the 2100 metre (7,000 foot) level on the mountain where views of the Bow Valley are even more exceptional than the roadside panorama below. Trails lead out from Parking Lot #3 below the lodge to the summit of Stoney Squaw, the Cascade Amphitheatre and Elk Lake.

Lake Minnewanka Loop Drive. 13.5 kilometres (8.4 miles) from the Banff Traffic Circle back to the Trans-Canada Highway near Anthracite. This is the longest tour in the Banff vicinity (actually closer to 25 kilometres round-trip from the townsite), and one of the most popular since it visits the largest lake in Banff park.

The road branches from the traffic circle three kilometres east of Banff (the town's east exit on the Trans-Canada Highway) and runs north along the base of 2998 metre (9,836 ft) Cascade Mountain, the highest peak in the Banff vicinity. The waterfall which gives the mountain its name plunges over a towering cliff of Palliser limestone just beyond the traffic circle.

At Kilometre 2.9 (Mile 1.8) a long abandoned mining town is commemorated at a roadside point-of-interest. In the valley below the road, the coal mining town of Bankhead flourished from 1904 to 1923, digging anthracite from the Cretaceous Kootenay Formation beneath the cliffs of Cascade Mountain. All that remains of the town, which once housed around 1,000 residents, are a few concrete foundations.

As you look to the massive cliffs of Cascade Mountain, it is curious to note that the limestone which composes these massive walls is much older than the coal-bearing formation beneath it. During the uplift and deformation of the range some 70 million years ago the bedding was fractured by tremendous forces applied to the earth's crust, and shoved up and over the younger rock.

Only 500 metres beyond the Lower Bankhead point-of-interest, a gravel road branches left, leading to the parking area for Upper Bankhead and the trail to C-Level Cirque — a 3.9 kilometre (2.4 mile) hike to a small, bowl-shaped depression gouged into the lower cliffs of Cascade Mountain. Along the way, remnants of the old Bankhead coal mining operation are encountered in the form of concrete foundations and mounds of tailings.

At Kilometre 4.3 (Mile 2.7) the road passes the entrance to the Cascade Fire Road — a limited access road often used by hikers who wish to visit the remote eastern valleys of the park.

Lake Minnewanka is reached at Kilometre 5.5 (Mile 3.4). The loop drive continues to the right across the crest of the earth-filled dam, but a parking area across the road on the left provides a stopping point for those who would like to spend some time along the lakeshore or on one of the boat tours which run during the summer season. A five minute walk leads one past the boat concession to a pleasant picnic area beside the lake.

Just off the point of land from the picnic area the foundations of the small resort town of Minnewanka Landing lie in silence beneath the cold waters of the lake. The resort flourished during the early years of this century, but was abandoned with the construction of the reservoir.

Beyond the picnic area, at the end of the spur road, is a trail leading to Stewart Canyon, 0.8 kilometre (0.5 mile), and on along the north shore of Lake Minnewanka to its eastern end. The short hike to Stewart Canyon is of interest as this gorge once contained the tributary Cascade River before the dam backed Minnewanka's waters into it. Steeply tilted slabs of limestone comprise the canyon's walls.

Continuing the loop drive across the earth-filled dam, the road passes a viewpoint overlooking the lake. Though Minnewanka has always been one of the largest lakes in this section of the Rockies, thanks to the dam it is an even greater body of water today than before the coming of the white man. The lake was first raised by 3.5 metres (12 feet) in 1912 and by another 20 metres (65 feet) in 1941.

George Simpson, Governor of the Hudson's Bay Company, entered the Rocky Mountains by way of Devil's Gap at the eastern end of the lake in 1841, and, in passing along its north shore, named it Peechee's Lake in honour of his Indian guide who was said to make his home here. The lake was known as Devil's Lake or Devil's Head Lake by both Indian and white man just prior to the turn of the century, but was eventually changed to Minnewanka (meaning "lake of the water spirit") by the Department of the Interior.

The mountains across the lake to the north comprise the southern end of the Palliser Range, while the massive cliffs of Mount Inglismaldie (2964 m/9,725 ft) contain the lake to the south.

Upon leaving the Lake Minnewanka viewpoints, the road climbs over a ridge and descends to Two Jack Lake Picnic Area and Campground. South of Two Jack Lake the road follows along a canal used to funnel most of the outflow from Lake Minnewanka to the turbines of the Cascade Power Station.

The mining town of Bankhead.
Archives of the Canadian Rockies

Early sport on Lake Minnewanka — iceboating circa 1890.
Archives of the Canadian Rockies

Johnson Lake is the last stop of interest on the Minnewanka circuit. Situated on the east side of the road just 500 metres from the road's intersection with the Trans-Canada Highway, the lake is set on an open, dry, south-facing slope, surrounded by Douglas fir, and the usual stands of fire-succession lodgepole pine. The lake is often visited by waterfowl including the park's only nesting common loons, and muskrat are commonly seen swimming about in its waters. Magpies, gray jays and chickadees frequent the surrounding forest.

If you are returning to Banff townsite turn left on the Trans-Canada Highway at the junction and drive east for 500 metres to the intersection with the Tunnel Mountain Road.

Tunnel Mountain Drive. 6.8 kilometres (4.2 miles) one-way. This road is usually travelled as an extension of the Lake Minnewanka Loop tour, and it offers more points-of-interest and exceptional views than any other drive in the Banff vicinity.

From its intersection with the Trans-Canada Highway, the Tunnel Mountain Road crosses the CPR tracks and the Cascade River, then climbs the glacial outwash bench extending eastward from Tunnel Mountain. At Kilometre 2.3 (Mile 1.4) the road reaches the parking area for the Hoodoos nature trail — a short ten minute walk to a number of weirdly shaped pillars carved from the silts and gravels of the outwash bench. While much of the well-sorted and stratified material in this steep bank overlooking the Bow River is in the process of erosion, some of the gravel and sand has been cemented by lime mud, making it more resistant to weathering. Thus, the slope erodes leaving the consolidated material standing in the form of pillars called hoodoos.

A pull-off 600 metres (0.4 mile) beyond the Hoodoos nature trail gives an excellent perspective of Mount Rundle, Tunnel Mountain and the gap separating the two. At one time Tunnel Mountain was connected to Mount Rundle as a part of one long, continuous ridge, but during the Pleistocene ice advances water courses were altered. During this period of dramatic change either the Bow River or Spray River was diverted over the Mount Rundle ridge, and in time it cut down through the bedrock to create the gap we see here.

A short walk along these slopes will give the visitor a close-up look at a montane forest environment. As a south-facing slope, the hillside is open and dry, populated by isolated stands of aspen poplar, Douglas fir and lodgepole pine. Creeping ground cover such as shrub juniper and kinnikinnick help to consolidate the easily eroded soil, while woody shrubs such as buffalo berry and shrubby cinquefoil populate the partially shaded areas. True montane forest, such as this, occurs in only a few limited areas in the mountain parks.

Another tree growing on the slope is limber pine. A rare species in the mountain parks, limber pine differs from the more common lodgepole in that its needles grow from the branches in bundles of five (lodgepole produces its needles in pairs); limber pine cones are substantially larger than those of lodgepole, seldom measuring less than 7 centimetres (3 in.) in length. Limber pine is another indicator of the dry, montane environment.

TURN TO PAGE 65 —

Mount Rundle from the Vermilion Lakes.

Golden-mantled ground squirrel on Sulphur Mountain.

Banff from the summit of Sulphur Mountain.

Lake Minnewanka from the
trail to C-Level Cirque.

Autumn aspen in the Bow Valley.

Castle Mountain.

Fireweed in the Vermilion Pass burn.

Marble Canyon.

Sunrise on Mount Victoria and Lake Louise.

Moraine Lake in the Valley of the Ten Peaks.

Takakkaw Falls.

The Leanchoil Hoodoos.

At Kilometre 3.9 (Mile 2.4), opposite the main entrance to Tunnel Mountain Campground, there is another fine viewpoint for Mount Rundle, Tunnel Mountain and the Bow River gap. As the interpretive sign at the overlook states, this is an excellent place to study the Palliser limestone-Banff shale-Rundle limestone "sandwich" of formations in the slopes of Mount Rundle. The limestone formations show up as massive cliffs in the summit and near the base of the mountain, while the shale formation comprises a narrow band of eroded and more moderately inclined rock between the other two.

At Kilometre 4.5 (Mile 2.8), the road reaches an intersection in the midst of a chalet-condominium development. By continuing straight ahead, you will drop directly into Banff townsite, but dedicated sightseers will prefer to turn left and continue the drive up and onto the lower slopes of Tunnel Mountain.

A viewpoint 800 metres (0.5 mile) beyond the intersection looks out over the Bow Valley to the major mountains north of the townsite. Starting on the right is Cascade Mountain (2998 m/9,836 ft), the highest mountain overlooking Banff and certainly the most impressive from this vantage point; Stoney Squaw is the low mountain to the left of Cascade; and Mount Norquay, with the well-defined ski runs descending its slopes, rises beyond Stoney Squaw to the west. Across the road from this pull-out there is an outcrop of Mississippian age limestone — rock which was formed some 320 million years ago. Noisy and bold Clark's nutcrackers are common on these slopes throughout the year.

Clark's nutcracker.

Yet another pull-off on the slopes of Tunnel Mountain occurs further along. This overlook gives a more direct view down the Bow Valley to the west. It is easy to see the distinctive U-shape of the valley from here, a characteristic of all glacially carved valleys. The snow-capped peaks of the Massive Range stand up-valley on the far horizon. The trail to the Tunnel Mountain summit ridge strikes off into the trees on the opposite side of the road. A short climb of less than an hour brings the hiker to an excellent viewpoint for the Bow and Spary Valleys and the mountains ringing the town of Banff.

The road drops down from the viewpoint and passes above the Banff Centre campus. Before entering the townsite via Buffalo Street, there is one last viewpoint on the left — a fine overlook of the Bow Falls, Banff Springs Hotel and the long range of Sulphur Mountain.

Sulphur Mountain Road. 3.5 kilometres (2.2 miles) one way. To reach the road up Sulphur Mountain, start from downtown Banff, cross the Bow River bridge and turn left, keeping right at the next intersection to follow Mountain Avenue uphill past the Park Administration Building.

The road soon climbs past the last townsite homes and into a forest composed primarily of fire succession lodgepole pine. The drive along the lower slopes of the mountain is rather uneventful but for a few glimpses of the town and the Bow Valley through the trees on the left side of the road. Two large parking areas at the end of the road serve the two main attractions of the drive — the Upper Hot Spring and the Sulphur Mountain Gondola Lift.

Of the eight distinct springs along the face of Sulphur Mountain, the Upper Hot Spring is the warmest, with a maximum temperature near 47°C (117°F). Like all hot mineral springs in the Canadian Rockies, the Upper Hot Spring is the result of snow melt and rain runoff seeping into joints and fractures in the limestone bedrock. The waters work their way down several thousand metres beneath the earth's surface where they are heated and percolated upward to where they emerge in the springs. The mineral content of the water is acquired from the bedrock which the waters pass through on their round-trip journey from the surface. In addition to substantial amounts of calcium and magnesium (minerals contained within limestone and dolomitic bedrock), the springs exhibit a slight radioactivity, a factor which has led people to believe in their medicinal value. The distinctive smell of the water is due to the presence of hydrogen sulfide. The Upper Hot Spring bathhouse facilities are open on a year-round basis.

Just below the Upper Hot Spring parking lot is the Sulphur Mountain Gondola Lift. The gondola conveys visitors to the summit ridge of Sulphur Mountain — at nearly 2300 metres (7,500 ft) above sea level, the outstanding vantage point in the Banff vicinity.

From the summit teahouse, you can look down on the town of Banff and trace the courses of rivers both past and present. The gap cut by the Bow River between Tunnel Mountain and Mount Rundle is particularly evident from this angle, and it is easy to see how the river must have once run on the opposite side of Tunnel Mountain, flowing out of the mountains via the broad valley which now contains Lake Minnewanka (the lake is just visible in the distance to the northwest). Glacial damming probably played a role in forcing the Bow into this strange new course, perhaps by creating a lake whose outlet poured over the long, unbroken ridge of Mount Rundle and thereby initiating the cutting action which eventually created the gap.

Other mountains across the valley from the Sulphur Mountain summit are Cascade Mountain with its distinctive limestone-shale-limestone sandwich structure, and Mount Norquay with the grassy ski runs descending its slopes. The long ridge of peaks paralleling Sulphur to the southwest is the Sundance Range, distinguished by the many bowl-shaped cirques carved into its slopes by the plucking action of alpine glaciers during ice ages past.

The summit of Sulphur Mountain also displays life forms typical of a timberline environment. Trees thin out and become more stunted, particularly on the southwest side of the ridge which is exposed to the prevailing winds of the region. Timberline forest species such as the five-needled whitebark pine and the deciduous alpine larch grow here. Flowers are affected by altitude and exposure too, with typical subalpine forest species such as heart-leaved arnica, fringed grass-of-parnassus, golden fleabane, and asters thriving on the cooler, more protected northeast slope. Meanwhile ground-clinging alpine plants such as white mountain avens and the heathers inhabit the dry, open, southwesterly exposure.

Animal inhabitants of the summit ridge include both Columbian and golden-mantled ground squirrels, chipmunks, and the occasional band of bighorn sheep. Birdlife includes the ubiquitous gray jays and Clark's nutcrackers as well as varied thrushes, Swainson's thrushes, ruby-crowned kinglets, and white-crowned sparrows.

Golf Course Loop Tour. 11.3 kilometres (7 miles) round trip. A favourite trip for cyclists around the pleasantly forested roadway which circles through the Banff Springs Golf Course and travels through the gap between Tunnel Mountain and Mount Rundle. In fact, the road is not recommended for motorists beyond the Bow Falls viewpoint.

The golf course loop road is reached from downtown Banff by crossing the Bow River Bridge and turning left onto Spray Avenue. Follow the avenue for 800 metres (0.5 mile), turning left at the sign indicating Bow

Falls and Golf Course. This side road leads downhill and to the right, reaching the Bow Falls parking area in 500 metres (0.3 mile).

Waterfalls in the mountains always seem to form where a river has been recently (geologically speaking) forced out of its channel. The Bow Falls would appear to be no exception, probably having been diverted from its channel on the north side of Tunnel Mountain during the last ice age when the valley was dammed by glacial debris to form a large lake. Forced to find a new outlet, the water pushed around this side of Tunnel Mountain and cascaded over a cliff of Triassic age limestone. With the passage of time, the cliff eroded back to form the cascades seen here today. Also, notice how steeply tilted the bedrock is on either side of the falls.

From the Bow Falls viewpoint the road crosses the Spray River bridge and officially enters the Banff Springs Golf Course grounds. The road winds down to the end of the 18-hole course, continuing on until it is turned back by the Bow River. Views of the towering ramparts of Mount Rundle are outstanding from the road, as are those to the vertical east wall of Tunnel Mountain, a popular training ground for rock climbers.

The valley-bottom grasslands outside the golf course fence make excellent winter grazing for elk herds. Of course, the rich, exotic grasses on the fairways and greens are a welcome delicacy for these animals whenever they are clever enough to discover a breach in the fences.

An early log drive above Bow Falls, ca. 1890.
Archives of the Canadian Rockies

POINTS OF INTEREST WITHIN BANFF TOWNSITE.

Park Information Bureau. A large stone building located in the 200 block of Banff Avenue houses the Parks Canada Information Bureau. An excellent place to stop if you have any questions about the park, or simply need directions to find your way around the townsite. The bureau distributes all government-produced literature on the park as well as a complete selection of topographical maps. Slide presentations on mountain natural history are offered continually throughout the day. Open seven days a week throughout the summer season and on a somewhat more limited schedule during the winter.

The Peter and Catharine Whyte Foundation. A beautiful and unique building set within the trees between Bear Street and Bow Avenue just a half block north of the post office. The facility is divided into four main parts — the Public Library, the Peter Whyte Gallery, the Archives of the Canadian Rockies and the Banff Heritage Homes. The gallery presents an on-going series of shows usually centred upon painting and crafts of both regional and national origin. The Archives of the Canadian Rockies is a storehouse of information on anything and everything to do with the mountain west and, in addition to its own collections, houses the Alpine Club of Canada Library on world mountaineering. The heritage homes which are dotted about the grounds provide a glimpse of the lifestyle of early Banff. Facilities in the main building are open year around, and tours of the heritage homes are provided during the summer season.

Park Museum. Centrally located in the town park on Banff Avenue just before the Bow River bridge. The museum keeps an excellent collection of mounted specimens covering most of the common animals and birds found in the mountain parks. Open throughout the year.

The Luxton Museum. This replica of an early fur trade fort is reached by crossing the Bow River bridge and turning right onto Birch Avenue along the banks of the Bow. Founded by one of the town's early residents, the museum concentrates on the history of the Rocky Mountains and the adjacent plains, displaying relics from the fur trade era, artifacts from the local Indian cultures and some preserved specimens of indigenous wildlife. Open daily throughout the year.

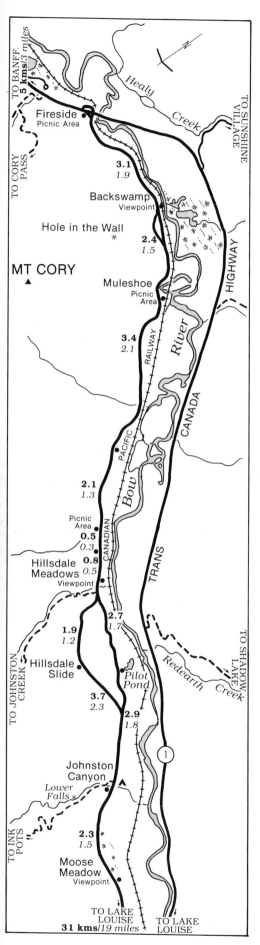

Bow Valley Parkway

The Bow Valley Parkway is an excellent alternative to the Trans-Canada Highway through Banff National Park.

The Parkway is actually the original highway (with some modifications) which ran from Banff to Lake Louise and over the Kicking Horse Pass into British Columbia. With the completion of the Trans-Canada Highway through the Parks around 1958, approximately 65 kilometres (40 miles) of the old roadway were left to serve as a scenic alternative to the more congested, higher speed Trans-Canada route. For many years it was known as the 1-A (alternate) Highway.

Forty-eight kilometres (30 miles) of the Bow Valley Parkway, between Banff and Lake Louise, parallel the Trans-Canada on the northeastern side of the Bow Valley. Near the service centre at Lake Louise, the two roads cross paths, the Parkway climbing the southwest side of the valley to Lake Louise. It eventually ends its journey by crossing the Kicking Horse Pass and rejoining the Trans-Canada Highway near Wapta Lake in Yoho National Park.

Because it climbs and winds, the Bow Valley Parkway seems to allow a much better perspective of the scenery in this section of Banff Park than does the straighter, less varied Trans-Canada (of course, lower speeds and less traffic help a lot). The route does offer better views of the rugged peaks of the Great Divide which rise on the southwest side of the Bow Valley. All campgrounds in this part of the valley are located along the Bow Valley Parkway as well, and you must use the Parkway to gain access to Lake Louise and the Valley of the Ten Peaks.

Eastbound travellers turn to page 76 and work backwards, following distances in the right-hand margin.

WESTBOUND Kilometres *Miles*	BOW VALLEY PARKWAY	EASTBOUND Kilometres *Miles*
0.0	**Junction with the Trans-Canada Highway** 5.6 kilometres (3.5 miles) west of Banff.	**64.4** *40.0*
0.5 *0.3*	**Fireside Picnic Area.** At the intersection of the Bow Valley Parkway with the picnic area access road, there is an interpretive exhibit describing the formation of the Bow Valley and introducing visitors to the first 49 kilometres (30 miles) of the Parkway.	**63.9** *39.7*

This particular stop stands in the middle of some interesting geology. A couple of hundred metres east of the viewpoint the Bourgeau Thrust Fault (a major fracture in the bedrock along which formations have been displaced) cuts across the Bow Valley. Two lesser faults cut across the valley just west of the parking area. These thrust faults along with folding of the valley bedrock have caused the once horizontal strata to be tilted nearly vertical here and have placed many millions of years of geology together in one locale. The massive grey cliffs which rise from the edge of the Bow Valley Parkway a few metres west of this stop are Middle and Upper Cambrian limestones and dolomites (about 550 million years old); the higher cliffs which rise above these bluffs to the north are composed of Devonian-aged dolomites (approximately 350 million years old); and a short distance to the east, just across the Bourgeau Thrust Fault, are Triassic mudstone and shale formations which are only 200 million years old. All of these formations are jammed together like the pages of a book which has been turned up on edge.

Looking west from the viewpoint, the snowcapped mountains of the Massive Range dominate the horizon.

3.1
1.9
Backswamp Viewpoint. Below this elevated viewpoint, the Bow River winds eastward toward the town of **Banff**. Looking across the valley to the southeast (on your left), are the rugged mountains of the Sundance Range. Directly across the valley stands Mount Bourgeau (2931 m/9,615 ft), and further to the west, Mount Brett (2984 m/9,790 ft), and Massive Mountain (2435 m/7,990 ft).
61.3
38.1

Side-stream damming of the Bow Valley just east of here has caused a river overflow or "backswamp" condition in this part of the valley. Willow, dwarf birch, sedges, and stunted spruce trees populate the supersaturated flats visible across the river. The backswamp provides an excellent environment for moisture-loving plants and ideal habitat for moose.

5.5
3.4
Muleshoe Picnic Area. The picnic area receives its name from a curious horseshoe shaped lake which serves as an overflow arm of the Bow River. It may be that this lake was once a major bend in the main channel of the river which the eroding action of the stream has since cut off, allowing the river to by-pass this "bow". This is an excellent place to see migrating waterfowl such as mallard and harlequin ducks, Canada geese, and common mergansers.
58.9
36.6

Elk use the bark of aspen poplar trees as a winter food source.

A short nature trail strikes off across the road from the picnic area. The way is steep, but the open meadow at its culmination (one kilometre distant) provides an excellent view down to Muleshoe Lake. The trail is also a superb place to examine a dry, south-facing montane forest environment. Hikers should keep an eye out for the blue grouse which are common on this slope and listen for the numerous songbirds that are active here on summer mornings.

Looking east from the picnic area, you can also see the dark cavern of the Hole-in-the-Wall 600 vertical metres (2,000 ft) above in the cliff of Mount Cory. The cave penetrates the massive Palliser limestone for little more than 30 metres (100 ft), but the most amazing aspect of this high cave is that it was dissolved from the bedrock by the action of glacial ice and meltwater at a time when huge glaciers filled this valley from side to side to a level of some 2400 metres (8,000 ft) above sea level!

8.9
5.5
Experimental Range Study Plot. A pull-off on the southwest side of the road provides access to an interesting vegetation study area. Walk out onto the open flats beside the pull-off. Notice how the branches of willow and other low-growing shrubs have been snipped off, almost as clean as if a gardener with shears had trimmed them. The tips of these shrubs have been used by elk as an emergency winter food supply. Now walk over to the fenced-in range plot. Animals have been fenced out of this area since 1944, and you can get some idea of what the valley floor might look like without the presence of browsing animals.
55.5
34.5

Looking up-valley from the meadow, you can see the bastion-like cliffs of Castle Mountain. It was probably not far from this spot that Dr. James Hector of the Palliser Expedition first sighted the mountain during his explorations up the valley in 1858. Hector was so struck by the distinctive shape of the peak he named it Castle.

11.0   **Sawback Picnic Area.** An exhibit near the entrance to the picnic area   **53.4**
6.8   interprets the use of trees and bushes as a source of winter feed for elk.   *33.2*
The branches of willow and dwarf birch have been nibbled and pruned by these animals. Also, notice how the lower bark on the aspen trees has been eaten away to a uniform level of a little over one metre (4 feet) above the ground. Without this source of winter food, many of these animals would perish during hard winters. This meadow is one of the most popular winter feeding grounds for elk in this part of the valley.

Across the valley to the southwest towers Pilot Mountain (2954 m/9,690 ft), composed of nearly horizontal beds of limestone, dolomite, and shale. To the east rise the steeply tilted strata of the Sawback Range.

11.5   **Tree-in-the-Road.** Legend has it that when the Banff-Lake Louise Road   **52.9**
7.1   was being straightened and widened during the 1930's, the Park Superinten-   *32.9*
dent, Major P. J. Jennings, admired this western white spruce and instructed the engineers to spare the tree by building the roadway around it.

12.3   **Hillsdale Meadows Viewpoint.** The peaks which stand above the mead-   **52.1**
7.6   ows to the north and east — Mount Ishbel (2877 m/9,440 ft) and the other   *32.4*
summits of the Sawback Range, are known geologically as "sawtooth" mountains. The strata which compose the mountains has been tilted nearly vertical by the forces of orogeny (mountain building), and have since been eroded into the distinctive, inverted-V patterns you see here. The left-hand ridge of Mount Ishbel is a particularly good spot in which to see the slabs of limestone sweeping upward toward the sky.

The rolling, forested hills above the meadows to the north are actually composed of the debris of a gigantic rockslide which gradually slumped from the slopes of Mount Ishbel sometime after the last ice retreat.

Recent studies in this area indicate the meadows may have been the traditional campground of Indian hunting parties on their forays into the mountains. Likewise, there are indications the area has been burnt over on several occasions, contributing to the establishment of this meadow in the midst of a forested valley.

Pileated woodpeckers, the largest of the Canadian woodpecker clan, are often heard and seen in the aspen woodlands that fringe these meadows.

Hillsdale Meadows with the steeply tilted strata of Mount Ishbel creating a dramatic sawtooth range.

14.2   **Hillsdale Slide.** West of the Hillsdale Meadows, the roadway splits for
8.8   3.9 kilometres (2.4 miles), and westbound travellers suddenly find themselves climbing over a forested ridge which extends out into the valley from the north. An interpretive sign at a small pull-out describes how this hilly terrain was created by a slump of rock debris from near the lower slopes of Mount Ishbel as the last tongue of glacial ice retreated from this section of the Bow Valley over 10,000 years ago.

Pilot Pond. Eastbound travellers contour around the toe of the Hillsdale   **49.4**
Slide, but have a different stop of interest from those who are travelling   *30.7*
west. From this interpretive exhibit, a 400 metre (¼ mile)-long trail leads to a beautiful, small lake hidden in the forest. From the slopes above the

pond there is an outstanding view of Pilot Mountain (2954 m/9,690 ft). Forest species around the pond include aspen poplar, western white spruce, and lodgepole pine.

Pilot Pond was known locally as "Lizard Lake" at one time since long-toed salamanders were found here in great numbers. Heavy stocking of trout in the pond has resulted in the depletion of this rare amphibian.

17.7 **Johnston Canyon Trail.** A parking area on the east side of Johnston   **46.7**
11.0   Creek serves as a starting point for this very popular hike.   *29.0*

The three main points of interest on the canyon trail are the Lower Falls, 1.1 kilometres (0.7 mile), the Upper Falls, 2.7 kilometres (1.7 miles), and the Ink Pots, 5.8 kilometres (3.6 miles). The canyon in the vicinity of the two falls exhibits the effects of erosion and solution of the limestone bedrock. Canyon walls are smoothed and potholed (rounded depressions in the rock) by the scouring effect of pebbles and rocks which are carried and tumbled within the waters of Johnston Creek.

Along the walls of the canyon you sometimes see slate-grey birds flying or perching just above the surface of the water; or, perhaps, one will be standing on a rock in the middle of the rushing torrent, calmly bobbing up and down like a man doing deep knee-bends. This is the dipper or water ouzel, a bird which lives and nests at the very edge of turbulent mountain streams. In feeding, the dipper will swim, dive, and even walk on the bottom of the stream.

Birdwatchers should also look for the black swifts that nest on the canyon walls throughout the summer. Johnston Canyon is one of only two known breeding sites for this species in Alberta.

The Lower Falls of Johnston Canyon.

Located in an open meadow beyond the canyon, the Ink Pots are a group of seven cold water springs. Two of the pools are noted for their unique, murky, blue-green colour — a hue created by the bubbling of water up through quicksand, and the subsequent stirring of the fine, silty material through the pools.

The Johnston Canyon Campground is across the road from the trail head parking area.

17.9 **Johnston Canyon Lodge** provides accommodation, meals, groceries,   **46.5**
11.1   and gasoline during the summer season.   *28.9*

20.2 **Moose Meadows.** A broad, open meadow offers photographers the best   **44.2**
12.6   view of the sharp, spike-like summit of Pilot Mountain (2954 m/9,690 ft).   *27.4*
The mountain was named in 1884 by the pioneer geologist George M. Dawson because of its visibility as a landmark from far down valley.

The flats are dotted with a few spruce, aspen and lodgepole pine, and populated by colonies of Columbian ground squirrels. As might be expected, the ground squirrels are considered a delicacy by the local coyotes who may sometimes be seen browsing among the burrows.

The shrubby willow and dwarf birch which cover this meadow often conceal such summer inhabitants as clay-coloured, savannah, and white-crowned sparrows, willow flycatchers, common yellowthroats, and Brewer's blackbirds.

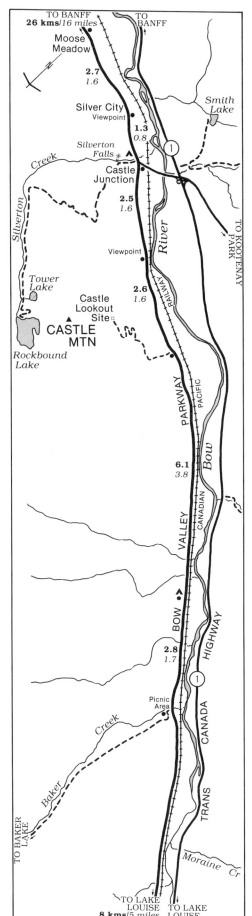

22.9
14.2
Silver City. Open meadow marks the site of a boom mining town whose heyday lasted but two short years. Named Silver City, the town blossomed overnight with the arrival of the railway in 1883, after ore from the surrounding slopes was assayed to contain significant quantities of copper and silver. At its height, the town could boast of a population of some 2,000, a half-dozen hotels, and four or five general stores. The mines never really panned out, however, as only marginal quantities of copper and lead ore were found, mainly on the slopes of Copper Mountain across the valley to the south. The involvement of two of the town's leading citizens in a disreputable mining claim helped to speed the demise of the boom, and by the close of 1885 Silver City was a ghost town. Only one miner, Joe Smith, kept the Silver City dream alive, living at the site of the old boom town and prospecting in the hills until his death in 1937.
41.5
25.8

23.4
14.5
Eisenhower Campground.
41.0
25.5

24.0
14.9
Castle Mountain Warden Station. A trail strikes off from a parking area beside the station and climbs for eight kilometres (five miles) to a pair of lakes — Tower and Rockbound, hidden in a hanging valley behind Castle Mountain. A branch only 300 metres (0.2 mile) up this trail leads to the beautiful Silverton Falls — a short hike which should take little more than 15 minutes to the falls.
40.4
25.1

A Canadian Youth Hostel is located directly across the road from the warden station.

24.2
15.0
Castle Junction. A short, one kilometre-long stretch of highway crosses to the southwest side of the Bow Valley to link up with the Trans-Canada Highway at a point nearly midway between Banff and Lake Louise. The junction also serves as the eastern terminus of the Banff-Windermere Parkway.
40.2
25.0

The junction, as well as the Bow River bridge area 500 metres to the west, provides superb, close-up views of the turreted peaks of Castle Mountain (2766 m/9,076 ft). From this angle it is easy to see why the mountain was named Castle by the first white man to pass this way — Dr. James Hector of the Palliser Expedition in 1858. The massive cliffs of the mountain are composed of Cambrian age limestones and dolomites. The large ledge system running like a catwalk midway up the face, is composed of a shale formation, however; since shale is less resistant to weathering than limestone, this section of the mountain has eroded into a gentle slope of broken talus.

An interpretive display at this junction provides travellers from the Trans-Canada Highway and Banff-Windermere Parkway with an overview of the Bow Valley Parkway both east and west of this point.

The Castle-Eisenhower Chalets at the junction provides gasoline, accommodation, meals, and groceries during the summer months.

26.7
16.6
Storm Mountain Viewpoint. From this elevated pull-off you can look directly across the Bow Valley to the low gap of Vermilion Pass (1650 m/5,415 ft). Situated between 3161 metre (10,372 ft) Storm Mountain on the left and 2758 metre (9,050 ft) Boom Mountain on the right, Vermilion is one of the major passes on the Great Divide and serves as the eastern gateway to Kootenay National Park. The Banff-Windermere Parkway climbs through the pass and drops into the East Kootenay region of British Columbia.
37.7
23.4

The first white man through the pass was geologist Dr. James Hector in 1858. Hector was in search of low, easily-traversed passes across the spine of the Rockies, but he did not feel Vermilion would be feasible as a future transportation route.

The last major glaciation in the Canadian Rockies occurred just over 8,000 years ago, and this viewpoint is very near to the furthest down-valley advance of glacial ice. Following that last surge, the glaciers retreated back to the high cirques of the Great Divide where they have remained to this day.

Silver City as it appeared shortly after the end of the boom in 1884.
Glenbow

29.3 **Castle Fire Lookout Trail.** A 4.0 kilometre (2.5 mile) hike leading off
18.2 through a forest of lodgepole pine on a broad, fire road, and eventually emerging onto the open meadowland high on the side of Castle Mountain. From the site where a lookout cabin once stood and the adjacent meadows, there are expansive views of the Bow Valley, Vermilion Pass, and the mountains of the Great Divide.
35.1
21.8

35.4 **Protection Mountain Campground.** From the mouth of the camp-
22.0 ground, you can look across the CPR tracks and the Bow Valley to the rugged mountains of the Bow Range — the peaks forming the main wall of the Great Divide. Behind the campground to the northeast runs the long, relatively low ramparts of Protection Mountain.
29.0
18.0

38.2 **Baker Creek Picnic Area.** The rugged wall of Panorama Ridge rises
23.7 across the valley to the west. Protection Mountain sprawls across the horizon to the east.
26.2
16.3

A trail leads off from the picnic area, climbing up the course of Baker Creek through a forest of lodgepole pine and spruce. The trail is a popular cross-country ski course in the winter, and in summer it serves as an alternate route into the Boulder Pass-Skoki Valley area.

Across the road from the picnic area, Baker Creek Bungalows provides meals and accommodation during the summer months.

All along the Bow Valley Parkway from Castle Junction to Lake Louise the forest is predominantly composed of pure, even-aged stands of lodgepole pine. Since pure stands of lodgepole pine can only be generated by a forest fire (the serotinous cones need to be heated above 45 degrees C or so before they open in profusion, and the seeds need the open, sunny conditions left in the burn to thrive), these forests are a good indicator of past conflagrations. Some of these fires were lightning caused and predate the coming of the white man, while others were caused by sparks thrown from old, coal-burning, steam locomotives or careless railway work crews. With improved methods of fire control introduced by the parks service, there have been few serious fires in the valley in the past 50 years.

43.7 **Outlet Creek Exhibit.** From this pull-off there is an excellent view
27.2 across valley to the massive bulk of Mount Temple. At 3544 metres (11,626 ft) above sea level, it is the third highest peak in the Banff Park and the highest in the range surrounding Lake Louise and Moraine Lake. The mountain is a part of the Main Ranges of the Rockies and is composed of nearly horizontal layers of quartz sandstone and limestone which were formed between 500 and 600 million years ago.
20.7
12.8

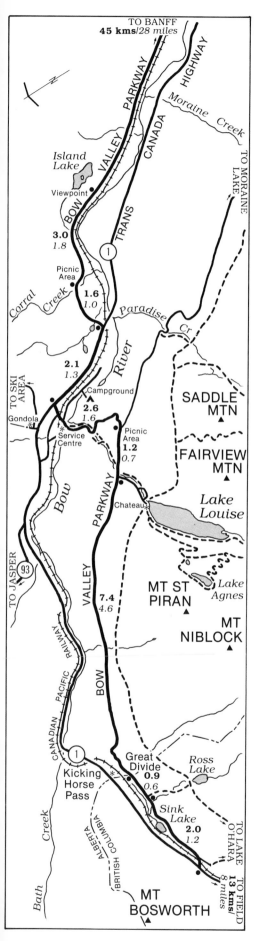

46.5 **Canadian Youth Hostel.** Located in the forest on the southwest side of **17.9**
28.9 the road. *11.1*

46.7 **Corral Creek Picnic Area.** A pleasant roadside stop situated in an open **17.7**
29.0 pine forest about 400 metres off the main road. Mount Temple towers *11.0*
above the valley to the southwest, the most prominent of many spectacular mountains in the Bow Range.

47.8 **Bow Valley Exhibit.** Here eastbound travellers on the Bow Valley **16.6**
29.7 Parkway are introduced to the valley and its geological past. The pull-off *10.3*
is also a good viewpoint for Mount Temple and the peaks to its north —
Mount Aberdeen, Sheol Mountain, Saddle Peak, and the rounded dome
of Fairview Mountain.

The orange-red rock outcropping near this stop is a part of one of the
oldest formations in the park. At the time this rock was being deposited
as sand and silt on the floor of a shallow, inland sea some 600 million
years ago, only the most primitive of life forms existed in the oceans.

48.3 **Junction with the Trans-Canada Highway.** The Bow Valley Parkway **16.1**
30.0 travels west with the Trans-Canada for 500 metres (0.3 mile) before *10.0*
branching off as the east exit to Lake Louise.

48.8 **Junction with the Trans-Canada Highway.** The Bow Valley Parkway **15.6**
30.3 travels east with the Trans-Canada for 500 metres (0.3 mile) before *9.7*
branching off to the northeast side of the Bow Valley.

50.0 **Lake Louise Campground Entrance.** The road travels through the **14.4**
31.1 trailer section of the campground for nearly 800 metres. *8.9*

50.5 **Trailer Drop-off.** Because of narrow, congested roads in the Lake **13.9**
31.4 Louise-Moraine Lake area, Parks Canada has designated a large parking *8.6*
area on the west side of the road as a trailer drop-off point.

50.9 **Lake Louise Road Junction.** A short spur road branches north at the **13.5**
31.6 junction to the lower Lake Louise service centre — a year-round facility *8.4*
providing meals, lodging, gasoline, groceries, post office, warden station, park information bureau, and police contingent.

52.9 **Moraine Lake Road Junction.** Intersecting from the south, this road **11.5**
32.9 winds for 12.4 kilometres (7.7 miles) to Moraine Lake and the Valley-of- *7.1*
the-Ten Peaks. (See Lake Louise and Vicinity, page 80 .)

53.1 **Paradise Picnic Area.** Across the road from the picnic area is a superb **11.3**
33.0 example of subalpine forest, composed primarily of spruce mixed with *7.0*
lodgepole pine and alpine fir. The alpine fir is the key species here,
preferring the cooler, damper environment of this northeast facing slope.
The bark of alpine fir is less scaly than either the spruce or pine, smoother
and whitish in colour with prominent resin blisters. The pungent balsam
aroma of the subalpine forest is due primarily to the presence of alpine
fir.

53.6 **Paradise Lodge.** Accommodation and groceries in the summer season. **10.8**
33.3   *6.7*

54.1 **Lake Louise Access Road Junction.** A short, 800 metre spur road **10.3**
33.6 branches from the Parkway and climbs to the parking area for Lake *6.4*
Louise. (See Lake Louise and Vicinity, page 77 .)

A service station operates at the junction in the summer season.

Between the Great Divide and the Lake Louise Road Junction, the
Parkway winds along the north-northeast facing slope of the valley. The
forest along the way is subalpine, composed of spruce, alpine fir, and
lodgepole pine.

61.5 **The Great Divide.** By walking down through the picnic area to the edge **2.9**
38.2 of the railway tracks, you can visit the monument erected on the water- *1.8*
shed divide in the historic Kicking Horse Pass. The pass stands at 1625
metres (5,333 ft) above sea level. The waters draining east from the
summit run down to the Bow River, into the Saskatchewan River system,
and on to Hudson's Bay; the waters flowing west form the Kicking Horse
River which runs into the Columbia, and on to the Pacific Ocean.

Dr. James Hector ascended the pass from the west with his Indian guides
in the late summer of 1858 while exploring with the Palliser Expedition
for routes through the Rockies. While struggling up the canyon toward
the summit, Dr. Hector was kicked in the chest by one of the pack horses.
Knocked unconscious, his guides took him for dead and nearly buried
him before he came to his senses. The incident led Hector to name the
pass Kicking Horse.

The trans-continental railway crested the summit of the pass during the
summer of 1884. The westbound tracks were joined with the eastbound at
Craigellachie. British Columbia, and the last spike was driven on
November 7, 1885. The earliest passenger trains travelled so slowly
through the Kicking Horse Pass that seats were attached to the cow-
catchers of the locomotives so travellers could savour every exhilarating
mile of the crossing. (Lady Agnes Macdonald, wife of Canada's first
Prime Minister, was one of the first to partake of this novel sport, riding
the cow-catcher of her train most of the distance from the Kicking Horse
Pass to the Pacific Coast.)

62.4 **Ross Lake Trail.** An excellent opportunity to visit a glacially-carved **2.0**
38.8 amphitheatre on the side of the Bow Range. A short 2.9 kilometre (1.8 *1.2*
mile) trail leads into one of the most perfect cirques imaginable and to the
shore of a beautiful, subalpine tarn. An outstanding trail for close-up
examination of a subalpine forest environment.

63.2 **Sink Lake Viewpoint.** A unique lake in that it has no visible outlet. The **1.2**
39.3 depression which the lake occupies may have been created by the melting *0.7*
of a detached block of ice on top of a thickness of silt and gravel during the
last retreat of the glaciers. Water drains from Sink Lake by flowing down
through the glacial outwash material (sand and gravel) which composes its
bottom, reemerging further down valley to flow into Wapta Lake.

64.2 **Lake O'Hara Road Junction.** A short spur road leads downhill to the **0.2**
39.9 gate and parking area for the Lake O'Hara Fire Road. This is a 10 *0.1*

kilometre (6 mile)-long, limited access road leading to the Lake O'Hara Lodge and the center of a beautiful day-hiking area. A shuttle bus service operates up and down the road throughout the day, transporting lodge guests and hikers to and from the parking area. (For information concerning bus schedules and fares, inquire at the nearby Wapta Lake Lodge or the information bureau at Lake Louise.)

64.4 **Trans-Canada Highway Junction.** The western terminus of the Bow   **0.0**
40.0 Valley Parkway, 2.9 kilometres (1.8 miles) west of the B.C.-Alberta boundary and 2 kilometres (1.2 miles) east of Wapta Lake on the Trans-Canada Highway.

WESTBOUND **Kilometres** *Miles*	BOW VALLEY PARKWAY	EASTBOUND **Kilometres** *Miles*

Lake Louise and Vicinity

During the summer of 1882 a packer for the CPR surveys named Tom Wilson was camped with a small band of Stoney Indians along the Pipestone River not far from its confluence with the Bow. It was a cold, drizzly day and the sounds of avalanches could be heard nearby. One of the Stoneys, Edwin Hunter, told Wilson the slides came from a snowy mountain above "the lake of the little fishes". When the following day dawned wet and cold, Hunter led Wilson into a hanging valley above the Bow and to the shore of the lake.

"For some time we sat and smoked and gazed at the gem of beauty beneath the glacier," Wilson later recalled. He named his discovery Emerald Lake, but it was later changed by the Geographic Board to Lake Louise, in honour of Princess Louise Caroline Alberta, wife of the Marquis of Lorne, Governor General of Canada from 1878 to 1883.

The scene Wilson and his Stoney guide surveyed in silence on that wet summer day nearly a century ago is today one of the most familiar mountain vistas in the world. The lake is just as emerald green and the avalanches still thunder off the broad, white face of Mount Victoria, but the shore where the two men first caught sight of the lake is now graced by the Canadian Pacific Railway's Chateau Lake Louise, a massive, luxury hotel which provides all the amenities throughout the year.

The first small chalet was built on the lakeshore by the CPR in 1890, and over the years it gradually evolved into a hotel of major proportions. In 1924, a fire swept through the structure, levelling the greater part of the hotel, and the subsequent reconstruction saw the erection of the present building.

During the 1890's, Lake Louise became the hub for exploration and adventure in the Canadian Rockies. Mountaineers from the United States and Great Britain came to scale the treacherous, unclimbed summits surrounding the lake, and horse parties struck off to the north to explore the untracked valleys leading to the Columbia Icefield.

Until the road was built from Banff to Lake Louise in 1920, all travel to the area was by train. Disembarking at the station (known as Laggan in those days), hotel guests would make the dusty, four mile trip to the hotel via horse-drawn tally-hos. From 1912 to 1930, a tramway was used to ferry guests and baggage to the hotel. In the 1930's, skiers began visiting the area in winter, trekking overland to a small lodge in the mountains east of the Bow Valley.

The mountains and glaciers. As you look down the lake from the shore in front of the Chateau, Mount Victoria (3464 m/11,365 ft) and the Victoria Glacier dominate the scene. Fairview Mountain (2744 m/9,001 ft) rises above the lake to the left, while The Beehive hems it in on the right. By following the trail around toward the north side of the lake, the snow-crested dome of Mount Lefroy (3423 m/11,230 ft) soon heaves into view beside Mount Victoria.

Tom Wilson on the shore of Lake Louise in 1930, nearly 50 years after his discovery.

Archives of the Canadian Rockies

The CPR station at Laggan in the 1890's.

Archives of the Canadian Rockies

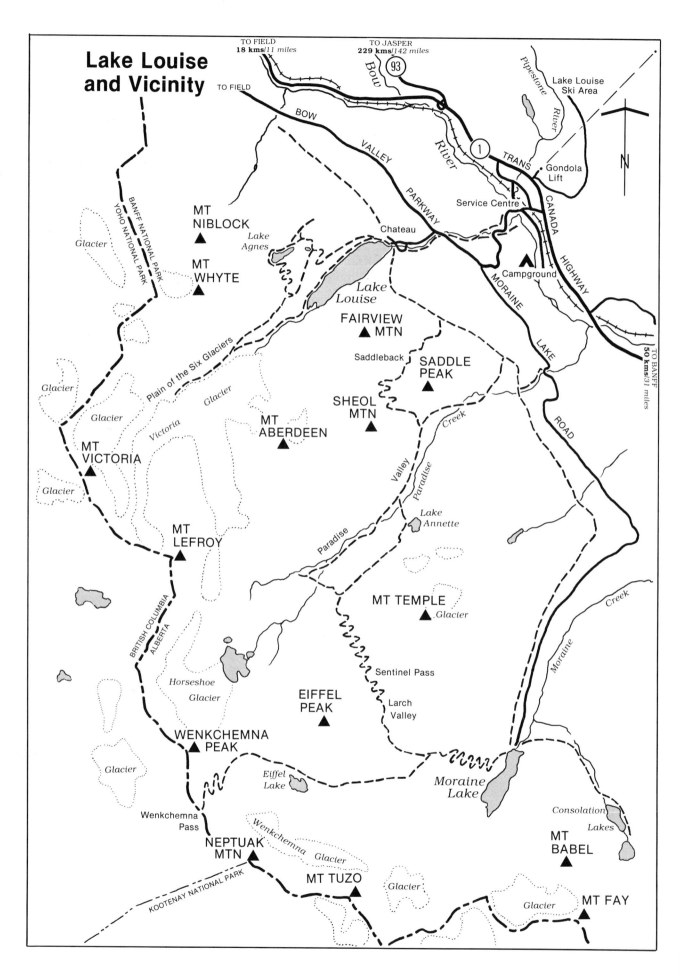

Lake Louise and Vicinity

TO FIELD
18 kms/11 miles

TO JASPER
229 kms/142 miles

TO FIELD

(93)

Bow

BOW

VALLEY

PARKWAY

River

(1)

TRANS

CANADA

HIGHWAY

Pipestone River

Lake Louise Ski Area

Gondola Lift

Service Centre

N

Campground

MORAINE

LAKE

ROAD

TO BANFF
50 kms/31 miles

BANFF NATIONAL PARK
YOHO NATIONAL PARK

MT NIBLOCK ▲

Lake Agnes

MT WHYTE ▲

Glacier

Chateau

Lake Louise

FAIRVIEW MTN ▲

Saddleback

SADDLE PEAK ▲

Creek

Plain of the Six Glaciers

Glacier

Glacier

SHEOL MTN ▲

Valley

Glacier

Victoria

Glacier

MT ABERDEEN ▲

Paradise

Paradise

MT VICTORIA ▲

Lake Annette

Glacier

MT LEFROY ▲

BRITISH COLUMBIA
ALBERTA

MT TEMPLE ▲ ·Glacier

Creek

Moraine

Horseshoe
Glacier

Sentinel Pass

EIFFEL PEAK ▲

Larch Valley

Glacier

WENKCHEMNA PEAK ▲

Eiffel Lake

Moraine Lake

Consolation Lakes

Wenkchemna Pass

Wenkchemna

NEPTUAK MTN ▲

Glacier

MT BABEL ▲

KOOTENAY NATIONAL PARK

MT TUZO ▲

Glacier

Glacier

MT FAY ▲

The Chateau sits atop the natural dam which has created Lake Louise. The dam is actually a ridge of rock and gravel debris deposited at the toe of the Victoria Glacier after it advanced to this point during a previous ice age. A glacier is something like a conveyor belt carrying rock debris; it is forever flowing forward, depositing the rubble at its toe. When the glacier is advancing or retreating, this material is spread more or less evenly across the landscape, but when it is stationary for a period of time, the debris accumulates in a ridge called a terminal moraine. If the ice does not surge forward again, but retreats, the moraine will survive, often helping to create a lake in the deep depression gouged out by the glacier. Such is what has occurred at Lake Louise, probably during the last major advance of the Victoria Glacier around 8,000 to 10,000 years ago.

The unique, greenish-blue colour of the lake is likewise directly attributable to the presence of glaciers. These bodies of ice are continually grinding away at bedrock, and as a result, meltwater is thick with silt, also known as glacial flour. The material is so fine, much of it remains suspended in the water after it pours into the lake, reflecting the green rays of the spectrum.

Lake Louise Chalet in 1909.
Archives of the Canadian Rockies

The subalpine forest. At 1731 metres (5,680 ft) above sea level, Lake Louise is set well into the zone of the subalpine forest. The climax forest species are spruce and alpine fir, with lodgepole pine growing where forest fires have burned. Rainfall and snowfall are heavier here than at the town of Banff, and temperatures are cooler — factors which affect the length of growing season and the species composition of both flora and fauna. The forest is dense and its floor well-shaded, making excellent habitat for small mammals such as chipmunks and red squirrels; small birds like chickadees, red-breasted nuthatches, and winter wrens appreciate the dense character of these woods as well, joined by such old standbys as the gray jays and Clark's nutcrackers. A mature climax forest is not a favourite of the larger mammals, though some marshy, spruce bogs scattered through the area attract moose.

Plain-of-the-Six Glaciers Trail. A 6.6 kilometre (4.1 mile) trail following the shoreline on the north edge of the lake and through the gap beyond the inlet. The route continues to climb to a spectacular overlook of the Victoria Glacier, with close-up views of Mount Victoria (3464 m/11,365 ft), Mount Lefroy (3423 m/11,230 ft) and Abbot Pass (2925 m/9,598 ft). A teahouse situated near trail's end serves lunches and refreshments during the summer season.

Lakes-in-the-Clouds Trail. A trail branching uphill from the lakeshore just beyond the Chateau Lake Louise dormitories. The track climbs steadily to Mirror Lake, 2.6 kilometres (1.6 miles), and Lake Agnes, 3.4 kilometres (2.1 miles), with extensions ascending to viewpoints on the Big and Little Beehives. Features along the way include the beautiful hanging valley containing Lake Agnes, the alpine larch-studded summits of the Beehives, and outstanding views down to Lake Louise and the Bow Valley. A teahouse at Lake Agnes serves light meals throughout the summer season.

Saddleback Trail. A trail leading from behind the boathouse to a high pass between Fairview and Saddle Mountains, 3.7 kilometres (2.3 miles) distant. Excellent views of the Bow and Paradise Valleys and the towering north face of Mount Temple (3544 m/11,626 ft). Later in the season, more adventurous hikers can trace a faint trail to the top of Fairview Mountain — at 2744 metres (9,001 ft) above sea level, the highest viewpoint reached by trail in the area.

MORAINE LAKE AND THE VALLEY OF THE TEN PEAKS.

Lake Louise is not the only area of exceptional beauty locked within the Bow Range. Just 1.1 kilometres (0.7 mile) east of the Lake Louise Access Road on the Bow Valley Parkway, opposite the Lake Louise Picnic Area, another side road branches to the south, reaching Moraine Lake and the Valley of the Ten Peaks in 12.4 kilometres (7.7 miles).

The geological story. The emerald green lake, somewhat smaller than Lake Louise, is set before a backdrop of sharp, glaciated summits called the Wenkchemna Peaks (Wenkchemna is the Stoney Indian word for ten, hence the Valley of the Ten Peaks). Above the lake to the north looms yet another spectacular peak, Mount Temple (3544 m/11,626 ft) — the highest mountain in the Bow Range and the third highest in the park.

Like most mountains within the Main Ranges, these are composed of quartz sandstones and limestones formed during the Cambrian Period nearly 600 million years ago. The sandstones are found in the lower half of the surrounding mountains, lending a reddish-orange hue to the slopes; grey cliffs of limestone comprise the upper levels near the summits.

While most mountain lakes are created by the direct action of glaciers gouging deep basins then damming their outlets with morainal material, Moraine Lake would appear to be the creation of a rockslide from the Tower of Babel, rising immediately above the northeast end of the lake. The lake received its name from its first visitors, who mistakenly thought the large pile of boulders near the outlet to be a terminal moraine. This great mound of quartz sandstone boulders makes a fine, elevated viewpoint for the lake.

A lodge at the lake offers accommodation and meals throughout the summer months. Canoe rentals are also available.

Larch Valley—Sentinel Pass Trail. A trail leading out from behind the Moraine Lake Lodge and climbing steadily for 2.4 kilometres (1.5 miles) to the open, subalpine meadows at the foot of Sentinel Pass. The meadows are laced with stands of stunted Engelmann spruce, alpine fir and alpine larch, and dotted by several small lakes. In autumn, the larch needles turn to yellow-gold prior to dropping from the trees, making the high valley a popular spot for photographers. By continuing another three kilometres or so along the trail, you can climb above timberline to the 2611 metre (8,566 ft) summit of Sentinel Pass. More energetic hikers can continue down the opposite side of the pass into Paradise Valley, eventually emerging near the Paradise Creek bridge at Kilometre 2.7 (Mile 1.7) on the Moraine Lake Road (you'll have to hitch-hike back to Moraine Lake if you didn't arrange transportation in advance).

Eiffel Lake Trail. A branch cutting away from the Larch Valley trail at Kilometre 2.4 (Mile 1.5) and leading along a high, open ridge to a rockbound tarn known as Eiffel Lake, 5.6 kilometres (3.5 miles). By continuing on through the tumbled boulder field of a large landslide, the trail eventually climbs to the 2600 metre (8,531 ft) summit of Wenkchemna Pass, 9.7 kilometres (6.0 miles) from Moraine Lake.

Consolation Lakes Trail. Descend through the picnic area and cross Moraine Creek just below the lake, following the trail around the flanks of the Babel rockslide. The trail reaches Lower Consolation Lake after a pleasant 2.9 kilometre (1.8 mile) walk through a cool, damp, subalpine forest. Like Moraine Lake, Lower Consolation Lake is partially contained by a large rockslide off the slopes of Mount Babel. Exceptional views from the lakeshore to the glacier-clad peaks of Mount Quadra (3173 m/10,410 ft) and Bident Mountain (3084 m/10,119 ft).

Banff Windermere Parkway

The Banff-Windermere Parkway (also known as the Banff-Radium Highway) was the first roadway across the central Rockies from Alberta to British Columbia. For its part in funding the construction of the road, the federal government received a strip of land five miles wide on either side of the highway from the Province of British Columbia to use as a national park. Thus, in the year 1920, Kootenay National Park was created, and on June 23, 1923 the highway was officially opened.

In addition to being one of the most scenic drives in the mountain parks, the 104 kilometre (64 mile)-long highway serves as the only route for those wishing to visit Kootenay National Park.

The eastern terminus of the highway is at Castle Junction on the Trans-Canada Highway in Banff National Park, while its western terminus is near the mouth of Sinclair Canyon and the village of Radium in eastern British Columbia. In between, the road follows along the Vermilion and Kootenay Rivers, passing such features as the Vermilion Pass burn, Marble Canyon, the Paint Pots, and the red rock and hot springs of Sinclair Canyon. The highway is also one of the best roads from which to view wildlife, with elk, black bear, mountain goat and coyotes often seen along the right-of-way.

If you are eastbound, travelling from Radium Hot Springs to Banff Park, turn to page 89 and work backwards, following the distances in the right-hand margin.

WESTBOUND Kilometres *Miles*	BANFF WINDERMERE PARKWAY	EASTBOUND Kilometres *Miles*

0.0 / **Castle Junction.** Here, the Banff-Windermere Parkway intersects with the Trans-Canada Highway at a point nearly midway between Banff and Lake Louise (see Trans-Canada Highway, page 38). — **103.7** / *64.4*

Dense stands of lodgepole pine border the sides of the highway on the five kilometre (three mile) grade between Castle Junction and Storm Mountain Lodge. The grassy margin along the road is often carpeted with the crimson flowers of Indian paintbrush in mid-summer.

5.2 / *3.2* **Vemilion Pass Fire Viewpoint.** A pull-off at the top of the long grade dropping to Castle Junction and the Trans-Canada Highway, and directly across the road from Storm Mountain Lodge. Across the Altrude Creek valley to the south stands Storm Mountain (3161 m/10,372 ft), a typical peak of the Main Ranges composed of 600 million year old quartz sandstones. — **98.5** / *61.2*

The viewpoint is of particular interest as it presents an excellent panorama of the Vermilion Pass burn — a fire started in July, 1968 by a bolt of lightning. In the course of four days the fire burned over 6,000 acres of forest, before being brought under control by fire-fighters and cool,

Castle Mountain dominates the view from near Storm Mountain Lodge in the photograph taken by Byron Harmon shortly after the opening of the Banff-Windermere Highway in 1923.

Archives of the Canadian Rockies

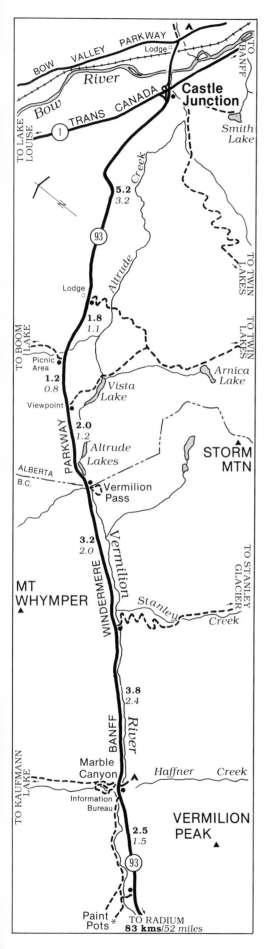

damp weather. The conflagration swept eastward from the Marble Canyon area of Kootenay Park, over the Great Divide, and onto the lower slopes of Storm Mountain.

East from the edge of the burn, you can see two distinct forest types: on the ridge extending eastward from Storm Mountain, the dark green forest indicates the climax species of the region, spruce and alpine fir; the lighter green further down on the slopes indicates a pure forest of lodgepole pine which was generated by a previous fire in the area. Since pure lodgepole pine forests always follow a forest fire (their cones usually stay tightly sealed until heated by a passing fire), the Vermilion Pass burn will one day be repopulated with these trees. Then, if no further fires occur over the next 200 years or so, the lodgepole forest will be replaced by the dark green foliage of the more tolerant spruce-fir climax forest.

Storm Mountain Lodge was opened for business in 1923. It was known as Castle Mountain Bungalow Camp in those days and was one of the Canadian Pacific Railway's early outlying lodges. It was sold to private interests in 1935, and though it has undergone some modernization in the intervening years, the main lodge still retains much of the charm that typified early tourist accommodation in the parks.

7.0 **Boom Creek Picnic Area.** Though the Vermilion Pass fire passed very   **96.7**
4.3 close to this roadside stop, the cool, damp environment of the spruce-   *60.1*
alpine fir forest survives here. This is an excellent spot in which to examine the climax, subalpine forest at close range.

The trail to Boom Lake, 5.1 kilometres (3.2 miles) strikes off at the bridge near the rear of the picnic ground.

8.2 **Vista Lake Viewpoint.** An excellent vantage point for the Vermilion   **95.5**
5.1 Pass burn and Storm Mountain as well as Vista Lake which lies in the   *59.3*
valley below. To the east, rising beyond the broad Bow Valley, are the jagged summits of the Sawback Range and the broad buttresses and towers of Castle Mountain.

A trail descends from the viewpoint to Vista Lake, providing a pleasant hour's outing. More energetic hikers may continue up the steep slope beneath Storm Mountain to Arnica Lake, 5.3 kilometres (3.3 miles), or Twin Lakes, 7.6 kilometres (4.7 miles), both favourite spots for local fishermen.

10.2 **Vermilion Pass (1651 m/5,416 ft).** This is the summit of the Great   **93.5**
6.3 Divide. Waters east of the divide flow into the Bow River and eventually   *58.1*
into Hudson's Bay via the Saskatchewan and Nelson Rivers; waters to the west run to the Columbia River and on to the Pacific Ocean. The pass also serves as the boundary between Banff and Kootenay National Parks, as well as Alberta and British Columbia.

A short, self-guiding nature walk called the Fireweed Trail leads on a loop hike through a portion of the Vermilion Pass burn. Here is an excellent opportunity to view a fire-ravaged forest at close range. The fire burned over 6,000 acres in a four day period during the summer of 1968, yet a great diversity of life has already moved back into the area. Many small mammals and birds inhabit the charred forest, while the flood of sunlight now reaching the forest floor creates a veritable garden of wildflowers every summer.

After viewing the forest, it is hard to judge fire as either good or bad, but rather, it is merely a fact of life in the mountains as it has been for thousands of years — an important part of the subalpine ecosystem.

The mountains rising around Vermilion Pass include Storm Mountain to the south, Mount Whymper to the west, and Boom Mountain directly to the north.

Avalanche Slope. Along this section of highway, snowslides have swept down from the south-facing slopes of Mount Whymper, snapping off the burnt spars from the Vermilion Pass fire and depositing them along the banks of the Vermilion River. The Vermilion Pass fire may have actually contributed to more extensive snowslides on this slope since dense forest cover used to arrest many avalanches well above the highway.

Vista Lake surrounded by the weathering spars left in the wake of the Vermilion Pass burn.

13.4   **Stanley Glacier Trail.** Looking above this roadside parking area to the   **90.3**
8.3   south, several high, distinct valleys are sandwiched between the snow   *56.1*
and glacier-capped peaks. These steep-walled amphitheatres are called cirques and were carved out of the bedrock by the plucking action of alpine glaciers during past ice ages. The Stanley Glacier trail leads up into the very heart of one of these cirques and, at its terminus, offers a close-up view of an alpine glacier at work.

The first two kilometres or so of the trail pass through the Vermilion Pass burn where lodgepole pine trees are springing up in the wake of the 1968 fire. Other greenery and flowers flourishing in the burn include Labrador tea, fireweed, harebells, yellow columbine, and heart-leaved arnica.

17.0   **Marble Canyon Campground.**   **86.7**
10.6   *53.8*

17.2   **Marble Canyon Nature Trail.** A short but interesting nature hike along   **86.5**
10.7   the rim of Marble Canyon, 2 kilometres (1.2 miles) round-trip.   *53.7*

Marble Canyon is typical of several extremely narrow and deep gorges worn into the limestone strata at different locations in the mountain parks. The canyon was carved by the action of water flowing through narrow joints or cracks in the bedrock. Slowly, over a long period of time, the water dissolved the minerals and widened the cracks to form the present canyon. From its head to its mouth, Marble Canyon is approximately 600 metres (0.4 mile) long. While its breadth varies from only three to eighteen metres, it reaches a depth of some 60 metres (200 feet). The nature trail bridges this chasm in several spots to provide a dizzy glimpse into the canyon depths.

In several sections of the canyon, evidence of the abrasive action of rocks and boulders being swirled in the current can be seen in the smoothed, concave indentations and rounded potholes formed in the bedrock.

The canyon receives its name from the white marble outcropping throughout the area. The entire valley of Tokuum Creek lies along the strike of a major fault (a fracture in the strata), and due to the extreme pressures and movement which have occurred in the vicinity of the fault plane, the limestone bedrock has been transformed (metamorphosed) into marble. This marble is probably best displayed at the upper end of the canyon where a small waterfall tumbles over great slabs of the white rock.

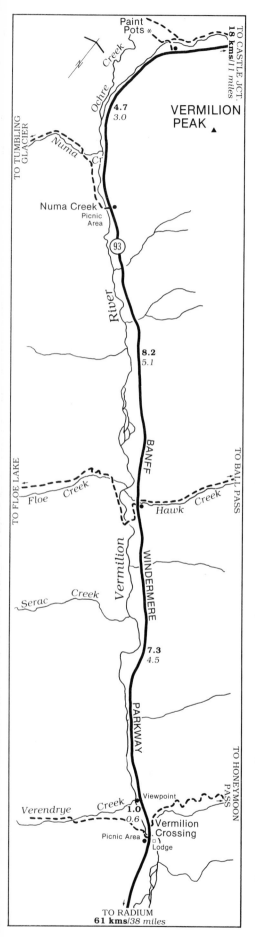

17.6
10.9
Marble Canyon Warden Station. The trail to Tumbling Glacier and Ottertail Pass starts at the bridge across from the station.
86.1
53.5

19.7
12.2
Paint Pots Nature Trail. Also known as the Ochre Beds; a short trail leads to an unique area of brilliantly coloured earth across the Vermilion River.
84.0
52.2

The red and yellow clays of the region have been stained by mineral spring water containing significant quantities of iron. The three Paint Pot pools near the end of the trail are actually the cold, mineral springs, which provide much of the iron-laden water. Before the arrival of the white man, Indian tribes from both sides of the mountains came here to collect the ochre clay for body paint; to these peoples, the springs were a place of "great medicine" inhabited by animal spirits. After its discovery by the white man, the ochre was mined for a short period and shipped to Calgary for use as a base for paint.

24.4
15.2
Numa Creek Picnic Area. The Numa Creek trail, leading to such distant points as Tumbling and Numa Passes, starts from the bridge beside the picnic area.
79.3
49.2

Between Vermilion River Crossing and the Numa Creek Picnic Area, there are many well-defined avalanche paths on the steep slopes above the Vermilion River. Looking like ski runs cut through the trees, the paths mark the descent of powerful winter snowslides. Under certain conditions, avalanches can reach speeds near 300 kilometres (200 miles) per hour, snapping large trees like matchsticks.

32.6
20.3
Floe Lake and Hawk Creek Trails. A parking area on the west side of the highway serves as a starting point for two trails. The hike to Floe Lake, 10.5 kilometres (6.5 miles), begins beside the trail map at the edge of the parking area; the trail to Ball Pass and Banff Park begins on the opposite side of the highway. The trail to Floe Lake bridges the Vermilion River less than a kilometre from here, and the short trip to this mini-canyon makes a pleasant nature walk.
71.1
44.1

39.9
24.8
Mount Verendrye Viewpoint. A roadside pull-off offering good views up the course of Verendrye Creek to the towering ramparts of Mount Verendrye (3086 m/10,125 ft) and the sheer, limestone cliffs of the Rockwall. The Rockwall is actually the eastern escarpment of the Vermilion Range — a line of peaks running for some 40 kilometres (25 miles) along the western boundary of Kootenay Park, composed of limestones and dolomites that were formed during the Cambrian age some 500 million years ago.
63.8
39.6

40.9
25.4
Vermilion River Crossing. Both a lodge and a picnic area are located on opposite sides of the road from one another near where the highway crosses the Vermilion River. From the picnic area, a 4.5 kilometre (2.7 mile)-long trail leads up Verendrye Creek to the avalanche slopes at the foot of Mount Verendrye. The lodge offers accommodation, groceries and gasoline during the summer months.
62.8
39.0

43.2
26.8
Mount Assiniboine Viewpoint. From a small, roadside pull-off, Mount Assiniboine is seen as little more than the tip of a pyramid sticking above the mountains to the southeast, but this is the only point on any highway from which the "Matterhorn of the Rockies" can be viewed. At 3618
60.5
37.6

metres (11,870 ft) above sea level, Mount Assiniboine is the highest mountain in this section of the Rockies.

44.8 **Avalanche Slopes.** One of the few points on the Banff-Windermere
27.8 Parkway where avalanche paths cross the roadway. The highway is sometimes blocked in winter by slides down these snow chutes.

46.8 **Mount Shanks Fire Lookout and Simpson River Trail.** A bridge
29.1 across the Vermilion River marks the starting point for these two lengthy and infrequently travelled trails. The Simpson River trail serves as one of the routes to Mount Assiniboine Provincial Park.

47.5 **Simpson Valley Viewpoint.** A monument at the pull-out commemorates
29.5 the journey of George Simpson, Governor of the Hudson's Bay Company, in the summer of 1841. Searching for a more southerly route for his fur traders to follow in crossing the Rockies, Simpson entered the mountains from the east via the Devil's Gap, passed the site of present-day Banff, and crossed an obscure pass on the Great Divide which today bears his name. He descended the valley which stretches away to the west from the viewpoint, and upon reaching the Vermilion River followed more or less along the route of today's Banff-Windermere Parkway, crossing Sinclair Pass and descending to the Columbia River Valley. Simpson found the route impractical for either fur traders or settlers, and had to be satisfied with the traditional passes of Athabasca and Yellowhead further north.

48.6 **Animal Lick.** Some riverside locales provide muds and clays which are
30.2 high in mineral content and attractive to wildlife. Moose, elk and deer are often seen licking the muds found along this stretch of the Vermilion River.

49.1 **Rocky Springs.** A major, freshwater spring gushes from an underground
30.5 passage at the pull-off, offering a refreshing drink for thirsty travellers. As summer progresses, the spring's flow decreases until it finally runs dry in late summer or early autumn.

50.7 **Wardle Creek Picnic Area.**
31.5

55.3 **Hector Gorge Picnic Area.**
34.4

56.2 **Rocky Mountain Goat Range.** At the point where the Vermilion River
34.9 flows through the narrow gap between the south end of the Vermilion Range and the north end of the Mitchell Range, Rocky Mountain goats are often seen on the lower slopes of Mount Wardle, just above the highway to the north. Mountain goat are distinguishable from mountain sheep by their distinctive white coat and short black horns. An adult billie will weigh in around 80 kilos (180 lbs.), 45 kilos (100 lbs.) or so lighter than an adult, bighorn sheep ram. Unlike sheep, goats are seldom seen so near the valley bottoms, but the easily ingested mineral soil found in this roadcut is an attraction which overcomes the animal's normal shyness.

58.9
36.6

56.9
35.3

56.2
34.9

55.1
34.2

54.6
33.9

53.0
32.9

48.4
30.0

47.5
29.5

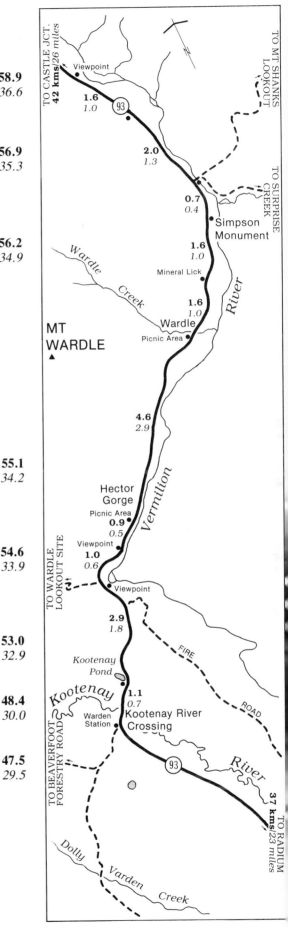

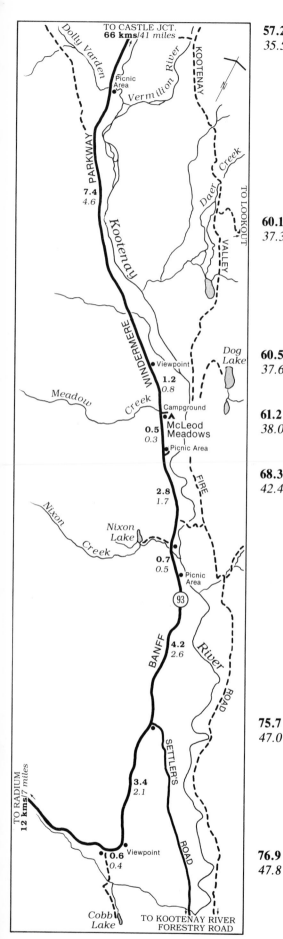

57.2
35.5
Hector Gorge Viewpoint. A lofty pull-off offering an excellent view down the course of the Vermilion River as it flows toward the south and a junction with the Kootenay River. This section of the river is known as Hector Gorge, named for Dr. James Hector, a geologist who explored the valley in the late summer of 1858. The peaks of the Mitchell Range border the river to the left, while back across the highway to the north stands Mount Wardle (2810 m/9,218 ft), the southernmost peak of the Vermilion Range. The narrow gap between the two ranges is quite obvious from the overlook, and there is a strong possibility the ranges were once connected at this point, the Vermilion River eroding the gorge which now separates them.
46.5
28.9

60.1
37.3
Kootenay Pond Picnic Area. Geologists believe Kootenay Pond to be a "kettle", that is, a depression made by the melting away of a detached piece of glacier ice which had been either wholly or partially buried in the glacial sands and gravels near the end of the last ice age. As the ice melted, the sands and gravels slumped to form the depression. Water levels in the steep-sided pool vary from season to season, as the water percolates down through the alluvial material on the pond's bottom.
43.6
27.1

60.5
37.6
Kootenay River Bridge.
43.2
26.8

61.2
38.0
Kootenay River Crossing Warden Station.
42.5
26.4

68.3
42.4
Dolly Varden Picnic Area.
35.4
22.0

This section of the Kootenay River valley is a popular grazing area for elk throughout much of the year. In fact, of all roads in the mountain parks, the Banff-Windermere is the one from which these animals are most frequently observed. The elk, or wapiti, is one of the largest members of the deer family, with males often weighing near 450 kilos (1000 lbs.). Elk are easily distinguished from mule and whitetail deer not only by relative size, but also by their prominent light rump patch and reddish-brown coat. Bulls have large "racks" of spreading antlers from late summer into early spring. The animals migrate up to higher elevations in mid-summer, but are quite often found grazing along the highway in early summer and autumn. It is estimated that around 300 of these animals range through Kootenay Park during most of the year.

75.7
47.0
Mount Harkin Viewpoint. A roadside stop allowing a fine perspective of the Mitchell Range to the east and the Brisco Range across the highway to the west. The most prominent mountain in the Mitchell Range is Mount Harkin (2981 m/9,780 ft), named for the first Commissioner of National Parks, James B. Harkin — a man who was one of the most vocal proponents of national parks and the park ideal in the first half of the century.
28.0
17.4

76.9
47.8
McLeod Meadows Campground. The open character of the McLeod Meadows is the result of repeated forest fires which have swept this section of the Kootenay Valley since the arrival of the white man in the late 19th Century. From this point south, the valley becomes less and less a typical Rocky Mountain subalpine forest, and increasingly akin to the interior Douglas fir forest of southeastern British Columbia.
26.8
16.6

A bridge at the rear of the campground serves as the trail head for a short walk to Dog Lake, 2.7 kilometres (1.7 miles); the bridge crosses the Kootenay River and also allows access to the fire road on the east side of the river, along which extended hikes or ski trips can be made.

77.4
48.1 **McLeod Meadows Picnic Area.** The open meadow surrounding the picnic area is dotted with the burrows of Columbian ground squirrels. The Columbian is one of the larger of the ground squirrel clan, measuring up to a foot in length. When not foraging for food amongst the grasses and flowers, these squirrels are often seen sitting upright near the mouth of their burrows, on the alert for intruders. A sharp, chirping bark warns other colony inhabitants of danger. At lower elevations such as this, the Columbian ground squirrel is an early hibernator, often disappearing before the end of August.
26.3
16.3

The trail to Dog Lake, 2.7 kilometres (1.7 miles) starts from the edge of the meadow.

80.2
49.8 **Nixon Creek Trail.** A short one kilometre (0.6 mile) woods walk to a small lake locked in the forest.
23.5
14.6

80.9
50.3 **Kootenay River Picnic Area.** A viewpoint providing an outstanding panorama of the Mitchell Range northward to Hector Gorge and the Vermilion Range beyond. Across the highway to the west is the Brisco Range — its most prominent peak Mount Kindersley (2692 m/8,831 ft). The Brisco Range is a part of the Western Ranges of the Rocky Mountains and is composed of limestones, dolomites, sandstones, and shales which were formed during the Ordovician and Silurian geological periods 400 to 500 million years ago.
22.8
14.1

85.1
52.9 **Settler's Road Junction.** A gravel road travelling above the Kootenay River in a southeasterly direction for around seven miles to the park's southern boundary. The road continues beyond the park to the valley's intersection with the Rocky Mountain Trench near Canal Flats, British Columbia.
18.6
11.5

88.5
55.0 **Kootenay Valley Viewpoint.** One of the most expansive views from the Banff-Windermere Parkway. The broad Kootenay Valley stretches from north to south for 80 kilometres (50 miles) or more. Opposite the viewpoint is the long ridge of the Mitchell Range.
15.2
9.4

Just 150 metres (500 ft) or so north along the highway, a few isolated western larch trees can be found. Western larch is a rather rare tree in the Rocky Mountain parks, being found more frequently in the Columbia Valley and the ranges to the west. The larches are the only coniferous trees in Canada to lose their needles in the autumn. In summer, their foliage is soft and light green in colour, but in October the needles turn to yellow-gold before falling from the branches.

89.1
55.4 **Cobb Lake Trail.** A short, 2.7 kilometre (1.7 mile) walk to a small lake on the lower slopes of Mount Sinclair. Much of the forest along the trail is fire succession pine — lodgepole pine which grew up in the wake of a previous conflagration. A few old Douglas fir survive from before the blaze, however. With its thick, furrowed bark, Douglas fir is a fire resistant species, and though many of the trees are charred around their bases from the passing fire, the heartwood remains protected and healthy.
14.6
9.0

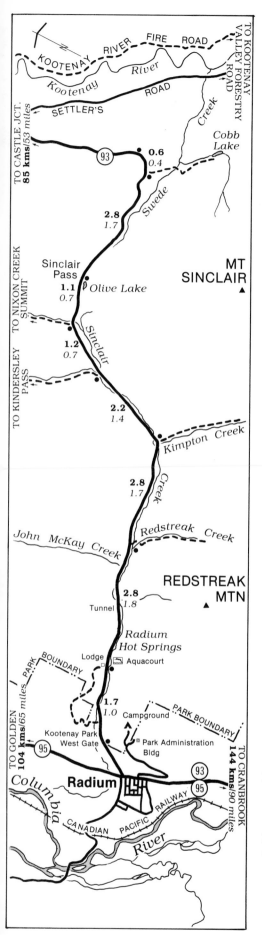

91.9
57.1
Sinclair Pass (1486 m/4,875 ft). In the summer of 1841, a Metis named James Sinclair led a group of Red River emigrants over the pass and down Sinclair Canyon to the Columbia River valley. The group travelled on to the Oregon Territory where its members eventually settled. Sinclair's path across the mountains was a rugged one, crossing from the Bow Valley to the western slopes via White Man Pass, then ascending to this rugged gap between the Brisco and Stanford Ranges.
11.8
7.3

A picnic area is located near the summit, just east of Olive Lake.

Olive Lake. A beautiful, green lake set in the dense forest of Sinclair Pass. The lake is at the top of the steep grade descending to Radium Hot Springs and the Columbia Valley.

93.0
57.8
Sinclair Creek Trail. A trail leading up the narrow gorge of Sinclair Creek for approximately 6 kilometres (4 miles) to the stream's source near the spine of the Brisco Range.
10.7
6.6

94.2
58.5
Kindersley Pass Trail. A trail leading up to the watershed divide on the Brisco Range and the high meadows beyond. The trail eventually crosses a 2375 metre (7,800 ft) ridge to connect with the Sinclair Creek Trail in the adjoining watershed. This high country is home to the Sinclair Canyon herd of mountain sheep in late summer.
9.5
5.9

94.7
58.8
Sinclair Creek Picnic Area.
9.0
5.6

96.4
59.9
Kimpton Creek Trail. A 4.8 kilometre (3.0 mile) hike along the forested drainage of Kimpton Creek.
7.3
4.5

99.2
61.6
Redstreak Creek Trail. A short, 2.6 kilometre (1.6 mile) hike up the Redstreak Creek canyon.
4.5
2.8

The 10 kilometre (6 mile) section of Sinclair Canyon running from near the aquacourt to the summit of Sinclair Pass is surely one of the most pleasant and beautiful areas of its kind in the mountain parks. Sinclair Creek tumbles down along the road at a steady drop of over 50 metres per kilometre (250 feet per mile). In some shaded sections along the stream, particularly where the creek is running on the south side of the canyon, western red cedar grows in the cool, damp environment. Where the stream banks are more open and exposed to sunlight, pink fireweed stands on tall stalks beside the sparkling water. Several picnic areas and pull-offs present a chance to stop and enjoy this exceptional area, while short nature trails probe many of the side-canyons along the way.

101.2
62.9
Iron Gates Tunnel.
2.5
1.5

101.5
63.1
Iron Gates Parking Area. A roadside stop surrounded by the red cliffs which have given this section of the canyon its name. The limestone and dolomite breccia cliffs have been stained by iron oxides contained in the hot, mineral spring waters which have bubbled to the surface in this locale for thousands of years. The cliffs lie in the plane of a major fracture in the strata called the Redwall Fault. The fault extends thousands of metres beneath the earth's surface and it is along its plane that the hot mineral waters rise to their present outlets in the aquacourt area.
2.2
1.3

Bighorn sheep are often seen on the north side of the canyon between the Iron Gates and the mouth of the canyon. It is estimated that as many as 100 of these animals inhabit the hot springs area during the spring and fall, but the herd moves into the alpine country above the canyon in mid-summer.

The pool at Radium Hot Springs, ca. 1910.
Archives of the Canadian Rockies

102.0 **Radium Hot Springs Aquacourt.** On the south side of the highway is
63.4 the main aquacourt complex with its hot pool, swimming pool, bath-house and restaurant facilities. Above the highway to the north, stands the Radium Hot Springs Lodge. Parking areas adjoin both facilities. Motorists should drive slowly and with caution since this is a very busy and crowded area during the summer months.
1.7
1.0

Radium Hot Springs. The springs feeding the pool bubble to the surface at temperatures which range from 35°C (95°F) to 47°C (117°F), depending upon the spring and season of the year. The springs receive their name because of their relatively high radioactivity compared to other mineral springs in the Rockies. As with other hot mineral springs, it is believed surface water seeps down into the earth's crust via a system of fractures and joints in the rock. At a level several thousand metres beneath the surface, the water is heated and percolated upward to appear in the form of hot springs. The mineral content of the water is acquired from the bedrock along the way.

As might be expected from the composition of the surrounding strata, the springs contain a rather high percentage of calcium (limestone is calcium carbonate) as well as quantities of sodium, magnesium, potassium and other minerals. Generally, however, the waters of the Radium Hot Springs have a lower mineral content than similar springs in the Rockies.

It is interesting to note that the day following the Alaska earthquake in the spring of 1964 the waters of the springs displayed a distinct reddish-brown discolouration. It is assumed that the muddiness was caused by minor movements along the Redwall Fault which released small quantities of the oxidized breccia into the spring water.

103.1 **Sinclair Canyon.** At the mouth of the canyon, the walls of limestone
64.1 have been split by the eroding waters of Sinclair Creek to form a narrow gap through which the highway runs. Faults or fractures in the rock can be seen in the canyon's walls, as different kinds of rock are brought together on opposite sides of dipping fault planes.
0.6
0.3

103.5 **Juniper Trail.** An interesting 3.2 kilometre (2.0 mile) nature walk
64.3 leading up to the lip of Sinclair Canyon and down to the aquacourt area.
0.2
0.1

103.7 **Kootenay Park Entrance Gate.** An information office and rest rooms
64.4 are located just inside the park gates on the south side of the highway.
0.0

WESTBOUND
Kilometres
Miles

BANFF WINDERMERE
PARKWAY

EASTBOUND
Kilometres
Miles

Icefields Parkway

Hector Lake.

Of the many exceptional roadways in the mountain national parks, the Icefields Parkway must be considered the preeminent for scenic grandeur and variety of interesting features.

The Parkway is by far the longest tour in the four contiguous parks, stretching for 230 kilometres (143 miles) from the Trans-Canada Highway on the south to the townsite of Jasper on the north. The course which the road follows is unusual as well, tracking along in the shadow of the Great Divide in a general north-south direction rather than just cutting across the range east to west in the manner of the other main park highways.

The Icefields Parkway crests two passes which are the highest traversed by public road in the parks: the crossings of Bow Summit (2069 m/6,787 ft) and Sunwapta Pass (2035 m/6,675 ft) take visitors to the very edge of the treeless, alpine tundra.

All the terrain which the highway traverses has been heavily glaciated, and the features left in the wake of these ice age advances are a highlight of the tour. Not all the glaciers have disappeared either, with well over 100 visible from the roadway between Jasper and Lake Louise.

The Parkway is also one of the best roads for viewing wildlife; it is not uncommon to sight black bear, moose, elk, mule deer, mountain sheep, goat and coyote on any given excursion.

Of course, the focal point of the Parkway for most travellers is the Athabasca Glacier — a tongue of the 325 square kilometre (130 square mile) Columbia Icefield. Not only is this the only glacier in the parks accessible by road, it is a part of the largest body of ice in the Rocky Mountains. The features surrounding the Icefield are of grander proportion than anywhere else, too, with huge rock and gravel moraines rimming the valleys, glacially-carved amphitheatres gouged into the sides of mountain peaks, swollen, silt-laden rivers pouring from ice caves, and mountains that rise to over 3600 metres (12,000 feet) above sea level.

Some people make only half the trip along the Icefields Parkway, venturing south to the Athabasca Glacier from Jasper or north from Lake Louise, then returning the way they came. Yet, the fullest and most rewarding trip is to travel the route in its entirety, moving at a leisurely pace and taking time to explore some of the scenic trails that wander off through subalpine forest and flowered alpine tundra. Or better yet, spending a week or more travelling the Parkway by bicycle, staying at the conveniently spaced youth hostels along the way.

Travellers southbound from Jasper, turn to page 119 and work backwards, following distances in the right-hand margin.

0.0   **Junction of the Icefields Parkway with the Trans-Canada Highway,**   **230.3**
1.6 kilometres (1.0 mile) west of the Lake Louise service centre exit and   *143.1*
7.0 kilometres (4.4 miles) east of the Great Divide.

Slabs of orange-red rock are tilted steeply toward the sky in a roadside
outcrop at this junction. The slate-like rock is among the oldest found in
the parks, having been deposited as sediment over 600 million years ago
on the floor of a Precambrian ocean.

0.8   **Icefields Parkway Interpretive Exhibit.** At the top of the grade just a   **229.5**
0.5   short distance from the Trans-Canada Highway junction is a Parks   *142.6*
Canada interpretive exhibit designed specifically for northbound travellers starting the Icefields Parkway tour. In addition to giving an excellent preview of the 230 kilometre journey which lies ahead, this roadside
stop allows a close-up look at one of the typical forest types encountered
on the trip — a dense stand of fire succession lodgepole pine.

3.0   **Herbert Lake.**   **227.3**
1.9   *141.2*

3.3   **Herbert Lake Picnic Area.** A beautiful, roadside lake set within a forest   **227.0**
2.0   of lodgepole pine. From the lakeshore below the parking area, you can   *141.1*
look south to the cluster of high peaks that comprise the Bow Range —
the mountains which surround Lake Louise. The highest of these peaks is
ice-capped Mount Temple (3544 m/11,626 ft), visible furthest to the
south. The closest mountains in the range, rising directly across the lake
to the southwest, are Mount St. Piran (2649 m/8,691 ft), Mount Niblock
(2976 m/9,764 ft), and standing behind them, Mount Whyte (2983
m/9,786 ft). Looking to the west, just north of the Bow Range, is the
broad, low gap of the Kicking Horse Pass which carries the Trans-Canada
Highway and the Canadian Pacific Railway across the Great Divide.

Like many small, valley-bottom lakes in the Rockies, Herbert Lake has
no visible outlet stream. Known as a "sink" lake, the depression which it
occupies was probably formed by the wasting away of a detached block of
ice in a bed of silt and gravel near the end of the last ice age.

Between the Hector Lake Viewpoint and Herbert Lake, northbound
travellers have good views to Mount Hector, while southbound travellers
look upon the massive north wall of Mount Temple and the peaks of the
Bow Range surrounding Lake Louise. The Waputik Range follows along
on the western horizon for much of the distance between the two viewpoints, exhibiting superb examples of cirques (glacially-carved, bowl-
shaped depressions) between peaks and avalanche paths descending into
the forest from the ridges above.

17.0   **Hector Lake Viewpoint.** Hector Lake is named for Dr. James Hector, the   **213.3**
10.6   geologist with the Palliser Expedition who was the first white man to pass   *132.5*
up this valley in the autumn of 1858. The range of mountains surrounding
the lake and trailing away to the south is called the Waputik Range
(Waputik is the Stoney Indian name for "white goat").

The mountain rising above the near end of the lake is Pulpit Peak (2725
m/8,940 ft). On its slopes grow some of the most northerly stands of

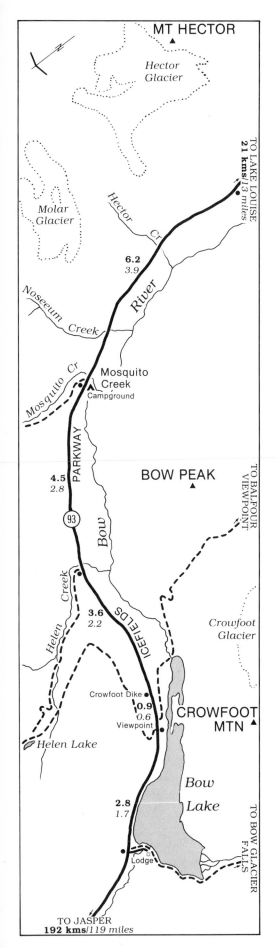

alpine larch found in the Rockies. The larches are the only deciduous conifers found in Canada. In autumn, their needles turn from pale green to gold, giving a splash of colour to the slopes of Pulpit Peak before they dry up and fall from the branches. As with all the slopes of the Waputik Range, distinct avalanche paths can be seen fingering down from the upper ridges of Pulpit Peak and into the forest below.

Many bowl-shaped depressions are visible along the slopes of the mountains above Hector Lake and the Waputik Range to the south. These cirques were carved by the eroding and plucking action of alpine glaciers which once occupied the slopes (some still do). Probably the most beautiful example of these glacially-carved bowls is that nestled on the northwest slope of Pulpit Peak, directly above Hector Lake. This cirque contains a small tarn called Turquoise Lake. The lake's outlet stream tumbles over the cliff at the mouth of the cirque and down into Hector Lake. Cirques like this are also known as "hanging valleys." While the Turquoise Lake cirque was being carved into the slopes of the Waputik Range, a larger glacier carved the valley which contains Hector Lake. When the ice retreated, the cirque was left "hanging" on the side of the Hector Lake valley.

Mount Hector looms above this viewpoint to the east. Looking up-valley, Bow Peak is the first mountain north of Hector Lake, while the castellated towers of Dolomite Peak rise near the head of the valley beyond.

17.9 *11.1*	**Hector Lake Trail.** A short hike down to the shores of the Bow River. Strong hikers can ford the river at the point where the trail reaches it and carry on for another 800 metres to the pleasant shores of Hector Lake.	**212.4** *132.0*

23.0 *14.3*	**No See Um Creek.** No See Ums are small blackflies noted for their vicious bite.	**207.3** *128.8*

24.1 *15.0*	**Mosquito Creek Campground.** By wandering around to the open areas of the campground or down to the open flats by the Bow River, good views can be had of the complete circle of peaks in this section of the valley. Across the Bow River to the west rise the reddish-orange quartz sandstone cliffs of Bow Peak (2868 m/9,409 ft), its bedding dipping away to the west. The rugged cliffs of Mount Hector (3394 m/11,135 ft) dominate the southeast skyline.	**206.2** *128.1*

Further north, beyond Bow Peak, stands Dolomite Peak. The strata in Dolomite Peak are nearly horizontal causing it to weather into a castellate or layer-cake type of mountain. The many towers along the mountain's ridgeline are typical of this form of natural sculpting.

Across the highway from the campground, the Mosquito Creek trail strikes off to the northeast, climbing through the subalpine forest of the narrow valley and onto the alpine tundra of Molar Pass 10 kilometres (6 miles) distant.

28.6 *17.8*	**Helen Creek Trail.** This trail climbs up the Helen Creek drainage for 6.0 kilometres (3.7 miles) onto the alpine meadows surrounding Helen Lake — an area particularly rich in wildflowers during the month of July. A continuation of the trail reaches Katherine Lake at Kilometre 8.0 (Mile 5.0) and Dolomite Pass at Kilometre 8.9 (Mile 5.5).	**201.7** *125.3*

From the parking area by the creek, walk south on the highway for approximately 150 metres to where a major avalanche has swept a path down through the forest to the very edge of the pavement. This slide occurred during the heavy-snow winter of 1971-72.

32.2   **Igneous Rock Outcrop.** Igneous formations — rock which has been   **198.1**
20.0   formed from molten magma — are quite uncommon in the Canadian   *123.1*
Rockies. In fact, this outcrop of dense, greenish rock by the side of the road is the only known occurrence of igneous rock in Banff Park. Known as the Crowfoot Dike, it is a diorite intrusion which, when in a molten state, forced its way through and across the bedding of the surrounding sedimentary strata.

33.1   **Crowfoot Glacier Viewpoint.** Perched on the sheer face of Crowfoot   **197.2**
20.6   Mountain is the cold, blue ice of Crowfoot Glacier. Throughout the   *122.5*
decades of the Twentieth Century, glaciers in the Rockies have been retreating, and Crowfoot is no exception. Early in this century, when the first pack trains wound their way northward from Lake Louise, this glacier resembled the foot of a crow with three large "toes" of ice hooked across the face of the mountain. But, in the past 50 years, the third toe, which had descended over the lowest cliff, has disappeared. Only the well-defined ridges of terminal moraine debris on the slope below the cliff bear witness to the extent of the glacier's last advance.

Below the viewpoint, the turquoise waters at the southern tip of Bow Lake narrow to form the Bow River. Beyond Crowfoot Glacier to the southeast, separated from Crowfoot Mountain by a low col, is Bow Peak (2868 m/9,409 ft).

Crowfoot Glacier as it looked shortly after the turn of the century (above) and as it appears today (below).

The forest in this section of valley is subalpine, composed of Engelmann spruce, alpine fir, and a few stands of lodgepole pine. The open meadows which finger through these stands are filled with wildflowers during July and August.

A trail starts across the highway from the viewpoint and climbs around the shoulder of Cirque Peak to Helen and Katherine Lakes, and the treeless, alpine tundra of Dolomite Pass — all within 9 kilometres (5.5 miles).

34.5   **Bow Lake Viewpoint.** One of the most beautiful lakes in the mountain   **195.8**
21.4   parks, Bow Lake serves as the headwaters of the Bow River and, hence,   *121.7*
the South Saskatchewan River. Across the lake to the northwest is the red-roofed Num-ti-jah Lodge. The walls of Crowfoot Mountain glower from across the narrow southern arm of lake.

35.9   **Num-ti-jah Lodge Road.** The first lodge was built here in the 1920's by   **194.4**
22.3   the pioneer outfitter and guide Jimmy Simpson. Before the construction   *120.8*
of the Icefields Highway, the lodge was accessible only by a long, twisting horse trail from the railway station at Lake Louise.

At the head of the valley which contains Bow Lake, the tumbled icefall of the Bow Glacier can be seen cascading over the upper cliffs of a huge rock amphitheatre. Below the glacier toe, a hidden, meltwater lake feeds a large waterfall which pours over a 150 metre (500 ft) wall of Cambrian age quartz sandstone.

A 5 kilometre (3 mile)-long trail leads off from the parking area adjacent to the lodge road, follows the lakeshore past the lodge, and eventually emerges at the foot of the Bow Glacier Falls. It is a fine, half day outing which offers the hiker a close-up look at the outwash plain of a major

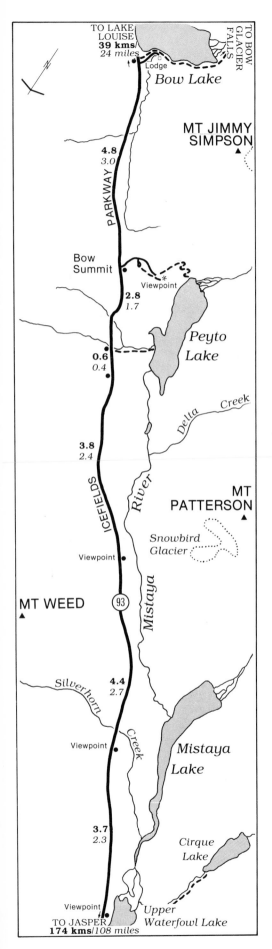

icefield. Near the falls, there is a narrow canyon with a natural bridge. Beneath the falls, a huge, rock-filled bowl is contained by the terminal moraines of the last major glacial advance.

Num-ti-jah Lodge is open year around with meals and accommodation. Parking at the lodge is limited, however, so hikers and sightseers should park at the access road entrance.

Between the Num-ti-jah Lodge Road and Bow Summit, the Parkway passes through an area of willow-covered meadowland. While trees grow on either side of this shallow valley, the meadow can be thought of as belonging to the alpine zone. This anomaly provides an excellent example of the influences of microclimate on forest vegetation. A combination of factors may account for the lack of trees in this area: excessive moisture, the slope's exposure to winds funnelling down from the nearby Wapta Icefield, heavy accumulation of snow in winter, and temperature inversions which tend to seal cold air in the valley bottoms. Watch for these and other microclimatic variations as you travel along the Parkway, particularly as they affect the upper limit of tree growth from one mountain slope to another.

These meadows with their brushy growth of willow and dwarf birch are a good place to spot such birds as the solitary sandpiper, water pipit, savannah sparrow, and even the occasional mountain bluebird.

40.7   **Bow Summit (2069 m/6,787 ft).** This pass serves as the watershed   **189.6**
25.3   divide for the North and South Saskatchewan River systems. Waters that   *117.8*
split on this divide do not meet again until the prairies of central Saskatchewan. There, the two branches join to flow on toward Hudson's Bay.

A spur road branches from the Parkway on the pass, climbing for 500 metres to the parking area for the Peyto Lake Viewpoint. The viewpoint has as much to offer in the way of interesting features and scenic vistas as any other point-of-interest in the mountain parks. A short walk of some 400 metres from the parking area concludes at a spectacular overlook for Peyto Lake — a turquoise, glacial meltwater lake 240 vertical metres (800 ft) below.

The lake is fed by the meltwaters of the Peyto Glacier which is visible to the southwest. The glacier is a tongue of the extensive Wapta Icefield, and like similar bodies of ice, it is continually grinding and pulverizing the bedrock over which it flows. The finely ground glacier flour, which is produced by this perpetual abrasion along the sole of the glacier, washes out with the meltwater and into Peyto Lake. A broad, alluvial fan is slowly filling the lake at its inlet as this silt settles out. One day the lake may disappear when it has completely filled with silt.

The glacial rock-flour is also responsible for the distinctive blue-green colour of the lake. At the inlet, the waters pouring into the lake are heavy with silt — an obvious murky grey. But, much of the finer material disperses through the lake and is held in suspension in the water. The light reflecting off these suspended particles is responsible for the unique greenish hue.

Though the Peyto Glacier is presently retreating (it has receded nearly a mile in the last century), it once advanced well down the Mistaya Valley. A glacier carries a great deal of rock material on its surface and locked within its ice. This material is deposited along the edge of the tongue as lateral moraine and near the point of furthest advance as terminal moraine. A terminal moraine left after one of these glacial advances is responsible for the formation of Peyto Lake, having dammed the lake near its present outlet.

Glacial advances down the Mistaya Valley during the Pleistocene age are also responsible for the distinctive U-shape of the valley. Valleys carved by stream erosion have a sharper, V-shape appearance.

Peyto Glacier and Lake are named for the pioneer packer and guide Bill Peyto. Bill guided some of the early packtrains northward from Lake Louise around the turn of the century, and he was noted for his colourful, outspoken manner. One of the campsites on the trail north was here at Bow Summit, and legend has it that Bill would often pack up his bedroll in the evening and head down to the lake to spend the night, noting as he left that "it's just too crowded around here for me." Hence, the lake came to be known as Peyto's Lake.

The forest at the viewpoint is typical of the upper reaches of the sub-alpine zone. Engelmann spruce and alpine fir are the common species, stunted in size by the altitude and exposure to the elements. Some of these small, twisted trees have dead limbs and needles; these branches, left uncovered by winter snows and unable to gain moisture from the frozen ground, are destroyed by the desiccating effect of cold, winter winds.

Another tree indigenous to the exposed slopes near timberline is white-bark pine. Whitebark is a five-needled pine, its needles growing in fascicles, or bundles, of five rather than in pairs like the lodgepole pine.

In July and August, the meadows along the viewpoint trail are covered with wildflowers — the distinctive ground covers of white mountain avens and the red and white heathers; the white-flowered western ane-mone and globeflower growing in the damper environments; the tiny, blue alpine forget-me-not and cream coloured androsace clinging to the open hillsides.

This is a good area for the study of timberline birdlife. In addition to the noisy Clark's nutcrackers which are continually fluttering about in search of a handout, the meadows are home to white-tailed ptarmigan — a member of the grouse family which turns white in winter and a mottled grey-brown in summer to blend perfectly with the surroundings. Other species commonly seen on these slopes at various times of the year include hermit thrushes, crossbills, fox sparrows and grey-crowned rosy finches.

A steep trail descends from the Peyto Lake Viewpoint for 2½ kilometres (1½ miles) to the edge of the lake, allowing exploration along the lakeshore and across the alluvial deposits at the lake's inlet.

Peyto Lake and the Mistaya Valley.

Bill Peyto.
Archives of the Canadian Rockies

43.5 **Peyto Glacier Viewpoint.** Off to the southwest, the tongue of the Peyto **186.8**
27.0 Glacier descends from the expansive Wapta Icefield névé. The large *116.1*
mountain hemming the glacier in on the left is Mount Thompson (3084 m/10,119 ft), while Peyto Peak (2989 m/9,805 ft) stands to the right. The Mistaya Valley drops away from this viewpoint toward the north and its rendezvous with the North Saskatchewan River 32 kilometres (20 miles) distant.

A short 1.6 kilometre (1.0 mile) trail down to the shores of Peyto Lake takes its head just south of this pull-off, near the end of the guard rail on the opposite side of the road. An enjoyable walk (though boggy and wet at times) through a dense, subalpine forest to a small, gravel beach on the lakeshore.

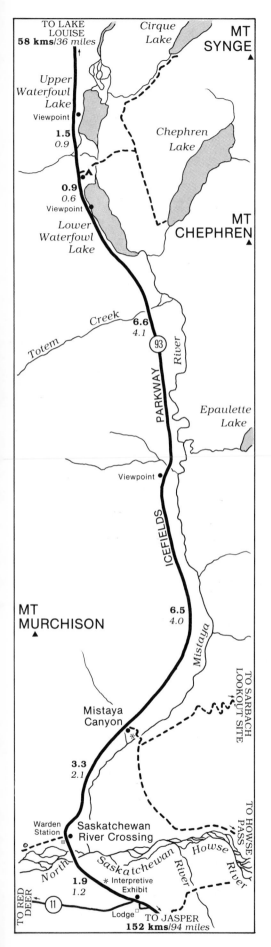

44.1
27.4
Rock Slide. Here a large slide of reddish-orange quartz sandstone has tumbled down from the slopes to the east.
186.2
115.7

47.9
29.8
Snowbird Glacier Viewpoint. Above the highway to the west, spread across the face of Mount Patterson like a white angel, is the beautiful Snowbird Glacier. The glacier is all the more interesting for the well-defined moraines beneath the cliffs of Mount Patterson. Showing up as two, high ridges of rock and gravel debris, these moraines indicate the extent of a previous glacial advance.
182.4
113.3

52.3
32.5
Barbette Glacier Viewpoint. This alpine glacier is set within a deep cirque on the northwest side of Mount Patterson (3197 m/10,490 ft). From this hanging valley, the glacier's meltwaters drop over 300 metres into Mistaya Lake. Though the lake is one of the largest in the valley, and less than a mile from the roadway, few visitors have ever seen it, since it is so well hidden by the surrounding forest.
178.0
110.6

56.0
34.8
Upper Waterfowl Lake Viewpoint. Two well-defined cirques stand out across the valley from this viewpoint. Both of these steep-walled amphitheatres were carved into the slopes of the Great Divide by the plucking action of glaciers over many thousands of years, and the mouths of both have been dammed by morainal deposits to form lakes — Cirque Lake hidden in the left-hand bowl and Chephren Lake in the right.
174.3
108.3

Here, probably more than at any other point in its long, twisted course, the Great Divide takes on the appearance of a sheer barrier of rock. In fact, so wall-like is the divide behind the Cirque Lake bowl, it is almost impossible to distinguish where one mountain ends and the other begins (the main mountain rising behind the cirque is Stairway Peak). Two very well-defined and spectacular peaks dominate the Chephren Lake cirque, however: behind the bowl towers the snow and ice-crusted head of Howse Peak (3290 m/10,793 ft) while the distinctive, leaning pyramid of Mount Chephren (3266 m/10,715 ft) stands to the north near the mouth of the amphitheatre.

Upper Waterfowl Lake is one of a series of lakes which the Mistaya River flows through on its journey to the North Saskatchewan River. The lake is in the process of silting-up from its south (inlet) end. The Mistaya breaks into several channels, flowing across the flats in a braided pattern before entering the lake. The valley's low, marshy aspect makes excellent moose habitat.

57.5
35.7
Waterfowl Lakes Campground. At the rear of the campground, near where the Mistaya River enters Lower Waterfowl Lake, a trail leads to the amphitheatres containing Cirque and Chephren Lakes. Both are excellent examples of glacially-carved cirques, with remnant glaciers clinging to their vertical headwalls and well-defined morainal deposits indicating the extent of previous glacial advances.
172.8
107.4

58.4
36.3
Lower Waterfowl Lake Viewpoint. Mount Chephren (3266 m/10,715 ft) is the dominant peak across the lake from this pull-off. If you look closely, you might discern that the upper half of the mountain is composed primarily of grey-coloured rock, while the lower half exhibits bedding of a reddish-orange hue: the grey formations are mainly Cambrian age limestones, and the orange, slightly older quartzites. Howse Peak (3290 m/10,793 ft) rises just as proudly to the left of Chephren, displaying the same geological structure.
171.9
106.8

TURN TO PAGE 105 —

Herbert Lake.

Bow Lake (top) and Peyto Lake (bottom).

98

The alpine meadows near Bow Summit are home to numerous species of wildflowers as well as white-tailed ptarmigan (below).

Athabasca Glacier.

*The Columbia Icefield Chalet
and Dome Glacier.*

Mount Athabasca from near the Icefield Chalet.

Dome Glacier.

*Mountain goat (top) and bighorn sheep (below) are commonly
seen near Sunwapta Pass.*

*Mount Athabasca from the
Sunwapta Gorge viewpoint.*

Mount Kitchener from the Sunwapta River valley.

The Athabasca Valley with Mount Christie and Brussels Peak.

65.0 **Kaufmann Peaks Viewpoint.** The Kaufmann Peaks, rising to 3109 **165.3**
40.4 metres (10,200 ft) and 3094 metres (10,150 ft) above sea level, are named *102.7*
after Christian Kaufmann, an early Swiss climbing guide who partici-
pated in the first ascent of the mountain in 1902. The massive cliffs of
Mount Murchison rise above the pull-off to the east.

71.5 **Mistaya Canyon Trail.** A short nature trail of only 300 metres (0.2 mile) **158.8**
44.4 drops down from a roadside pull-off to the gorge of the Mistaya Canyon. *98.7*
Here the rushing waters of the Mistaya River have cut deeply into
limestone bedrock to form a narrow, twisting gorge with sheer vertical
walls. It is interesting to see how the action of water has sculpted the
canyon, dissolving the limestone to widen the gorge and, with the help of
rocks and boulders carried in the current, eroding rounded, pothole
depressions into the walls. (Mistaya is the Cree word for "grizzly bear".)

A bridge spans the gorge, and trails carry on to the old Sarbach Lookout
site, 5.1 kilometres (3.2 miles) and Howse Pass, 26 kilometres (16 miles).

The braided channels of the Howse River with the towering pyramid of Mount Outram on the right.

74.8 **Saskatchewan River Warden Station.** **155.5**
46.5 *96.6*

75.1 **Saskatchewan River Bridge.** **155.2**
46.7 *96.4*

76.4 **Howse Valley Interpretive Exhibit.** The best views of the Howse Valley **153.9**
47.5 are available by walking through the forest behind the interpretive exhibit *95.6*
trailer to the lip of the glacial outwash bench. Here the broad, historic
Howse Valley stretches away toward the Great Divide and the earliest
pass used as a regular route of travel across the Rocky Mountains. In
1807, the North West Company sent fur trader David Thompson up the
North Saskatchewan River from its outpost of Rocky Mountain House in
the foothills. His mission was to cross the Rockies, establish a trading
post on the western slope, and if possible, explore and survey a route to
the Pacific Coast. Thompson and his small party, travelling by canoe and
horse, reached these flats on the Howse in early June. Near the bend in
the valley (visible about 10 kilometres distant), they set camp to await the
melting of snow on the Howse Pass. To these prairie traders, some of the
earliest white men in the Rockies, the scene was understandably awesome. Wrote Thompson:

"Here among the stupendous and solitary Wilds covered with eternal
Snow, and Mountain connected to Mountain by immense Glaciers, the
collection of Ages and on which the Beams of the Sun make hardly any
Impression when aided by the most favourable weather. I staid for 14
Days more, impatiently waiting the melting of the Snows on the Height of
Land."

Thompson crossed the pass, which lies hidden in the distance behind the
peaks of the Waputik Mountains, and established a post on the Columbia
River near the present-day town of Invermere, British Columbia. Over
the next three years, he spread his company's trade down into the valleys
of Montana and Idaho as well. Howse Pass served as the main trade route
across the Rockies until 1811, when the Piegan Indians threw up a
blockade west of Rocky Mountain House to prevent the traffic in guns to
their enemies on the western slope. The pass and river receive their
names from Joseph Howse, a trader with the rival Hudson's Bay Company, who trailed Thompson across the Rockies in 1810 to assess the
chances of establishing a competitive trade.

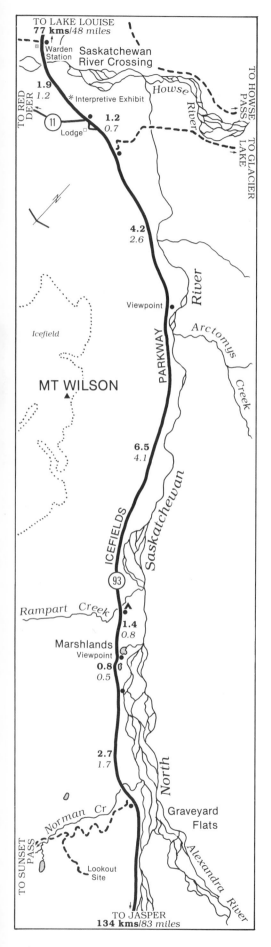

From this excellent lookout point, a broad panorama of mountains opens up to the south and west. Rising nearby to the left is Mount Sarbach (3127 m/10,260 ft). The prominent peak standing between the Howse Valley and the Glacier River valley to the right is Mount Outram (3252 m/10,670 ft), named for a British mountaineer who made many first ascents of major peaks in the Rockies in the first decade of this century. Just visible behind and to the right of Mount Outram is the pyramid-tip summit of Mount Forbes at 3612 metres (11,852 ft), the second highest peak in Banff Park. Further north is Survey Peak (2676 m/8,781 ft) with the broad, high summit of Mount Erasmus (3265 m/10,711 ft) rising behind.

The interpretive trailer is open during the summer months with displays explaining the natural and human history of this part of the park.

76.7 **David Thompson Highway Junction.** This highway leads eastward and **153.6**
47.7 out of the mountains along the North Saskatchewan River. The park *95.4*
boundary is 8 kilometres (5 miles), Rocky Mountain House 180 kilometres (112 miles), and Red Deer 257 kilometres (160 miles).

77.0 **Saskatchewan River Crossing-Parkway Lodge.** The two most impres- **153.3**
47.8 sive mountains seen from the parking area at Saskatchewan River Cross- *95.3*
ing are without a doubt Mount Wilson (3240 m/10,631 ft) and Mount
Murchison (3333 m/10,936 ft), situated to the north and south respectively. Since Saskatchewan River Crossing is near an elevation of 1433
metres (4,700 feet) above sea level, these two mountains have an incredible vertical rise above the valley floor of well over a mile. It is little
wonder the Indians once thought Mount Murchison to be the highest
mountain in the Rockies.

Both Mounts Wilson and Murchison are part of the western arm of the
great Castle Mountain Syncline — a downfold in the strata which runs
continuous from Castle Mountain near Banff to Mount Kerkeslin near
Jasper. The bedding of the mountains can be seen dipping eastward
toward the axis of the syncline. Both peaks are carved from Cambrian and
Ordovician limestones, shales and quartz sandstones that are around 500
million years old.

The Parkway Lodge is open throughout the year, offering meals, groceries, accommodation and gasoline.

77.9 **Glacier Lake Trail.** A 8.9 kilometre (5.5 mile) trail that leads westward **152.4**
48.4 through rolling forest of pine and spruce to the shores of an exquisite 3- *94.7*
kilometre-long, glacier fed lake. Beyond the west end of the lake is the
tumbled icefall of the Southeast Lyell Glaciers.

Immediately opposite this trail head is Mount Wilson. The cliffs above
tree-line on this mountain are one of the best spots along the Icefields
Parkway to see mountain goats. However, you will need binoculars since
the goats are only a white speck at this distance.

82.1 **Mount Erasmus-Mount Wilson Viewpoint.** Massive cliffs of lime- **148.2**
51.0 stone rise above the highway to the east, composing the lower slopes of *92.1*
Mount Wilson. Across the Valley of the North Saskatchewan stand
Survey Peak and Mount Erasmus. On the lower slopes of Survey Peak is a
broad patch of burnt timber which was destroyed by a major fire which
swept the North Saskatchewan Valley in July of 1940 — the year that the
Banff-Jasper Highway was completed. Down the highway to the south is
the broad Mount Murchison massif and, to the right, Mount Sarbach with
the ship's prow of Mount Chephren jutting out behind.

88.6 **Rampart Creek Campground.** Looking down-valley from the camp-
55.1 ground entrance road, the massive cliffs of Mount Wilson (3240
m/10,631 ft) contain the left side of the valley; on the right rises Survey
Peak, its lower slopes denuded by a past forest fire. Further down-valley
stands Mount Sarbach with the sharp pyramid of Mount Chephren
leaning out from behind.

The North Saskatchewan Valley displays typical glacier-fed, river bottom
terrain, with broad gravel flats populated by sparse stands of spruce,
shrub willow and birch.

88.8 **Rampart Creek Youth Hostel.**
55.2

90.0 **Marshlands Viewpoint.** This low, wet marshland is created by the
55.9 alluvial fan of Rampart Creek which has pushed the North Saskatchewan
River to the west and nearly blocked the valley. This wetland makes
excellent moose habitat, and it is not uncommon to see one of these
animals grazing on the succulent underwater plants near dawn or at dusk.

90.8 **Mount Amery-Mount Saskatchewan Viewpoint.** A slightly elevated,
56.4 roadside pull-off which allows a very good perspective on the braided
stream pattern of the North Saskatchewan River. At this point, the river is
less than 30 kilometres (20 miles) from its source at the Columbia
Icefield. Its waters are thick with silt and gravel washed out in the
meltwater streams from this huge body of ice. Much of the material is
deposited in these downstream areas, and as it accumulates the bed of the
river is broken into several channels which are constantly shifting and
wandering on the broad alluvial flats. The gravel choked valley bottom
with its shifting, braided river of many channels is typical of all glacier-
fed rivers.

Across the valley to the west towers 3335 metre (10,940 ft) Mount
Amery, a deep, bowl-shaped depression carved into its face by the
quarrying action of an alpine glacier. The snow-capped peak to the
northwest, with the small glacier clinging to its slopes, is Mount Saskatchewan (3342 m/10,964 ft). The sedimentary beds in these two
mountains lie nearly horizontal, a factor contributing to their massive,
"layer-cake" appearance.

93.5 **Graveyard Flats.** The Alexandra River flows in from the west, adding its
58.1 own silt-ridden waters to those of the North Saskatchewan. The Alexandra takes its headwaters from the Alexandra Glaciers and the Castleguard River, some 20 kilometres (12 miles) west of this confluence on
the Great Divide.

These broad flats opposite the mouth of the Alexandra River were used as
a campsite for hunting parties during the early years of the century.
Animals were often packed to the camp and skinned, and many bones
and skulls were discarded here. In time, the campsite came to be known
as Graveyard Flats.

At the edge of the forest, on the east side of the road, a trail leads to the
old Sunset Fire Lookout site (4.5 km/2.8 mi.) — a spectacular viewpoint
for the North Saskatchewan and Alexandra Valleys. A branch at Kilometre 2.9 (Mile 1.8) leads over Sunset Pass and down to the shores of
Pinto Lake, 13.7 kilometres (8.5 miles) from the trail head.

141.7
88.0

141.5
87.9

140.3
87.2

139.5
86.7

136.8
85.0

*Travelling to the Columbia Icefield in
1924, a horse outfit fords the North
Saskatchewan River.*

Archives of the Canadian Rockies

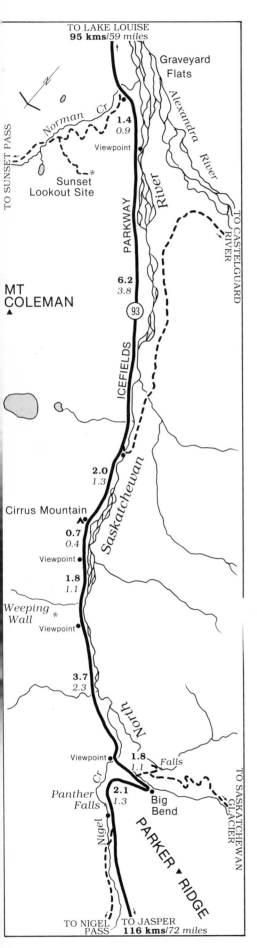

TO LAKE LOUISE
95 kms/59 miles

94.9 **Castelets Viewpoint.** The Castelets are just visible up the Alexandra **135.4**
59.0 River to the west, so named because the twin summits resemble two *84.1*
small castles. Directly across the valley stand the broad and bulky cliffs
of Mount Amery (3335 m/10,940 ft).

101.1 **North Saskatchewan River Viewpoint.** The river flows through a **129.2**
62.8 narrow gorge on the west side of the highway. A bridge across the river *80.3*
marks the head of the Alexandra River fire road — a 23 kilometre (14
mile)-long trail leading to the headwaters of the river, with a branch trail
to the Castleguard Meadows.

103.1 **Cirrus Mountain Campground.** Huge cliffs of grey-coloured lime- **127.2**
64.1 stone rise behind the campground, forming the lower ramparts of Cirrus *79.0*
Mountain.

103.8 **Cirrus Mountain Viewpoint.** Undoubtedly, the dominant feature in this **126.5**
64.5 section of the valley is the massive wall of Devonian age limestone rising *78.6*
600 vertical metres (2,000 ft) above the highway to the east. These cliffs
compose the base of Cirrus Mountain (3267 m/10,720 ft), and in spring
and summer dozens of waterfalls cascade off the upper lip of the precipice.

Looking up the highway to the north, Nigel Peak pokes its head above a
notch in the skyline, displaying a distinct syncline (downfold) structure
in its bedding.

105.6 **Weeping Wall Viewpoint.** Here, the flow of water over the sheer **124.7**
65.6 limestone cliffs of Cirrus Mountain is at its greatest. Throughout the *77.5*
summer, the grey wall is stained dark by the constant flow; in winter,
huge sheets and columns of blue ice cling to the cliff.

This is one of the best viewpoints for the Castle Mountain Syncline to be
found along its entire length. A syncline is a downfold or bend in the
layers of sedimentary rock caused by the extreme forces applied to the
beds during the uplift and deformation of the mountain range. This
particular syncline is one of the best known in the Rockies, since it runs
continuous from Castle Mountain on the south to Mount Kerkeslin on the
north. Looking up-valley to the north, you can see this distinct downward
bend in the rock layers of Parker's Ridge and Nigel Peak beyond.

109.3 **Nigel Creek Canyon.** A pull-off at the north end of a high bridge allows **121.0**
67.9 a glimpse down into the deep gorge cut by Nigel Creek into the dolomite *75.2*
bedrock (dolomite is essentially a limestone containing magnesium, i.e.
calcium magnesium carbonate).

109.8 **North Saskatchewan Canyon Viewpoint.** The elevated pull-off is an **120.5**
68.2 excellent place to stop for a perusal of the North Saskatchewan Valley and *74.9*
the surrounding mountains. Hemming the river to the east is the sheer,
limestone wall of Cirrus Mountain (3267 m/10,720 ft). Though still a part
of the Main Ranges, Cirrus Mountain contains rock which is much
younger than that normally associated with the central section of the
Rocky Mountains. In fact, the formations in the mountain are identical
with those found in the Front Range mountains surrounding Banff
townsite, 160 kilometres (100 miles) to the south. The cliffs in the top and
bottom of Cirrus are composed of massive limestone, while the gentle,
sweeping talus slopes halfway to the summit are formed of easily
weathered shale.

The great syncline or downfold which runs through the strata of the valley is quite obvious from this viewpoint. Cirrus Mountain lies near the axis of the fold, the massive limestone beds in its summit nearly horizontal. The mountain's lower cliffs begin to rise as a part of the west arm of the syncline, while the bedding on the right side of the valley sweeps steeply toward the sky, completing the U-shaped bend in the layers of rock.

110.4 **Saskatchewan Glacier Trail.** This is an unofficial pull-off created by the **119.9**
68.6 junction of the old Banff-Jasper road with the present-day highway. An *74.5*
old concrete bridge below the junction, blocked to vehicular traffic due to its dilapidated condition, marks the beginning of two easy hikes — one a short half hour jaunt to an impressive cataract, and the other a trip of less than two hours to the toe of the Saskatchewan Glacier.

The first option follows the old highway downhill from the bridge for 400 metres to a series of waterfalls which thunder down a narrow gorge that originates high on the glacier-clad north face of Mount Saskatchewan. These impressive falls used to be a popular point-of-interest on the old road, but they are seldom visited today.

The route to Saskatchewan Glacier cuts right from the old Banff-Jasper right-of-way about halfway down to the falls and follows a long-abandoned gravel road to the broad outwash flats below the Saskatchewan ice tongue. (This old road was constructed by the U.S. Army during World War II as a route of access to a mountain warfare training camp below the glacier.) From the end of the road it is easy to pick your way across the stony terrain to the edge of the glacier.

A pack train crossing the Saskatchewan Glacier in 1924.
Archives of the Canadian Rockies

111.1 **Big Bend.** This long, sweeping switchback in the highway helps to hold **119.2**
69.0 a reasonable grade on what has been traditionally known as the "Big *74.1*
Hill". From the top of the grade to the bottom, a distance of some 11 kilometres (7 miles), the Parkway drops a total of 425 vertical metres (1400 ft).

Looking to the west, you can see the North Saskatchewan River tumbling through a narrow canyon which it has cut through the rock. Though it plunges toward the valley floor in a very spirited fashion, it is a mere "trickle" compared to the broad and mighty river which leaves the park just 40 kilometres (25 miles) further downstream.

Across the valley to the south, a veritable gusher of water thunders down a long chute in the bedrock to join the North Saskatchewan — one of that river's first tributaries.

112.7 **North Saskatchewan Valley Viewpoint.** A pull-off which offers excel- **117.6**
70.0 lent views down-valley to the massive cliffs of Cirrus Mountain (3267 *73.1*
m/10,720 ft) and the narrow canyon of the North Saskatchewan River. A distinct U-shaped bend can be seen in the rock composing Cirrus Mountain and the slopes across the valley from it: a cross-section of the Castle Mountain Syncline which runs from just north of Banff townsite to just south of Jasper.

The slender, silver thread of Bridal Veil Falls can be seen across the Nigel Creek gorge.

113.2 **Panther Falls.** A short one kilometre (0.6 mile)-long trail leads from the **117.1**
70.3 lower edge of this large roadside parking area to the foot of Panther Falls. *72.8*
(There is no sign, but the trail is obvious and well graded.) Though few

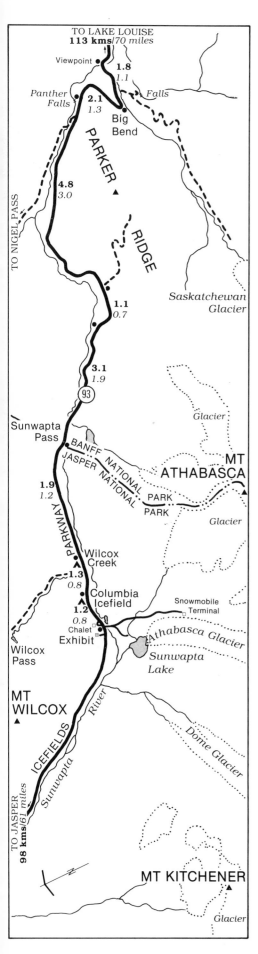

travellers take the time to visit this attraction, it is probably the most impressive roadside waterfall in Banff Park.

Bridal Veil Falls is the thin, graceful column of water visible directly across the valley.

114.1   **Nigel Peak Viewpoint.** Nigel Peak (3211 m/10,535 ft) appears as the   **116.2**
70.9   prominent mountain up the highway to the northwest. The layers of rock   *72.2*
in the mountain are bent into a trough-shaped fold which geologists call a syncline.

The high, subalpine valley of Nigel Creek leads away to the north and the low gap of Nigel Pass. Starting from the old road just below the viewpoint, a trail runs out along this valley, through the pass, and down into the Brazeau River drainage and the remote southwest corner of Jasper Park.

The name Nigel which has attached itself to so many of the features in the vicinity is for Nigel Vavasour, a packer who accompanied the first major climbing expedition to this area in 1898.

118.0   **Parker's Ridge Trail.** An excellent trail from which to examine the   **112.3**
73.3   upper limits of the subalpine forest and the treeless alpine tundra. For the   *69.8*
first 800 metres or so, the trail climbs through an open forest of spruce and alpine fir which becomes progressively more sparse and stunted as elevation is gained. The trail ascends above the upper limits of tree growth at around 2100 metres (7,000 ft) above sea level — the average elevation for timberline in this part of the Rockies.

The open tundra above the tree-limit is carpeted with wildflowers from mid-summer on, with violet-coloured alpine vetch, tiny blue alpine forget-me-nots, red and white mountain heather, the pink-flowered moss campion, and white mountain avens all common.

The growing season at this elevation is only a matter of a few short weeks; the frost-free period can be as little as seven days. Life is precarious, as plants cling close to the surface of the tundra, seeking out moisture in an environment that can be desert-dry during the growing season. All living things at this elevation have made special adaptations which allow them to survive the cold, dryness, and wind.

The trail crosses the top of Parker's Ridge and, at Kilometre 2.4 (Mile 1.5), reaches the viewpoint for the Saskatchewan Glacier. This great, long tongue of the Columbia Icefield is the source of the North Saskatchewan River.

If you do decide to hike this short nature trail, take care not to short-cut straight down through the switchbacks on your return. Stay on the trail. The delicate alpine tundra erodes easily, as can be seen where less considerate hikers have created deep furrows, and damage at this elevation will take decades to mend itself.

The ridge is also an excellent place to look for alpine birds such as white-tailed ptarmigan, grey-crowned rosy finches, Clark's nutcrackers, water pipits, and horned larks.

Visitors hiking on the meadows of Parkers Ridge in early summer, before the last snowbanks have melted away, may notice a distinct pinkish colouring in the snow. This "red snow" is actually a specialized form of algae which has adapted to living on snowfields and glaciers. The red coloration is protective adaptation, screening the chlorophyll cells from destructive wavelengths of intense sunlight at high altitudes. "Red snow" is found nearly everywhere in the Canadian Rockies where snowfields linger into summer.

118.7   **Hilda Creek Youth Hostel.**   **111.6**
73.8   *69.3*

119.1   **Hilda Creek Viewpoint.** A deep, bowl-shaped depression has been   **111.2**
74.0   carved into the slopes of Mount Athabasca to the west. Called a cirque by   *69.1*
geologists, a glacier still occupies its headwall, continuing the work of "plucking" rock from the side of the mountain and deepening the amphitheatre. Ridges of gravel and rock debris near the mouth of the cirque are moraines, deposited by the glacier during a previous advance.

The sharp, spike-like Hilda Peak above the cirque is called a "horn" — a mountain which has had at least three glaciers quarry into its sides, leaving a jagged spire in their wake.

Heavy accumulation of snow on the north slope of Parker's Ridge helps to depress the upper limit of tree growth.

122.2   **Sunwapta Pass (2035 m/6,675 ft).** This pass serves as the watershed   **108.1**
75.9   divide between the Athabasca River drainage to the north and the North   *67.2*
Saskatchewan system to the south. Waters flowing northward from this summit eventually reach the Arctic Ocean via the Mackenzie River, while those flowing south cross the prairies via the Saskatchewan and Nelson drainages to Hudson's Bay.

Sunwapta Pass also serves as the boundary between Banff and Jasper National Parks.

124.1   **Wilcox Creek Campground.** The glacier-clad summit of Mount   **106.2**
77.1   Athabasca (3491 m/11,452 ft) dominates the horizon across the valley.   *66.0*
Behind the campground stands 3211 metre (10,535 ft) Nigel Peak. The rock formations found in Nigel Peak are identical to those found in the Front Ranges near both Banff and Jasper townsites — 160 kilometres (100 miles) south and 105 kilometres (65 miles) north respectively.

125.4   **Columbia Icefield Campground.**   **104.9**
77.9   *65.2*

126.6   **Columbia Icefield Chalet.** The parking area for the chalet also serves as   **103.7**
78.7   an excellent viewpoint for the tongue of the Athabasca Glacier. Mount   *64.4*
Athabasca (3491 m/11,452 ft) totally dominates the skyline to the left of the glacier, while down-valley, the broad, glacier-capped dome of Mount Kitchener rises to a very respectable 3475 metres (11,400 feet) above sea level.

Roads branch from near the chalet to a parking area beside Sunwapta Lake and the toe of the Athabasca Glacier, as well as up along the lateral moraine beneath Mount Athabasca to the station for guided snowmobile tours onto the glacier. The Icefield Chalet offers meals, accommodation, and gasoline throughout the summer season, and a park information bureau is located along the highway 300 metres northwest of the chalet.

Columbia Icefield and Athabasca Glacier. Covering an area of some 325 square kilometres (130 square miles), the Columbia Icefield is the largest body of ice in the Rocky Mountains. The Icefield feeds a number of large glaciers which radiate out from the central névé, one of which is the Athabasca Glacier.

The Icefield Chalet and Dome Glacier.

The extent of the Athabasca Glacier in 1917 (above) and as it is today (below).

Glaciers are formed in areas where winter snowfalls never totally melt. As snow accumulates year by year, the grains become more closely compacted, finally forming ice. It takes great depths of snow, however, to create the pressures necessary to form a glacier, and the Columbia Icefield receives as great an annual snowfall as any other area in the Rockies — often in excess of 7 metres (23 feet).

Glacier ice has all the properties of a liquid, that is, it is continually "flowing" downhill. Thus, the Athabasca Glacier is flowing downhill from the central core of the Icefield beyond the horizon. Yet, despite the forward flow of the ice, the glacier is currently retreating — an indication that the rate of wasting away at the toe is greater than the rate of forward flow. In the first half of the 19th Century, the toe of the Athabasca Glacier advanced as far as the present-day Icefields Parkway, but since then it has been withdrawing, having retreated nearly a mile in less than a century.

A glacier carries great quantities of rock debris on its surface and locked within the ice along its sole; when it retreats, much of the broken rock is left behind in deposits called moraines: where the glacier has hesitated in its retreat, low ridges of rock debris called recessional moraines have been deposited along the stationary ice front; lateral moraines are deposited along the flanks of receding glaciers as narrow, sharp ridges of rock debris; and rolling, random deposits spread in the wake of the retreating tongue are ground moraines.

Looking at the Athabasca Glacier from the chalet, or preferably, the meadows above, one gets a good perspective of the entire length of the glacier. From the toe to the horizon, where it intersects with the main body of the Icefield, the Athabasca Glacier is around 7 kilometres (4½ miles) long. The glacier flows over three cliffs on its descent from the Icefield, visible as steep, broken icefalls. Any irregularities in the bedrock which the ice flows over will cause it to buckle creating deep crevasses, the largest in the Athabasca Glacier being just over 30 metres (100 feet) deep.

The maximum thickness of the ice in the Athabasca Glacier is around 300 metres (1,000 feet) below the lowest icefall. The Icefield névé beyond the horizon reaches thicknesses of up to 365 metres (1200 feet). The elevation of the névé is much greater than that of the Athabasca Glacier, averaging around 2750 metres (9,000 feet) above sea level.

Heavier snowfalls in the Rockies and cool, cloudy summers could trigger an advance of the Athabasca Glacier. Yet, it may take as long as twenty years for such a trend to show up as an advance at the toe of the glacier.

126.9
78.9
Columbia Icefield Information Bureau and Interpretive Centre. This Parks Canada facility provides interpretive slide shows and exhibits on the Columbia Icefield region, and dispenses information on nearby nature walks as well as more lengthy hikes.
103.4
64.2

Bighorn sheep are frequently observed close to the road throughout this section of the Sunwapta Valley. They are very tame due to their constant association with people, but please don't feed them. Many are killed on this road in search of handouts, while others suffer malnutrition from a constant diet of snack foods.

133.0
82.6
Sunwapta Canyon Viewpoint. This lofty overlook sets precariously on the lower slopes of Mount Wilcox with the Sunwapta River plunging through its canyon in the depths below. Just south of the viewpoint, the river makes a great plunge to the canyon floor after cutting through an old rockslide.
97.3
60.5

Looking upstream on the Sunwapta, you can see the massive, ice-clothed slopes of Mount Athabasca (3491 m/11,452 ft) framed by the walls of the valley — a truly inspiring view of this great mountain. Directly across the valley stands ice-capped Mount Kitchener (3475 m/11,400 ft).

The viewpoint is situated at the summit of a 4 kilometre (2.5 mile)-long grade which descends 300 metres (1,000 feet) to the bottom of the Sunwapta Valley.

134.2 **Tangle Falls.** Opposite a small, roadside picnic area, Tangle Creek **96.1**
83.4 plunges in a series of steps over cliffs of 500 million year old limestone. *59.7*

135.8 **Stutfield Glacier Viewpoint.** A tongue of the Columbia Icefield, the **94.5**
84.4 Stutfield Glacier pours down over the headwall of a huge cirque, falling *58.7* over 900 vertical metres (3,000 ft) in a series of icefalls and cliffs. Hemmed in on the south by Mount Kitchener (3475 m/11,400 ft) and on the north by Stutfield Peak (hidden behind the avalanche-swept ridge to the right), the Stutfield Glacier continues to pluck rock from the headwall of this great amphitheatre, eroding even deeper into the Icefield plateau.

Diadem Peak (3371 m/11,060 ft) can be seen down-valley to the north-west, while the Sunwapta River braids its way in several channels across the broad, gravel flats below.

141.0 **Avalanche Path.** By pulling to the side of the highway on this long, **89.3**
87.6 riverside straight-away, you can look across the broad, gravel flats of the *55.5* Sunwapta River to where an avalanche has ripped a narrow swath down through the forest to the valley floor. The timber and other debris which the snowslide swept ahead of it have been left in a pile on the river flats.

141.5 **Beauty Creek and Stanley Falls.** Looking across the gravel flats which **88.8**
87.9 border the highway to the east, watch for the old Banff-Jasper roadbed *55.2* skirting the forest. A bridgeless gap in this road indicates the mouth of Beauty Creek Canyon. By hiking the old road to this gap and then following an old footpath up into the canyon, one will encounter a series of eight cascades in little more than a kilometre. The last and most picturesque of these cataracts is Stanley Falls.

Stanley Falls is yet another beauty spot which has been bypassed by progress in the guise of a new highway. It is totally unmarked and few people visit it today.

144.4 **Beauty Creek Youth Hostel.** **85.9**
89.7 *53.4*

146.0 **Sunwapta River Viewpoint.** Spectacular mountains rise to the south and **84.3**
90.7 west — the peaks of the Columbia Icefield region. Looking across the *52.4* Sunwapta River to the west, there is an excellent example of a glacier-carved cirque or hanging valley; above the cirque towers Diadem Peak (3371 m/11,060 ft) with alpine glaciers clinging to its rugged east face. The massive flanks of Tangle Ridge (3001 m/9,845 ft) appear to block the highway to the south. Between these two giants, yet a greater mountain looms in the distance — 3475 metre (11,400 foot)-Mount Kitchener.

From this roadside stop, you can see how the valley bottom is choked with silt and gravel. The Sunwapta River flows across broad flats via

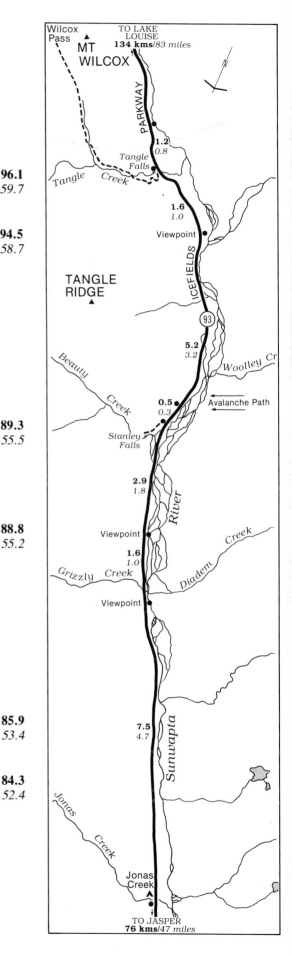

A large slide of sandstone boulders between Jonas and Poboktan Creeks.

several intertwining channels in what is known as a braided stream pattern. These features are typical of a glacial-fed river. The Sunwapta is forever depositing silt and gravel washed out from the glacier, and forever shifting its course as a result.

153.5 *95.4*	**Jonas Creek Campground.**	**76.8** *47.7*

155.3 *96.5* **Quartz Sandstone Rock Slide.** On both sides of the highway, piles of pinkish boulders lie strewn over a vast area. Looking up at the ridge to the east, a great rock slide can be seen descending all the way down the mountainside. Above the boulder field, near the top of the ridge, a distinct pink scar indicates where a huge slab of Cambrian age quartz sandstone broke away and slid into the valley.   **75.0** *46.6*

From this section of highway you can look up-valley to the southeast and see Sunwapta Peak (3315 m/10,875 ft) — a "writing-desk" type of mountain with a long, even slope on the right and a sheer face dropping away on the left. Its dipping strata contrast with the essentially horizontal bedding of Tangle Ridge seen near the head of the valley. The mountain which fed the quartz sandstone rock slide is similar in structure to Sunwapta Peak.

158.6 *98.6* **Poboktan Creek Warden Station.** A trail leading up Poboktan Creek from near the warden station, extends deep into the park's southeast wilderness to the Brazeau Lake region; another branch swings north over Maligne Pass to Maligne Lake.   **71.7** *44.5*

Poboktan is the Stoney Indian word for "owl". In 1892, geologist A. P. Coleman descended this creek with a small exploration party. Coleman later wrote: "We named the pass and creek Poboktan, from the big owls that blinked at us from the spruce trees . . ."

169.7 *105.4* **Bubbling Springs Picnic Area.** This small picnic area is enclosed within a dense forest of lodgepole pine, an indication that this section of the Sunwapta Valley was once swept by a forest fire. Lodgepole pine will only regenerate in a large stand with the help of fire. Its cones are sealed shut with resin and do not readily open until heated to around 45 degrees C (113°F); lodgepole seedlings also need the open, sunlit slopes provided by a recent fire, being unable to thrive under a shaded forest canopy. You will find lodgepole pine stands throughout most of the major valleys of the mountain parks.   **60.6** *37.7*

These woods are home to numerous species of birds that are typical of the pine-spruce forests in Banff and Jasper Parks. Watch and listen for gray jays, Swainson's thrushes, yellow-rumped warblers, dark-eyed juncos, and chipping sparrows.

The picnic area is named for a small, cold-water spring which bubbles to the surface in its midst.

175.7 *109.2* **Sunwapta Falls Junction.** A road entering the Icefields Parkway from the southwest, leads to the parking area for Sunwapta Falls in 600 metres.   **54.6** *33.9*

The Sunwapta Canyon has been eroded at a point where the river makes an abrupt turn from a northwesterly to southwesterly flow. Since it is entering the main Athabasca Valley at this point (it joins that river less than three kilometres downstream), it seems possible the Sunwapta may have been dammed by a previous advance of a glacier down the Athabasca Valley, forcing it to change direction and pushing it over the lip of a cliff. Today, the falls have cut back into the bedrock eroding a deep canyon. The canyon displays the usual smoothing and potholing caused by the abrasive action of silt and gravel-laden waters.

Sunwapta is a Stoney Indian word for "turbulent river", a name adopted by the geologist and Rocky Mountain explorer A. P. Coleman when he bushwhacked down this valley in 1892.

The Sunwapta Bungalow Camp at the junction with the Icefields Parkway provides accommodation, meals, groceries and gasoline throughout the summer season.

178.0 **Buck Lake.** A short road branches to the northeast and the parking area **52.3**
110.6 for Buck Lake. This is one of several small lakes situated on the flats near *32.5* where the Athabasca and Sunwapta Valley glaciers once converged. It is likely the lakes were formed during the last recession of these glaciers when detached blocks of ice were left to waste away in the silt and gravel. As the ice melted, the glacial drift gradually slumped to form the kettle which contains the lake.

179.3 **Honeymoon Lake Campground.** The campground is situated on the **51.0**
111.4 shore of Honeymoon Lake. Across its waters, there is an outstanding *31.7* panorama of the Endless Chain Ridge — a long bastion of reddish-orange Cambrian quartz sandstone which dips steeply toward this viewpoint. One large boulder in the midst of the campground allows a close-up inspection of the predominant bedrock in this part of the valley.

179.9 **Athabasca Valley Viewpoint.** One of the best overlooks available for a **50.4**
111.8 broad, expansive view of the Athabasca Valley. Looking to the south, *31.3* beyond the 3170 metre (10,400 ft) summit of Mount Quincy, you can see nearly to the headwaters of the Athabasca; the valley exhibits the characteristic U-shape carved by the passing of a major glacier. The valley to the west (right) of Mount Quincy is the Chaba, leading to Fortress Lake — one of the largest lakes in the Canadian Rockies.

184.2 **Mount Christie and Athabasca River Viewpoint.** Here, the Athabasca **46.1**
114.5 River makes a tight horseshoe bend. Someday the river may erode its way *28.6* through the core of the bend, cutting the horseshoe off and leaving this channel dry.

Across the valley, Mount Christie (3103 m/10,180 ft) dominates the horizon. When Dr. James Hector of the Palliser Expedition visited the valley in 1859, he named the peak in honour of William Christie, Chief Factor for the Hudson's Bay Company at Fort Edmonton.

189.1 **Mount Christie Picnic Area.** A pleasant roadside stop situated by the **41.2**
117.5 broad, gravel flats of the Athabasca River and in a forest composed *25.6* primarily of lodgepole pine.

Views across the river are to Mount Christie and, to its north, Mount Fryatt.

Just 100 metres or so south of the picnic area along the highway, a small stand of aspen poplar have had the bark stripped from their trunks up to a

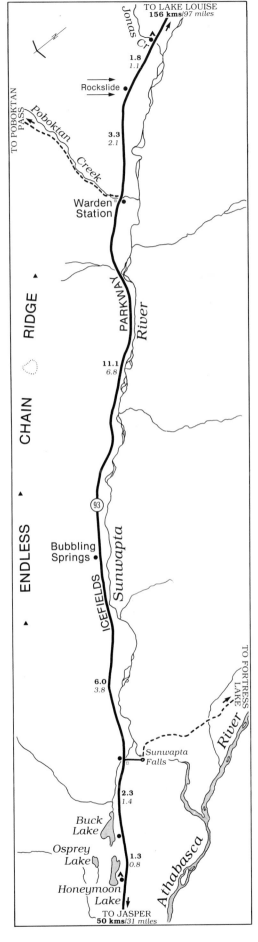

Mount Christie and Brussels Peak rise above the Athabasca River.

level of about four feet above the ground. The damage indicates the presence of elk in this part of the valley, these animals using the bark of aspen as an emergency winter food supply.

192.0 **Athabasca River Viewpoint.** A riverside pull-out exhibiting most of the **38.3**
119.3 same features described at the Goat Viewpoint (900 metres north). Views *23.8*
north to Mount Edith Cavell are more open, however, and the pull-off is usually a little closer to the point where the mountain goats cross the highway.

192.9 **Goat Viewpoint and Picnic Area.** Mountain goats inhabiting the sheer, **37.4**
119.9 quartz sandstone cliffs of Mount Kerkeslin to the east often abandon their *23.2*
lofty home to visit the steep banks of eroded glacial drift exposed beneath this viewpoint. Mountain goats, bighorn sheep, and other animals often seek out natural mineral licks in the mountain parks. These areas of exposed muds or earth contain minerals which the animals crave and need. It is surmised that animals visit these licks during the annual molt, acquiring the important nutrients necessary for renewing a thick, healthy coat.

This elevated picnic area also serves as one of the best viewpoints for this section of the valley. The murky waters of the Athabasca River swirl by, cutting away at the steep bank of silt, rock and gravel on which the viewpoint is situated. Down the valley to the south, two distinct peaks rise from the same mountain block — the pyramid-shaped summit of Mount Christie (3103 m/10,180 ft) and, immediately behind, the steamship funnel of Brussels Peak (3161 m/10,370 ft); the next great mountain mass to the north is Mount Fryatt (3361 m/11,026 ft); the lower mountain to the right of Fryatt is Whirlpool Peak; and finally, northwest of the Whirlpool River gap, the majestic, snow-capped summit of Mount Edith Cavell (3363 m/11,033 ft).

All of the mountains opposite the viewpoint display the effects of glaciation, including many cirques (bowl-shaped depressions) carved into their slopes. Alpine glaciers clinging to high mountains pluck rock from the steep faces, quarrying deeper and deeper into the slope with the passing centuries. The mouths of some of these cirques open out onto the Athabasca Valley, suspended high above the valley floor — thus the name "hanging valleys."

195.2 **Mount Kerkeslin Campground.** Situated in a forest of spruce, aspen **35.1**
121.3 and pine. The cliffs of Mount Kerkeslin tower across the valley to the *21.8*
east, composed of reddish-orange quartz sandstones which are around 600 million years old.

From the campground, you can walk down to the edge of the Athabasca River for views across valley to the slopes of Whirlpool Mountain, the Mount Fryatt massif further to the south, and Mount Christie and Brussels Peak — the twin summits further south yet. Mount Edith Cavell (3363 m/11,033 ft) rises snowily and majestically to the northwest.

198.0 **Park Warden Cabin.** **32.3**
123.0 *20.1*

198.4 **Canadian Youth Hostel.** Dense, even-aged stands of lodgepole pine **31.9**
123.3 indicate that this area was once burnt over by a forest fire. *19.8*

199.2 **Athabasca Falls—93 Alternate Highway Junction.** Here, the old high-
123.8 way branches off to allow an optional tour of 24.1 kilometres (15.0 miles) along the west bank of the Athabasca River; the road rejoins the Icefields Parkway 7.5 kilometres (4.7 miles) south of Jasper townsite. Among the features along the 93-A is a side-trip to the base of Mounta Edith Cavell and the Angel Glacier — one of the outstanding points-of-interest in the Jasper vicinity. (See 93-Alternate Highway, page 131.)

31.1
19.3

Only 400 metres west on the 93-A Highway is the viewpoint for Athabasca Falls. These falls, dropping over a lip of Precambrian quartz sandstone and thundering down into a narrow canyon, are among the most powerful and awesome to be found in the mountain parks. The entire force of the Athabasca River is funneled through this gap, and the walls of the canyon have been smoothed and potholed by the rushing waters and the abrasive rock and sand held within the current. By walking around the falls to the various viewpoints, this same smoothing, channelling and potholing effect can be seen in the forest bedrock — an indication that the river once flowed across a much broader area.

The canyon is very short, and by standing on the bridge below the falls, you can look down to its mouth and to where the Athabasca River spreads to its normal width once more. The broad river flats by the picnic area above the falls are covered with many rounded and smoothed rocks which have been tumbled in the waters of the Athabasca for many years before being deposited on this beach.

The red cliffs of Mount Kerkeslin (2984 m/9,790 ft) rise above the river to the east.

202.6 **Horseshoe Lake Parking Area.** A short walk to a small, horseshoe-
125.9 shaped lake situated within a rock slide beneath the cliffs of Mount Hardisty (2701 m/8,860 ft). There is also a spectacular view of Mount Kerkeslin (the next mountain to the south) from the parking area, displaying its great, down-folded cliffs of reddish-orange, Cambrian and Precambrian quartz sandstone.

27.7
17.2

204.8 **Whirlpool Valley Viewpoint.** Directly across the valley stands Mount
127.3 Edith Cavell — a sharp wedge of a peak which is 3363 metres (11,033 ft) above sea level. In the days of the early fur trade, Mount Edith Cavell was known as the Montagne de la Grande Traverse, for it was here the fur brigades would leave the Athabasca for the long, arduous ascent of the Whirlpool River to Athabasca Pass. The broad, low gap between Edith Cavell and Whirlpool Peak to the south is the valley of the Whirlpool running away to the southwest.

25.5
15.8

In some years, the forests on the slopes above the Athabasca Valley display a distinct reddish hue, usually in the form of a band at a height of some 450 metres (1500 ft) above the valley floor. Looking as if the trees have been attacked by a blight, it is actually a phenomenon called "red burn". In mid-winter, temperatures will sometimes rise quite dramatically, particularly during a temperature inversion (cold air trapped on the valley-bottom while a layer of much warmer air lies above). Needles on the trees begin to transpire as if it were spring, but unable to draw moisture from the frozen ground, they become desiccated and turn a reddish-brown. The colouration is only temporary, however, and "red burn" does not kill the trees.

215.3 **Wabasso Lake Trail.** A short 2.7 kilometre (1.7 mile) trail rolling
133.8 through a fire sussession forest of lodgepole pine and aspen poplar to a

15.0
9.3

TO LAKE LOUISE
180 kms/*112 miles*
Honeymoon Lake
0.6 *0.4*
Viewpoint
ICEFIELDS
93
4.3 *2.7*
Ranger
PARKWAY
Cr
Viewpoint
Creek
Lick
River
4.9 *3.0*
TO FRYATT VALLEY
Viewpoint
3.8 *2.4*
Glacier
Viewpoint
MT KERKESLIN
2.3 *1.4*
Mt Kerkeslin
4.0 *2.5*
Athabasca Falls
Picnic Area
3.4 *2.1*
93
Horseshoe Lake
Athabasca
93A
Leach Lake
HIGHWAY
2.2 *1.4*
MOAB LAKE ROAD
TO A ATHABASCA PASS
Viewpoint
Whirlpool River
93A
TO JASPER
21 kms/*13 miles*
TO JASPER

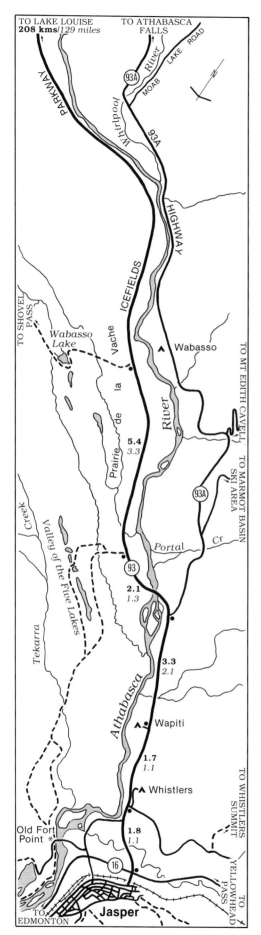

small lake near the eastern edge of the Athabasca Valley floor. The low, open grassland which is crossed on the way to the lake is part of Prairie de la Vache (Buffalo Prairie). When fur trader David Thompson passed up the valley in January of 1811 on his way over the Athabasca Pass, he abandoned his horses to winter on the grass here and noticed sign that buffalo had been feeding in the area.

220.7 **Valley-of-the-Five Lakes Trail.** A short 2.3 kilometre (1.4 mile) walk to   **9.6**
137.1 a series of five small lakes on the eastern edge of the valley. An excellent   *6.0*
trail from which to experience the unique environment of a relatively dry, low-elevation, lodgepole pine forest. A wide variety of wildflowers can be found along these valley-bottom trails, including the beautiful calypso orchid, the climbing vines of blue clematis, and the tiny, pink twinflower.

The lakes are home to many forms of wildlife including muskrat and moose. Common loons and Barrow's golden-eyes are the most common waterfowl on the lakes, and the wet terrain surrounding the water is the breeding ground for MacGillivray's and yellow warblers, northern water-thrushes, and yellowthroats. The pine and aspen forests along the approach trail shelter numerous ruffed grouse.

222.0 **Athabasca River Bridge.**   **8.3**
137.9   *5.2*

222.8 **93-Alternate Highway Junction.** A 24.1 kilometre (15.0 mile)-long   **7.5**
138.4 option paralleling the Icefields Parkway on the west side of the Athabasca   *4.7*
River and rejoining it further south near Athabasca Falls. The road to Mouth Edith Cavell branches from the 93-A 5.2 kilometres (3.2 miles) south of the junction. (See 93-Alternate Highway, page 120.)

223.0 **Icefields Parkway Interpretive Exhibit.** A short distance north of the 93-   **7.3**
138.5 A Highway junction is a Parks Canada interpretive exhibit designed   *4.6*
specifically for southbound travellers starting the Icefields Parkway tour. A good spot to stop and preview the journey ahead.

226.1 **Wapiti Campground.** Elk, also known as wapiti, frequent this low   **4.2**
140.5 valley from the autumn rutting season through the long winter. Though   *2.6*
you might not see elk in the area during mid-summer as they tend to move into higher country, many of the aspen poplar trees bear marks of their presence; elk strip the white bark of aspens to a height of one metre or more above the ground as a source of winter food.

Dense, even-aged stands of lodgepole pine contain the highway right-of-way. Stands of lodgepole pine are created by forest fires, and it is believed that these rather modest sized trees originated following a great fire which swept this part of the valley in 1889 — nearly 100 years ago!

227.8 **The Whistlers Road Junction.** A 4 kilometre (2.5 mile) side road   **2.5**
141.6 leading to The Whistlers Campground, the Parks Canada Hostel, and The   *1.5*
Whistlers Sky Tram. (See The Whistlers Road, page 145.)

228.2 **Junction.** An optional side road leading along the Athabasca River to   **2.1**
141.8 Jasper townsite. Also serves as an access route to the Old Fort Point-Lac   *1.3*
Beauvert Drive.

228.9 **Miette River Bridge.** A roadside pull-out at the south end of the bridge, **1.4**
142.2 provides a chance to walk along the banks of this historic river which *0.9*
takes its headwaters on the Yellowhead Pass 26 kilometres (16 miles) to
the west. Throughout the 19th Century, fur traders, gold seekers and
surveyors ascended the Miette to the Yellowhead Pass on their way to the
central heartland of British Columbia. The river is surrounded by a forest
of white spruce, lodgepole pine, and aspen poplar.

229.6 **Yellowhead Highway (Route 16) Junction.** The main highway which **0.7**
142.7 leads west through the Yellowhead Pass into British Columbia and east to *0.4*
the city of Edmonton. (See Yellowhead Highway, page 139.)

230.3 **Jasper Townsite.** **0.0**
143.1

NORTHBOUND   ICEFIELDS PARKWAY   SOUTHBOUND
Kilometres   **Kilometres**
Miles   *Miles*

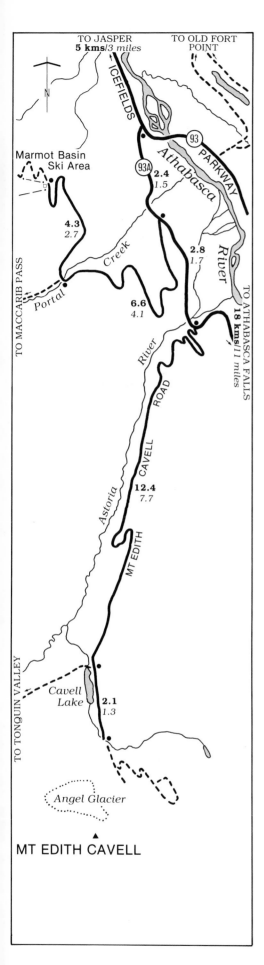

TO JASPER
5 kms/*3 miles*

TO OLD FORT
POINT

N

ICEFIELDS PARKWAY

Marmot Basin
Ski Area

Athabasca

93A   **2.4**
       1.5

93

4.3
2.7

Creek

2.8
1.7

River

TO MACCARIB PASS

Portal

6.6
4.1

River

TO ATHABASCA FALLS
18 kms/*11 miles*

CAVELL   ROAD

Astoria

12.4
7.7

MT EDITH

TO TONQUIN VALLEY

Cavell
Lake   **2.1**
        1.3

Angel Glacier

▲
MT EDITH CAVELL

93 Alternate Highway

The 93-A Highway is actually nothing more than the old Banff-Jasper Highway paralleling the new route for 24.1 kilometres (15.0 miles) on the opposite shore of the Athabasca River. The road diverges from the Icefields Parkway 7.5 kilometres (4.7 miles) south of Jasper townsite, winds along the forested west bank of the Athabasca River, and rejoins the new highway near Athabasca Falls. Yet, for all its proximity to the newer, faster and straighter Parkway, the 93-A provides access to several of the most important features of natural and human history in the park, including 3363 metre (11,033 ft) Mount Edith Cavell, the prime scenic attraction in the Jasper townsite vicinity.

Northbound travellers turn to page 131 and work backwards.

SOUTHBOUND Kilometres *Miles*	93-ALTERNATE HIGHWAY	NORTHBOUND Kilometres *Miles*
0.0	**Junction with the Icefields Parkway,** 7.5 kilometres (4.7 miles) south of Jasper townsite.	**24.1** *15.0*

As the road climbs and descends along the western slope of the Athabasca Valley, views open out to the long ridgeline of rounded summits to the east — the Maligne Mountains. A part of the Main Ranges, these mountains are composed of very old sedimentary rock deposited on the floor of a shallow ocean over 600 million years ago.

1.8 *1.1*	**Portal Creek Picnic Area.**	**22.3** *13.9*
2.0 *1.2*	**Portal Creek Bridge.**	**22.1** *13.8*
2.4 *1.5*	**Marmot Basin Road.** The 10.9 kilometre (6.8 mile)-long road to the Marmot Basin ski area intersects the 93-A Highway from the west. The drive to the ski area is short and not very scenic, but at the lodge it arrives at a point 1720 metres (5,640 ft) above sea level and a fine viewpoint for the Athabasca Valley. While the lifts at the ski area do not operate in summer, the open ski runs provide excellent opportunities for strong hikers to ascend to the alpine meadows on the upper slopes of Marmot Mountain.	**21.7** *13.5*

Another fine hiking option exists at the 6.6 kilometre (4.1 mile) mark on the Marmot Basin Road, at a point where the road switchbacks across Portal Creek. The Portal Creek trail departs from the parking area at this curve, leading to Maccarib Pass (12.4 km/7.7 mi) and Amethyst Lakes (21.3 km/13.2 mi). The first few kilometres of this trail make a pleasant nature hike, and the berry bushes along the way are usually filled with fruit in late August and early September.

TURN TO PAGE 129 —

Mount Edith Cavell from Cavell Lake.

Angel Glacier.

White Indian paintbrush and elephant head - typical wildflowers of Jasper's damp alpine meadows.

Gray jay.

Athabasca Falls.

Early morning mist on Maligne Lake.

Jasper Lake on the left and Talbot Lake on the right separated by a long, curving sand dune dike.

Talbot Lake and the Bosche Range.

Roche Miette.

Punchbowl Falls near Pocahontas.

5.0   Astoria River Bridge.
3.1

5.2   **Mount Edith Cavell Road Junction.** A narrow, 14.5 kilometre (9 mile)-
3.2   long road that winds up the Astoria Valley to the base of 3363 metre
(11,033 ft) Mount Edith Cavell — the highest mountain in this section of
the park.

Mount Edith Cavell from Cavell Lake.

A viewpoint at Kilometre 3.7 (Mile 2.4) offers an exciting glimpse down
into the steep-walled gorge of the Astoria River. Here, the river has cut
through great banks of silt and rock deposited by glacial outwash streams
over many thousands of years. The exposed drift is in a continual state of
erosion, and hints of hoodoo formations can be seen in some sections.
The roadside pull-off also provides views down the Astoria to the broad
Athabasca Valley.

Another viewpoint at Kilometre 12.4 (Mile 7.7) gives the visitor a
glimpse of the glacier-covered mountains near the headwaters of the
Astoria, some 15 kilometres (9 miles) to the west. Just 300 metres further
along is a trail leading to the Astoria headwaters and the beautiful
Tonquin Valley (19 km/11.8 mi). The Tonquin Valley is one of the most
popular hiking areas in the park, with the twin-jewel Amethyst Lakes
backed by the sheer wall of The Ramparts as the scenic focal point of the
region.

A shorter walk can be made along the Tonquin trail, however, dropping
from the roadside for 300 metres to the shores of Cavell Lake and a
favourite photographic view of the snow-clad heights of Mount Edith
Cavell. The waters of the lake are a brilliant greenish-blue, a colour seen
only in glacier country. Cavell Lake is fed by the meltwater stream of the
Angel Glacier, situated less than three kilometres above the lake. The
glacier grinds and pulverizes rock from the north wall of Mount Edith
Cavell, spewing this glacial flour forth in its meltwaters. Much of the fine
silt remains suspended in the water of Cavell Lake, reflecting light and
producing the unusual greenish hue.

The lake not only owes its colour, but its very existence to the presence of
glaciers; its waters have backed up behind a dam of rock and gravel debris
deposited as a terminal moraine at the toe of a glacier which advanced
down-valley to this point many centuries ago.

Mount Edith Cavell. At Kilometre 14.5 (Mile 9.0) the road ends at a
parking area near the base of Mount Edith Cavell. Few summits in the
mountain parks loom so ominously and impressively as that of Edith
Cavell above this viewpoint.

During the days of the early fur trade, the peak was known as the
Montagne de la Grande Traverse, for it was a landmark to voyageurs
entering the Whirlpool Valley for the arduous trek to Athabasca Pass and
the Great Divide. The mountain received a new name during the First
World War, however, commemorating a heroic nurse who was shot by the
Germans.

The mountain is composed of great thicknesses of Precambrian and
Cambrian age rock, much of which is quartz sandstone. These ancient
beds of rock dip ever so slightly toward the west.

From the parking area, a short paved trail leads out across the boulder
strewn outwash flats at the foot of the mountain's north wall to a remnant
of glacier ice and a small, powder blue, meltwater lake at its toe. On the
lower cliffs of Mount Edith Cavell, the beautiful Angel Glacier hangs.
The Angel once acted as a tributary to the valley glacier below, but its toe
has receded above the valley floor over the last century.

Angel Glacier.

The rock debris which covers this valley from side to side is left over from the last advance of ice. Note the distinct ridge of rock and gravel debris leading from the parking area to the foot of the mountain wall (an old footpath has been worn along its ridge). This is a lateral moraine which was deposited along the side of the main valley glacier after its last major advance around a century ago.

Part way along the nature trail, a branch trail forks uphill to the east and, in three kilometres (two miles), climbs to the open, alpine meadows directly opposite Angel Glacier. Along the trail, keep a sharp eye out for the boulder field inhabitants — the tiny rock pikas (listen for their loud squeak of warning) and the fat hoary marmots (a long shrill whistle is their trademark). Above the glacial outwash area, the meadows are alive with thousands of colourful wildflowers from mid-July into late August.

Motorists travelling to the end of the Edith Cavell Road are forewarned that this is a very congested area during the summer and traffic jams are common. Trailers are not allowed on the road and should be parked at one of the pull-outs along the 93-A Highway before the journey is undertaken.

9.2
5.7
Wabasso Campground. Wabasso is an Indian word meaning "rabbit".
14.9
9.3

11.2
7.0
Otto's Cache Picnic Area. The Otto brothers were early outfitters in the Jasper vicinity who led some of the first tourists into remote regions of the park.
12.9
8.0

11.4
7.1
Cavell Warden Station.
12.7
7.9

13.1
8.1
Athabasca Trail Exhibit. This roadside picnic area is located near the confluence of the Whirlpool and Athabasca Rivers. During the early 19th Century, westbound fur brigades would enter the mountains via the Athabasca River, ascending to this junction where they would ford the river and begin the 30 mile ascent of the Whirlpool to the Athabasca Pass on the Great Divide. The North West Company trader and surveyor David Thompson made the earliest recorded ascent of the valley during the winter of 1811, using dog teams to flounder through the deep snows in the pass. Because of Indian problems on the open prairies to the south the Athabasca Pass became the main trade route across the Rockies following Thompson's journey — a particularly advantageous route as it emerged on the western slope at the "Big Bend" of the Columbia River.
11.0
6.9

George Simpson, Governor of the Hudson's Bay Company, crossed the pass in 1824 and christened a small lake on its summit The Committee's Punch Bowl, thereby initiating a tradition among the traders who passed that way of drinking a toast in honour of the officers of the Company. After the Oregon Territory passed into American hands in the mid-1800's, the pass became less important as a trade route, and eventually it was completely abandoned in favour of the Yellowhead Pass to the north.

On a quiet day, it is possible to sit by the river and imagine the brigades of voyageurs splashing through the cold waters of the Athabasca with their horses, cursing and swearing at their balking animals, and ascending the Whirlpool Valley to a camp where the horses had to be abandoned; then, the men taking the burden on their own backs in ninety pound sacks for the trek through the glacier-rimmed defiles of the Athabasca Pass and down the "Grande Côte" to Boat Encampment on the Columbia.

15.2 *9.4*	**Whirlpool Fire Road.** The road enters the highway from the southwest, and access is allowed for 6.9 kilometres (4.3 miles) to within 500 metres of Moab Lake. A popular lake with fishermen, the Moab area is also excellent for a little low altitude botanizing. Twin-flowers and bunchberry carpet the forest floor, while the rare red variety of columbine can be found among the flowers and grasses of the open meadows. The fire road can be hiked beyond Moab Lake, eventually dwindling to a footpath which climbs to the summit of the historic Athabasca Pass, approximately 43 kilometres (27 miles) distant.	**8.9** *5.6*
15.4 *9.6*	**Whirlpool River Bridge.**	**8.7** *5.4*
19.6 *12.2*	**Leach Lake Picnic Area.** Small sink lakes such as this are common throughout the Rocky Mountains where major valleys intersect — in this case, the Whirlpool and the Athabasca. The lake was most likely formed near the end of the last ice age when the glaciers retreated up these two valleys, leaving detached blocks of ice buried within the silt and gravel. As the ice wasted away, the glacial drift slumped to form the basin containing the lake. These lakes seldom have an outlet stream, their waters draining down through the alluvial material in their basins.	**4.5** *2.8*
23.0 *14.3*	**Geraldine Lakes—Fryatt Valley Trail.** A locked gate at the entrance to an old fire road serves as a starting point for trips to the upper Fryatt basin, Geraldine Lakes and Geraldine Fire Lookout.	**1.1** *0.7*
23.5 *14.6*	**Athabasca Falls.** Here the Athabasca River pours over a cliff of Precambrian quartz sandstone and into a narrow gorge of its own making. (For a full description of this major point of interest, see the Icefields Parkway chapter, page 117.)	**0.6** *0.4*
23.7 *14.7*	**Athabasca Falls Picnic Area.**	**0.4** *0.3*
24.1 *15.0*	**Junction with the Icefields Parkway.** 31.1 kilometres (19.3 miles) south of Jasper townsite.	**0.0**

SOUTHBOUND **Kilometres** *Miles*	93-ALTERNATE HIGHWAY	NORTHBOUND **Kilometres** *Miles*

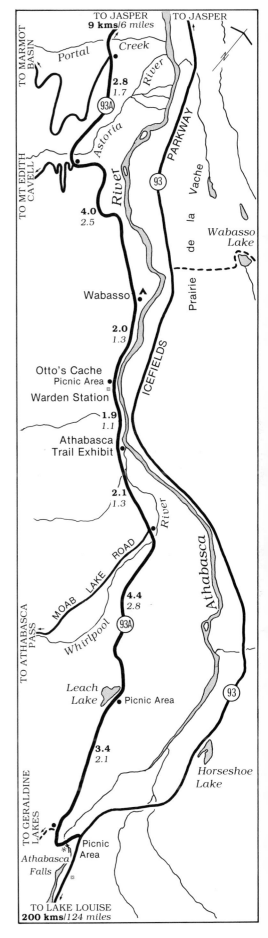

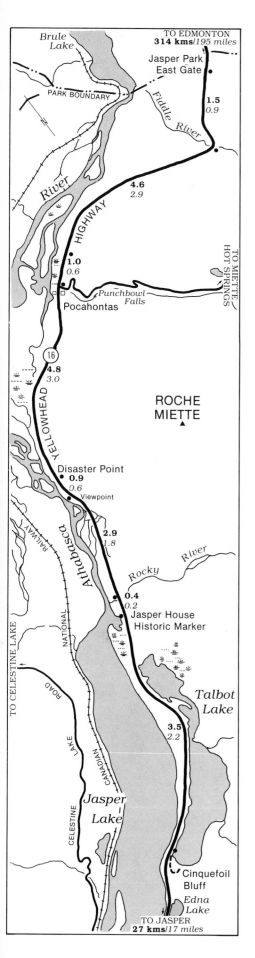

Yellowhead Highway

The Yellowhead Highway, also known as Route 16 and the Jasper-Edmonton Highway, is the main artery running east-west through Jasper National Park. Travelling 73.5 kilometres (45.7 miles) from Jasper East Gate to the West Gate near Yellowhead Pass, it is a relatively short route by mountain park standards, yet one which possesses unique natural features and a rich historical past.

Entering the park from the east, the highway follows upstream along the Athabasca River through one of the lowest and most arid valleys in the Canadian Rockies. The highway bends south with the river, passing the site of the old fur trade outpost of Jasper's House, the sand dune shores of Jasper Lake and the town of Jasper at Kilometre 48 (Mile 30.0).

West of Jasper, the scene changes totally as the highway leaves the broad, open terrain of the Athabasca Valley and climbs the last 26 kilometres (16 miles) to the Great Divide via the narrow, densely forested Miette Valley — the route of the old fur brigades travelling to New Caledonia (central British Columbia).

The Yellowhead Pass, at 1131 metres (3,711 feet) above sea level, is one of the lowest along the entire length of the Great Divide. As a route for trans-continental traffic and trade, it is one of the oldest in the mountain west.

As a major highway, the Yellowhead is relatively young, the first automobile reaching Jasper from Edmonton around 1921, and then only after an incredible journey following old abandoned railway grades and making use of horses and trains to negotiate the impassable sections. A gravel road was completed from Edmonton to the park's east boundary in 1928, but it wasn't until 1969 that the Yellowhead Highway was christened as a major through-route into British Columbia.

Eastbound travellers turn to page 141 and work backwards, following distances in the right-hand margin.

WESTBOUND Kilometres *Miles*	YELLOWHEAD HIGHWAY	EASTBOUND Kilometres *Miles*
0.0	**Jasper Park East Gate.** Pull-off on the wide berm just inside or outside the gate. Roche à Perdix rises above the highway to the east. A part of the Front Ranges of the Rockies, the mountain is filled with faults and tight folds, indicative of the tremendous forces which tortured, fractured and bent these once horizontal beds of sedimentary rock.	**73.5** *45.7*
1.5 *0.9*	**Fiddle River Bridge.**	**72.0** *44.8*

6.1   **Roche Miette Viewpoint.** The massive prow of Roche Miette (2316   **67.4**
3.8   m/7,599 ft) juts out above the Athabasca Valley to the south. The large   *41.9*
cliff which comprises the bulk of the mountain is formed from limestones
deposited on the floor of a shallow, inland sea some 350 million years
ago. The same massive, cliff-forming limestone is found throughout the
Front Ranges of the Rockies, even as far south as Banff townsite over 250
kilometres (160 miles) away.

There is an old legend dating back to the early decades of the 19th
Century as to how Roche Miette (Miette's Rock) got its name. As
recounted in 1846 by traveller and artist Paul Kane, the mountain "de-
rives its appellation from a French voyageur, who climbed its summit and
sat smoking his pipe with his legs hanging over the fearful abyss".

The Bosche Range lies across the valley to the northwest, while the long
ridgeline of the DeSmet Range seems to block the valley to the west.

There is a small slough beside the pull-off, a typical feature of the
Athabasca Valley bottom-land which is mostly muskeg and grasslands
with stands of spruce.

Roche Miette.

7.1   **Miette Hot Springs Road and Pocahontas.** A 17.5 kilometre (10.9   **66.4**
4.4   mile)-long road branches from the Yellowhead Highway and leads into   *41.3*
the mountains to the southeast and the Miette Hot Springs.

Up the Miette Hot Springs Road 150 metres or so, there is a paved area on
the right hand side of the road, just beyond the Pocahontas Visitor
Services development. A short walk up the nearby creek drainage will
bring you to a number of old foundations — remnants of the old mining
development of Pocahontas.

Two early prospectors, Frank Villeneuve and Alfred Lamoreau first
discovered "coal float" on the lower slopes of nearby Roche Miette in
1908. When the Grand Trunk Pacific Railway passed up the valley in
1911, a station was built here and a coal mine opened. The name
Pocahontas was given to the development by the American directors of
Jasper Park Collieries Ltd., in hopes that the mine would be as successful
as the coal field of the same name in southwestern Virginia. Entry to the
coal seam was made from the gravel terrace above. Coal cars were filled
in the tunnel, pulled to the top by horse, then lowered down the hill by
cable and hoisting engine to the tipple and siding below. After 10 years
operation, which saw 840,200 tons of coal produced, the mine was
closed down. The quality of coal was never as good as had been hoped
for, and when the railway tracks were moved to the other side of the
valley, the operation became economically infeasible.

Today, Pocahontas is a small, visitor service centre, providing accommodation, groceries and gasoline during the summer season.

By parking at the service centre and walking to the north side of the
Yellowhead Highway, one can visit an area known as the Pocahontas
Ponds — a typical Athabasca Valley wetland which is flooded each
spring by the river's overflow. Like most of these valley flood plains, this
area of sedge, willow and backwater is an excellent spot for birdwatching. In the spring and fall migratory birds such as mallards, teal, Canada
geese and great blue heron visit the ponds. White-throated sparrows and
savannah sparrows nest in the meadows during the summer, while osprey
nests can often be seen in the tops of white spruce snags.

The road to Miette Hot Springs climbs beyond Pocahontas, reaching
Punchbowl Falls at Kilometre 1.3 (Mile 0.8). The falls have formed

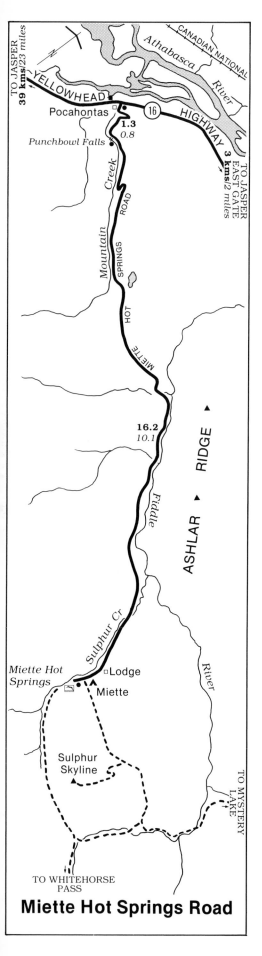

Miette Hot Springs Road

where Mountain Creek drops over a cliff of Cretaceous-age rock. The flow of water has cut a narrow cleft into the bedrock and eroded a rounded depression at the foot of the fall to form a picturesque pool. If you look closely at the bedrock, you will notice it is composed of many rounded, water-worn pebbles which have been cemented together with sand to form a solid body of rock. Known as conglomerate, the pebbly rock was probably formed in the bed of a fast moving stream which drained into this region from a range of mountains to the west approximately 130 million years ago.

The road continues to climb up and over a low ridge at the head of Mountain Creek, then drops sharply into the Fiddle River canyon. Across the river to the east, the steeply dipping limestone and shale beds of Ashlar Ridge have been eroded into a jagged range of sawtooth mountains.

Approximately 14 kilometres (9 miles) from Pocahontas, the road leaves Fiddle River and climbs the narrow Sulphur Creek drainage, arriving at the Miette Hot Springs area 3 kilometres (2 miles) further along.

Miette Hot Springs. Located on the banks of Sulphur Creek, the springs are renowned for being the warmest in the Canadian Rockies, the hottest of the three reaching temperatures of 54°C(129°F). As with other hot mineral springs in the range, these waters are believed to originate as rain and snow melt which has seeped down into joints and fractures in the bedrock. At a depth of several thousand feet below the surface, the water is heated and percolates back to the surface to emerge in the three springs. An estimated 250,000 gallons of water flow out of the springs each day.

The Miette Hot Springs are also noted for their high calcium content, the greatest to be found in any of the Rocky Mountain mineral springs. The mineral content of the water is acquired as it moves through the bedrock, and since most of the strata in the vicinity are comprised of limestone (calcium carbonate), a high calcium content is to be expected. Other minerals present in varying quantities include magnesium, iron and potassium, as well as traces of radium which lend the waters their slight radioactive properties. The distinct sulfurous smell at the springs is caused by the presence of hydrogen sulfide.

In addition to the pool and bathing facilities at the end of the road, a campground and resort motel are located nearby.

7.4	**Pocahontas Warden Station.**	**66.1**
4.6		*41.1*

11.9	**Disaster Point Animal Lick.** Mountain sheep populate the rugged	**61.6**
7.4	slopes of Disaster Point and often descend to these small pools to lick the	*38.3*

mineral-rich mud (high in calcium carbonate). It is thought this activity might be triggered by the summer molt, the minerals playing an important role in the production of a healthy, winter coat.

Before the arrival of the railway and dynamite, Disaster Point extended into the waters of the Athabasca River. Early travellers would often ford the river to pass the barrier, or, when the waters were high, make an arduous climb up and over the steep ridge. As might be expected, a number of "disasters" befell parties trying to circumnavigate this difficult point of land.

12.8	**DeSmet Range Viewpoint.** Across the Athabasca River to the west,	**60.7**
8.0	stands the high massif of the DeSmet Range — named for Father Pierre	*37.7*

DeSmet, a Belgian missionary who crossed the Rockies on several occasions during his work with the tribes of the mountain west. Down the highway to the southwest is the long line of mountains which comprise the Jacques Range — named for Jacques Cardinal, a Metis horse-keeper who worked for the Hudson's Bay Company during the mid-1800's. Looking far upstream to the horizon, the low ramparts of The Palisade and the distinctive triangle of Pyramid Mountain overlook the town of Jasper.

Directly across the Athabasca Valley, in the lower cliffs of the Bosche Range, is an excellent example of the tightly folded strata of the Front Ranges. By looking closely, you can see the distinct bends and swirls in the rock indicative of the tightly folded bedding.

Typical river-bottom gravel flats stretch out along the highway, outwash material spread across the valley floor by the glacier-fed waters of the Athabasca River.

| 15.7 | **Rocky River Bridge.** | 57.8 |
| *9.8* | | *35.9* |

| 16.1 | **Jasper House Point-of-Interest.** Located across the river from this | 57.4 |
| *10.0* | point, Jasper House was one of the earliest outposts of the mountain fur | *35.7* |

trade. The post was originally established by the North West Company at Brûlé Lake, 24 kilometres (15 miles) down-stream, shortly after David Thompson's epic journey over Athabasca Pass in the winter of 1810-11, and it received its name from one of the early post factors, Jasper Hawes. During the 1820's, after it came under the control of the Hudson's Bay Company, Jasper House was moved to this site near the northern end of Jasper Lake. Throughout its existence, the house served primarily as a supply station for fur brigades crossing the Rocky Mountains. While travelling through the valley in 1846, artist Paul Kane gave a colourful description of the tiny post:

Jasper House as photographed by Charles Horetzky in January, 1872.
B.C. Archives

"Jasper's House consists of only three miserable log huts. The dwelling-house is composed of two rooms, of about fourteen or fifteen feet square each. One of them is used by all comers and goers: Indians, voyageurs, and traders, men, women, and children being huddled together indiscriminately; the other room being devoted to the exclusive occupation of Colin [the chief factor] and his family, consisting of a Cree squaw, and nine interesting half-breed children."

The broad valley seen to the north between the DeSmet and Bosche Ranges is the Snake Indian Valley, a much-used route for trail riders and hikers going into the remote, northern wilderness of Jasper Park. Dr. James Hector, geologist with the Palliser Expedition, was told of how the valley got its name when he visited Jasper House in January of 1859:

"There was once a little tribe of Indians known as the Snakes, that lived in the country to the north of Jasper House, but which, during the time of the North West Fur Company, was treacherously exterminated by the Assiniboines. They were invited to a peace feast by the latter Indians, when they were to settle all their disputes, and neither party was to bring any weapons. It was held about three miles below the present site of Jasper House, but the Assiniboines being all secretly armed, fell upon the poor Snakes in the midst of the revelry, and killed them all . . . ."

| 19.6 | **Talbot Lake.** The lake has been created by a narrow ridge of drifting | 53.9 |
| *12.2* | sand dunes. The area containing the lake is protected from the prevailing, | *33.5* |

down-valley winds by the ridgeline of the Jacques Range to the south-

Jasper and Talbot Lakes as viewed from Cinquefoil Bluff. Roche Miette dominates the skyline.

west. But, just beyond the edge of that protecting ridge, the winds have created a long, narrow bar of sand to cut Talbot Lake off from the main body of the valley and Jasper Lake.

Like many of the more sheltered bodies of water in the Athabasca Valley, Talbot Lake is a good area for birdwatching. Waterfowl stop over on the lake in the spring and fall, ospreys nest in spruce snags across the lake, and bald eagles are sometimes seen wheeling above on the rising air currents. The best bird habitat is at the lake's northern end.

An excellent nature trail leads away from this roadside pull-off, through the sand dunes beside the Yellowhead Highway and up onto an open, grassy knoll called Cinquefoil Bluff. This is a fine viewpoint for this section of the Athabasca Valley, providing an expansive overview of the long sandbar which separates Jasper and Talbot Lakes. The broad, plateau-like summit of Roche Miette and the Miette Range dominates the skyline to the northeast.

22.6   **Jasper Lake Viewpoint.** A roadside stop providing excellent views   **50.9**
14.0   across the broad expanse of Jasper Lake. You can also see the sand dunes   *31.7*
which have drifted northeastward to cut Talbot Lake off from Jasper Lake. In summer, when water levels are high, Jasper Lake is filled to the brim, and the valley is lush and green; in winter, however, with little runoff or moisture in the form of rain or snow, the valley turns dry and brown, the lake shrinks, and the expanded shores are a cold desert of blowing winds and drifting sand.

At one time, it is believed, the entire Athabasca Valley was one huge lake. Evidence to support this theory can be seen throughout the valley in the form of terraces at various levels on the valley-sides. In fact, the sand and silt so prevalent throughout the lower Athabasca Valley was probably deposited here as sediment when the valley was filled by a huge 80 kilometre (50 mile)-long lake. Jasper Lake, Brûlé Lake, and the other smaller lakes which dot the valley are all that remain of this gigantic, prehistoric reservoir.

Osprey.

26.7   **Jacques Creek Trail.** A trail which leads backpackers to Jacques and   **46.8**
16.6   Merlin Passes and eventually to Jacques Lake, 32 kilometres (20 miles)   *29.1*
distant.

The first kilometre or so of this trail passes through a flat, brushy area known locally as "The Mushroom Patch." It is a good place for calling owls on spring nights and a densely populated nesting ground for various species of warblers and sparrows in early summer.

29.5   **Cold Sulphur Spring Point-of-Interest.** Pouring out from beneath a   **44.0**
18.3   cliff of steeply tilted limestones and shales, this cold water spring   *27.4*
contains significant amounts of hydrogen sulfide (note the distinctive sulfureous smell). The low temperature of the water indicates that, unlike hot mineral springs, it probably doesn't penetrate the strata to any great depth. The hydrogen sulfide content is probably acquired through dissolution of the bedrock as the water passes through oxygen-starved joints and channels underground.

In the Devonian age bedrock surrounding the spring, the fossils of brachiopods (an extinct bivalve resembling a clam) and stromatoporoids (an obscure, columnar-shaped animal resembling hydrozoans) can be found. It is against national park regulations to collect or displace any of these important geological features, however.

33.6 **Snaring River Bridge.** The river is named after a small tribe of Indians
20.9 which used to frequent the area, trapping small animals in snares for
food.

The highway is travelling between the steeply tilted limestone slabs of the
Colin Range on the east and the massive ramparts of The Palisade on the
west.

38.6 **Celestine Lake Road.** The road follows the course of the old Jasper-
24.0 Edmonton Highway for a short distance before turning into a controlled-
access gravel road. The narrow roadway winds northeastward above the
Athabasca Valley for another 34 kilometres (21 miles), paralleling the
Yellowhead Highway on the opposite side of the river before it comes to a
dead end at Celestine Lake and the mouth of the Snake Indian Valley.

The road offers a whole new perspective on the Athabasca Valley, rolling
through one of the finest examples of montane forest to be found
anywhere in the mountain parks. Forest cover is composed of lodgepole
pine and Douglas fir interspersed with large tracts of open grassland. In
the forested environs adjacent to the meadows, saw-whet and pygmy
owls are sometimes heard at dusk, and blue grouse and Townsend's
solitaires are often observed. The grasslands turn into a veritable wildflower garden in spring with blue flax and harebells, red Indian
paintbrush and yellow gaillardia and cinquefoil spreading colour across
the open, green expanses.

Along the way, the road passes the old Moberly cabins. Henry John
Moberly was in charge of the Hudson's Bay Company post of Jasper
House in the late 1850's. During his short tour of duty in the valley, he
took a young Iroquois girl, Suzan Cardinal, as his wife. When he left the
valley a few years later in search of greener pastures, he left his native
wife with two sons, Ewan and John. The brothers grew up and settled in
the valley, and Ewan built the cabins on this open stretch of ground
around 1898. When the national park was established a few years later,
Ewan sold his land to the Dominion government and moved on. But his
cabins were never demolished and remain along with the name "Moberly
Flats" a reminder of one of the valley's earliest settlers.

The Celestine Lake Road climbs high on the valley slopes to provide
vistas of Jasper Lake and the major ranges in this section of the park. At
Celestine Lake, a short hike takes the visitor to a fire lookout overlooking
the Athabasca Valley and provides a unique perspective on the massive
cliffs of Roche Miette across the river to the east. The Snake Indian
Valley trail also strikes off to the northwest from Celestine Lake, leading
to Snake Indian Falls, 21 kilometres (13 miles), and the remote northern
wilderness of the park.

This is not an idle side-trip, and any excursion up the Celestine Lake
Road should be planned as at least a full-day journey. First off, the road is
open only to one-way traffic, so certain hours of the day are reserved to
inbound traffic, other hours for returning traffic. Check the sign at the
entrance to the controlled access section or at the Park Information Office
in Jasper for the schedule. The road is also closed to trailers.

39.7 **Roadside Picnic Area.** The steeply dipping strata of the Colin Range
24.7 rises to the east of this pleasant picnic area, the highest peak in the range
Mount Colin at 2687 metres (8,815 ft) above sea level. Characteristic of
most mountains containing steeply tilted bedding, the Colin Range has
been eroded into a series of "sawtooth" peaks with distinctive summits
and slopes that exhibit a sharp, inverted-V pattern.

39.9
24.8

34.9
21.7

33.8
21.0

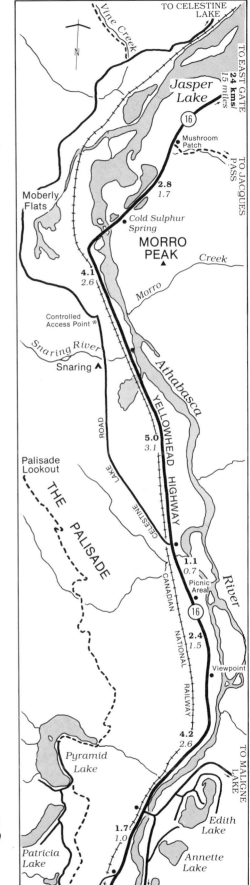

Swift's ferry on the Athabasca, seen here in 1911, was downstream from present-day Jasper.

Archives of the Canadian Rockies

To the west is the long, steadily rising cliff of The Palisade with the distinctive summit of Pyramid Mountain (2766 m/9,076 ft) standing beyond. The Palisade cliff lies within the Front Ranges of the Rockies and is composed of limestones which date back some 350 million years; Pyramid Mountain, on the other hand, is within the Main Ranges and composed of reddish-orange quartz sandstones which are over 600 million years old. A major thrust fault separates The Palisade and Pyramid Mountain, and the Front Ranges from the Main Ranges.

The picnic area is situated within a beautiful, open parkland of aspen and spruce, the grassland populated with the usual colony of Columbian ground squirrels. The most common rodent in the mountain parks, the Columbian ground squirrel lives in an extensive system of underground burrows and displays many characteristics of his cousin the prairie dog. At this elevation, the first of these animals comes out of hibernation in early April, returning underground as early as mid-August. During the summer months, ground squirrels forage about on flowers, roots, and stems, as well as seeds from grasses and forbs.

42.1 **Colin Range—Athabasca River Viewpoint.** Looking down on the **31.4**
26.2 Athabasca River, we can see broad gravel flats and a braided stream *19.5*
pattern, characteristics of a river fed by glacial meltwaters: gravel and silt
are forever transported and deposited, the stream channels forever wandering.

Above the river rise the steeply dipping slabs of the Colin Range, composed of limestones which once rested horizontally on the floor of a shallow, inland sea, but which have since been fractured and thrust up to this high angle by tremendous forces applied along the western margin of the continent. Up-valley, along the course of the highway, you can see the snow-dusted summit of Mount Edith Cavell, at 3363 metres (11,033 ft) above sea level the highest mountain visible from Jasper townsite and vicinity.

On both sides of the valley, along the foot of the mountains, well-defined terraces, or benches, are composed of sediment deposited by a great lake which filled this valley from side to side and for a length of some 80 kilometres (50 miles) near the end of the last ice age.

46.3 **Maligne Lake Road Junction.** A 44 kilometre (28 mile) road leading to **27.2**
28.8 one of the Rockies' most scenic lakes and passing Maligne Canyon and *16.9*
Medicine Lake along the way. (See Maligne Lake Road, page 146.)

48.0 **Jasper Townsite East Exit.** Many westbound travellers prefer to turn-off **25.5**
29.8 the Yellowhead Highway here, visit Jasper townsite, then rejoin the *15.9*
highway at its junction with the Icefields Parkway west of town.

50.3 **Signal Mountain Viewpoint.** An elevated pull-off directly above the **23.2**
31.3 Athabasca River provides one of the best 360 degree panoramas in this *14.4*
section of the valley.

Straight across the valley to the east is the low, forested summit of Signal Mountain — so-called because it was one of the earliest mountains to be outfitted with a lookout tower and a telephone. Rising beyond is the higher and more rugged peak of Mount Tekarra (2688 m/8,818 ft) named for an Iroquois hunter who accompanied Dr. James Hector of the Palliser Expedition up the valley in the winter of 1859.

Just across the river and slightly upstream, you can see a bridge and a low promontory standing beside it. This is Old Fort Point which commemorates the earliest fur trade outpost established in the Rocky Mountains. Named Henry's House for the North West Company fur trader William Henry who built it in 1811, the post was probably situated closer to this viewpoint than to Old Fort Point.

Beyond Old Fort Point, 24 kilometres (15 miles) up-valley, stands the broad, distinctive north face of Mount Kerkeslin (2984 m/9,790 ft). The mountain lies in the axis of a syncline, or downfold in the rock, and the downward bend in the bedding is discernable from here.

To the right of Mount Kerkeslin, towering majestically across the valley, is the highest mountain visible from Jasper townsite — 3363 metre (11,033 ft) Mount Edith Cavell.

Continuing the panorama to the right, the bulky, rounded mountain beyond the townsite to the southwest is The Whistlers, named for the hoary marmots which inhabit the summit and their distinctive, shrill whistle of warning. Notice the top terminal of The Whistlers Sky Tram, perched like a huge castle atop the mountain's summit ridge.

Across the highway to the northwest stands the familiar reddish-orange summit of Pyramid Mountain (2766 m/9,076 ft), its colouration coming from the quartz sandstone rock which composes its slopes.

And, finally down-river to the north, are the jagged, limestone peaks of the Colin Range — carved from steeply dipping layers of limestone that are some 350 million years old.

51.2 **Jasper Townsite Junction.** Turn off the highway to the west for Jasper **22.3**
31.8 townsite, east for Old Fort Point and Lac Beauvert. *13.9*

52.4 **Icefields Parkway Junction.** Serves as the west exit for Jasper townsite **21.1**
32.6 as well as the northern terminus for the Icefields Parkway. Eastbound *13.1*
travellers may wish to turn off the Yellowhead Highway at the junction, visit Jasper, then pick up the highway again east of the townsite. Two major campgrounds are located 2.4 kilometres (1.5 miles) and 4.5 (2.8 miles) south on the Icefields Parkway. (See Jasper and Vicinity, page 143, and Icefields Parkway, page 119.)

53.4 **Miette River Bridge.** The forest which fringes this section of the Miette **20.1**
33.2 River is one of the best areas for birdwatching in Jasper Park. Rufous *12.5*
hummingbirds, pileated woodpeckers and barred owls are common during the spring nesting season, and purple finches, vireos, redstarts and a variety of warblers frequent the brushy banks and forest margin.

60.2 **Roadside Picnic Stop.** A small, roadside pull-off lying just below the **13.3**
37.4 right-of-way for the old highway. The old roadbed was also used by one *8.3*
of two railways which ascended the valley prior to the First World War.

The orange-hued rock on the opposite side of the valley is Precambrian quartz sandstone — some of the oldest rock to be found in the mountain parks.

61.7 **Miette River Picnic Area.** This stop is in the heart of the rugged and **11.8**
38.3 rolling bottomland of the Miette Valley. Unlike the drier and more open *7.4*
landscape of the broad Athabasca Valley to the east, the Miette is closed-

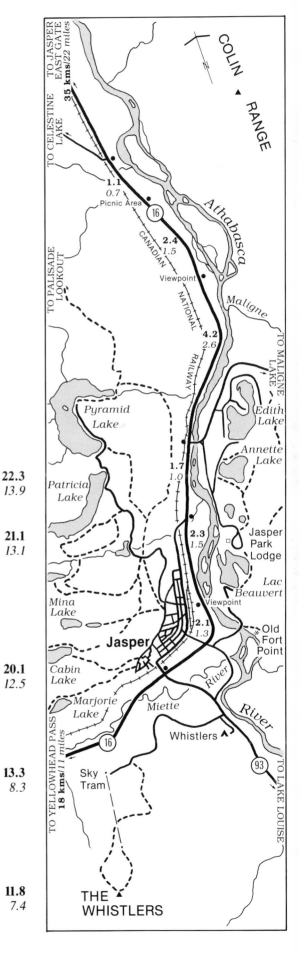

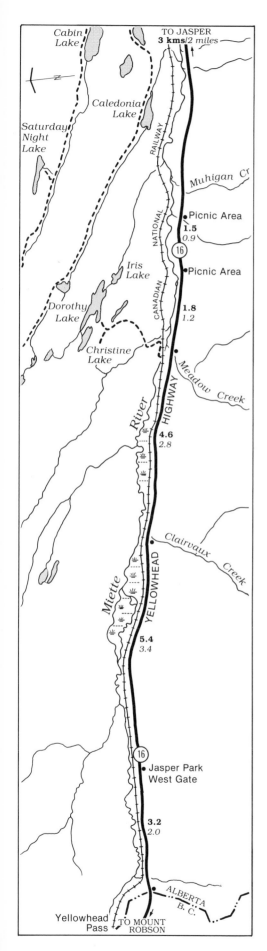

in, cooler and damper — a more typical subalpine forest. Species of trees on the valley floor include western white spruce, lodgepole pine, aspen and cottonwood poplars — a mixed composition which reflects the presence of riverbed alluvial deposits and past forest fires.

63.5 **Meadow Creek Bridge.** From a roadside pull-off on the west side of the   **10.0**
39.5   bridge, you can cross the CN tracks to the trail head for the three small   *6.2*
lakes of Virl, Dorothy and Christine which are situated beyond a low intervening ridge about 4.0 kilometres (2.5 miles) distant.

From the bridge-side pull-off, you can look down-valley toward where the Miette Valley opens into the broad Athabasca. A major glacier which once filled the Miette Valley also served as a tributary to an even larger mass of ice in the Athabasca Valley. On the right side of the valley looking downstream is Muhigan Mountain (2609 m/8,559 ft), and just beyond The Whistlers (2464 m/8,085 ft) with the upper terminal of the Sky Tram just visible on the summit ridge.

The many roadside, rock outcrops between the Yellowhead Pass and the junction with the Icefields Parkway are composed of massive, Precambrian quartz sandstones and argillites.

The wetlands created by the Miette River throughout this section of valley provide breeding habitat for Canada geese, belted kingfishers, ospreys, and many species of smaller birds.

68.1 **Clairvaux Creek Bridge.**   **5.4**
42.3   *3.4*

73.5 **Jasper Park West Gate.** By pulling off on the widened pavement on   **0.0**
45.7   either side of the entrance booth, you can get a good look at the surrounding countryside. Beyond the long, low forested ridge to the north rise the barren summits of the Victoria Cross Ranges — the two most prominent peaks being, from left to right, Elysium Mountain and Emigrants Mountain. Down the highway to the west three kilometres (two miles), lies the low, forested gap of the Yellowhead Pass.

Yellowhead Pass. At 1131 metres (3,711 feet) above sea level, the Yellowhead Pass is one of the lowest gaps to be found along the entire length of the Great Divide. Waters east of the divide flow to the Arctic Ocean via the Miette, Athabasca and Mackenzie Rivers; west of the divide, runoff feeds the headwaters of the Fraser River which snakes its way through the western cordillera to the Pacific Ocean.

The first white men to cross the pass were the fur traders of the early 19th Century. One of the first of these was a fair-haired Iroquois who gave his nickname to the pass as well as the town of Tete Jaune Cache further west in British Columbia. To many of the early traders, the gap was known as Leather Pass, since skins were shipped across it to the western posts.

During the early 1860's many emigrant parties passed over the pass on the westward trail to the Cariboo gold fields; green and inexperienced with the ways of the mountains, they suffered many hardships along the way. A decade later, the pass was proposed as a route for the Canadian Pacific Railway, and although the government ran surveys through the gap, it was eventually abandoned for the more southerly Kicking Horse Pass. It wasn't until 1912 and the construction of the Grand Trunk Pacific that the Yellowhead finally got its railway. Three years later, the Canadian Northern Railway paralleled the Grand Trunk through the pass, but the realities of war and a shortage of steel required the amalgamation of the two lines in 1916. The line was eventually nationalized to become the Canadian National Railway.

The watershed divide at the pass also serves as the boundary between Alberta and British Columbia, Jasper National Park and Mount Robson Provincial Park.

WESTBOUND **Kilometres** *Miles*	YELLOWHEAD HIGHWAY	EASTBOUND **Kilometres** *Miles*

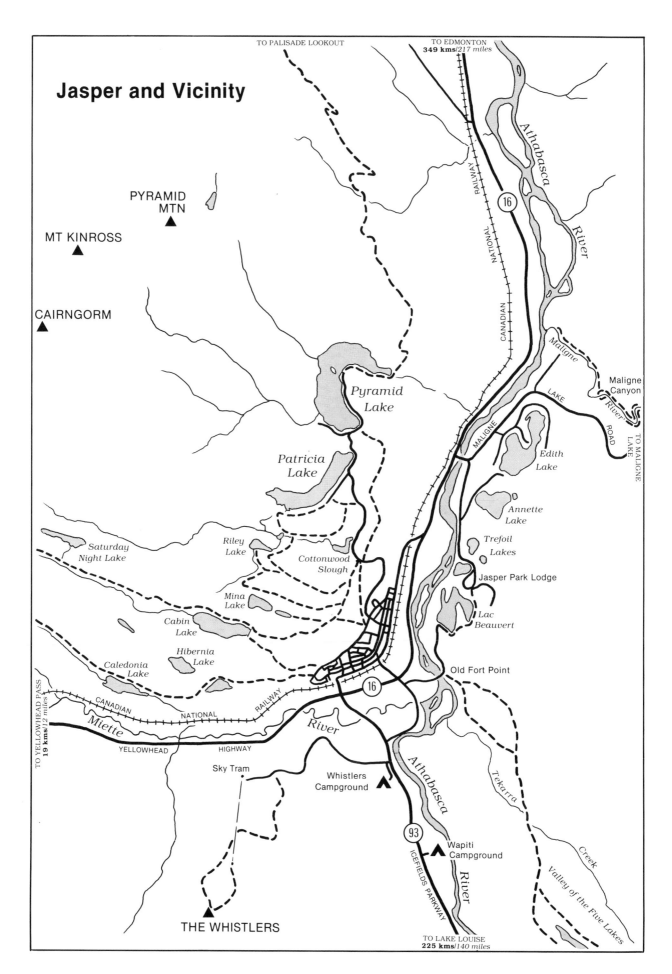

Jasper and Vicinity

TO PALISADE LOOKOUT

TO EDMONTON
349 kms/*217 miles*

▲ PYRAMID MTN

▲ MT KINROSS

▲ CAIRNGORM

Athabasca River

16

Pyramid Lake

Patricia Lake

RAILWAY

CANADIAN NATIONAL

Maligne

MALIGNE LAKE

Edith Lake

Maligne Canyon

Maligne River

TO MALIGNE LAKE

Saturday Night Lake

Riley Lake

Cottonwood Slough

Annette Lake

Trefoil Lakes

Jasper Park Lodge

Mina Lake

Cabin Lake

Hibernia Lake

Lac Beauvert

Caledonia Lake

Old Fort Point

16

TO YELLOWHEAD PASS
19 kms/*12 miles*

CANADIAN NATIONAL RAILWAY

Miette River

YELLOWHEAD HIGHWAY

Athabasca River

Tekarra

Sky Tram

Whistlers Campground ⛺

93

Wapiti Campground ⛺

ICEFIELDS PARKWAY

Creek

Valley of the Five Lakes

▲ THE WHISTLERS

TO LAKE LOUISE
225 kms/*140 miles*

Jasper and Vicinity

The section of valley in the immediate vicinity of Jasper townsite can boast a history as rich and varied as any in the Rocky Mountains. In fact, the earliest fur trade outpost in the central Rockies, Henry's House, was erected just a stone's throw from the present townsite. Established by one William Henry, probably in 1811, the post served as a way station for traders and brigades crossing the Athabasca Pass. As Jasper's House, located about 35 kilometres (22 miles) downstream, became a more important post, Henry's House fell into disuse. When the Yellowhead Pass came into use as a trading route in the 1820's, the junction of the Miette and Athabasca Rivers became the dividing point for parties travelling to the Columbia and New Caledonia (central British Columbia).

While the Jasper townsite vicinity remained essentially a wilderness throughout the remainder of the 19th Century, a great many travellers passed by on their way to and from the Athabasca and Yellowhead Passes: missionaries, geologists, railway surveyors, botanists, adventurers, gold seekers and even a pair of British spys returning from an intelligence mission to the Oregon Territory.

With the promise of a railway running through the Rockies via the Athabasca River and Yellowhead Pass, the Canadian government created Jasper Park in 1907. The actual development of the town was rather late in coming, however, having to await the arrival of the Grand Trunk Pacific Railway in 1911. The small town which the railway reached in that year was called Fitzhugh, but the name was changed to Jasper in 1913. A second railway, the Canadian Northern, was completed in 1915, paralleling the Grand Trunk through Jasper and over the Yellowhead Pass. As is obvious, the twin railways amounted to little more than a lot of wasteful competition. Attention focused upon this inefficiency during the First World War, and consolidation of the lines through Jasper Park began in 1916, eventually evolving into the Canadian National Railway.

In the meantime, Jasper served both as a division point on the railway and a burgeoning tourist centre. The first facilities for park visitors were established in 1915 in the form of a tent camp on the shores of nearby Lac Beauvert, with the Canadian National Railway completing construction of the Jasper Park Lodge on the site in the early 1920's. Hotels began to spring up within the townsite as well. In these early years, outfitters led horse tours to such remote beauty spots as Maligne Lake and the Tonquin Valley where tourists were first housed in tent camps, and, later, in log cabins and lodges.

Today, the town contains a resident population of some 3,000, and offers a complete list of visitor services including accommodation, restaurants, grocery stores, service stations and nearby campgrounds.

Pyramid Lake Drive. The eight kilometre (5 mile) road climbs northward out of the townsite to a pair of lakes at the foot of Pyramid Mountain. (The road skirts the western side of the townsite and can be picked up from any of the main avenues running crosstown.)

The Hotel Fitzhugh — luxury accommodation in the Jasper of 1912.
Archives of the Canadian Rockies

Early settlers in the Athabasca Valley, the Swift family built a cabin directly below the long cliff of The Palisade. 1911.

Archives of the Canadian Rockies

Climbing from the town onto an old bench of glacial till, the road winds through a forest composed primarily of fire succession aspen and lodgepole pine. While there have been many fires in this area over the past 200 years, the most severe and widespread was one which occurred around 1889, a blaze which engulfed much of this section of the Athabasca and lower Miette Valleys. Many of the lodgepole pine stands along this road date back to that burn.

Around two kilometres (1.2 miles) from the edge of town, the road passes beside an open wetland where the forest has been replaced by willow and sedge-fringed ponds. Footpaths lead out into this marshy flat known as Cottonwood Slough and into some of the best bird habitat near Jasper townsite. It is a particularly good area for some of the less frequently encountered species of waterfowl.

At Kilometre 4.0 (Mile 2.5), a side road cuts left to the Patricia Lake Bungalows, while the main road continues on, skirting Patricia Lake and arriving at the larger Pyramid Lake at Kilometre 6.5 (Mile 4.0). For the last 1500 metres of its run, the road clings closely to the eastern shore of Pyramid Lake, providing beautiful reflection views to Pyramid Mountain before terminating at a small, wooded picnic area not far from the lake's outlet.

Pyramid Mountain (2766 m/9,076 ft) is one of the best known landmarks near Jasper townsite, its distinctive shape recognizable from nearly every angle. The mountain displays a pronounced reddish-orange tint in its bedding, a clue to its composition of Precambrian age quartz sandstones.

When the glaciers withdrew from the Athabasca and Miette Valleys near the end of the last ice age, they left huge amounts of rock and gravel debris behind in the form of mounds and ridges along the valley bottoms. Many of the depressions set between the mounds and ridges became lakes, and two of the largest of these are Pyramid and Patricia.

The forest along the western shore of Pyramid Lake is still typical fire succession aspen and pine, but for some stands of old Douglas fir. Notice the thick, furrowed bark on these trees — an adaptation which undoubtedly saved them from the conflagration which once swept this section of valley. If you look closely, you will find some of the bark on the trees has been charred.

The trail to the Palisade Fire Lookout leads out from the gate at the end of the Pyramid Lake Road. The lookout offers some outstanding views of the Athabasca Valley, but the hike is a rather uninspiring 10.8 kilometre (6.7 mile) walk mostly on dusty (or muddy) fire road.

Old Fort Point—Lac Beauvert. A short but pleasant side trip to a fine viewpoint for this section of the Athabasca Valley and one of the prettiest lakes near the townsite. Particularly well suited to cyclists who can continue past the end of the road at Lac Beauvert and make a circuit back to the townsite via the Jasper Park Lodge Road.

The easiest way of reaching the road to Lac Beauvert is by turning across the CNR tracks and out of town at the point where Hazel Avenue intersects with Connaught Drive. In the first kilometre, the road crosses the Yellowhead Highway and reaches a left-hand turn-off to Old Fort Point and Lac Beauvert. In another kilometre the road crosses the Athabasca River at the foot of Old Fort Point.

Located near the confluence of the Athabasca and Miette Rivers, the name Old Fort Point commemorates Henry's House — the first fur trade post built in this section of the Rockies in 1811. (While an early version of the post may have been located near this knoll, the last site for the small outpost is believed to have been located near the east exit from Jasper townsite.) A trail leads up onto the open promontory and gives an excellent perspective on the Athabasca Valley and the complete circle of mountains surrounding Jasper townsite. The grassy slopes are also a favourite grazing area for mule deer.

After winding through the forest for another kilometre, the road reaches Lac Beauvert with Jasper Park Lodge situated picturesquely on the opposite shore. A good spot for a picnic or a pleasant stroll.

The Whistlers. Follow the Icefields Parkway south from Jasper for 2.4 kilometres (1.5 miles) and turn right at the Whistler Sky Tram sign. The road is only 4.0 kilometres (2.5 miles) long, climbing to the lower terminal of the sky tram on The Whistlers. While the lower terminal offers good views of the Athabasca and Miette Valleys along with Jasper townsite, the main purpose in visiting the area is the tram ride to the summit ridge of the mountain.

At an elevation of nearly 2300 metres (7,500 ft) above sea level, the upper terminal offers a most impressive panorama of the Jasper townsite environs as well as ranges of mountains up to 80 kilometres (50 miles) distant. This is a particularly good spot from which to view the many geological features surrounding the townsite. The valley-bottom lakes stretching beyond the town on the right-hand side of the Athabasca River are believed to be remnants of a much larger lake which once filled the valley from near present-day Jasper all the way to the park's east boundary. The lakes near the mouth of the Miette Valley, on the other hand, were created between mounds and ridges of rock debris deposited during the retreat of a large valley glacier.

The Colin Range rises beyond the townsite to the northeast, its peaks composed of steeply-tilted beds of limestone formed during the Devonian Period some 350 million years ago. Across the valley to the west, Pyramid Mountain stands above the twin lakes of Patricia and Pyramid, composed of reddish-orange Precambrian quartz sandstones which are 600 million or more years old. The great discrepancy in age between these two neighbouring mountain masses is the result of a major fault running between them — a fault which has thrust the older rock of the Main Ranges (Pyramid Mountain) adjacent to the younger formations of the Front Ranges (Colin Range).

Other vistas from this lofty overlook stretch far up the Athabasca Valley to the mountains surrounding the Columbia Icefield. Following the course of the Miette River westward toward the Yellowhead Pass, the peaks of the Victoria Cross Ranges march along in steady, measured ranks. And, on a clear day, the white pyramid of Mount Robson, the highest mountain in the Canadian Rockies at 3954 metres (12,972 ft) above sea level, can be seen away to the northwest.

A trail climbs from the upper terminal to the summit of The Whistlers at 2464 metres (8,085 ft) above sea level. This is an excellent walk over typical alpine terrain. Here tiny wildflowers burst into bloom during the few brief weeks of growing season in late July and early August. Many small animals make their home beneath the lichen-crusted boulders along the summit ridge as well, including the small, elusive bundle of fur called the pika; golden-mantled ground squirrels looking like large, overstuffed chipmunks; and hoary marmots, members of the woodchuck clan whose long, shrill whistle of warning gives the mountain its name.

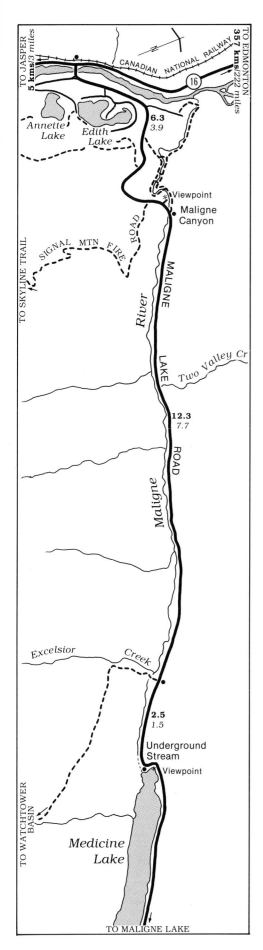

Maligne Lake Road

A journey along the Maligne Lake Road is an important side-trip for anyone visiting Jasper Park. Starting from its intersection with the Yellowhead Highway approximately 5 kilometres (3 miles) west of Jasper townsite, the road runs up the Maligne Valley for 44 kilometres (28 miles) to the northwest end of Maligne Lake, one of the exceptional beauty spots in the Canadian Rockies. With points of interest like Maligne Canyon and Medicine Lake along the way, it is an excursion worthy of a full day's outing.

Kilometres
Miles

0.0   **The Maligne Lake Road crosses the Athabasca River** immediately upon leaving the Yellowhead route, and, for the first few kilometres, climbs gradually through a forest of lodgepole pine.

The road to Jasper Park Lodge and Lake Edith cuts off to the right just beyond the Athabasca River bridge, and at Kilometre 2.3 (Mile 1.4) and Kilometre 3.1 (Mile 1.9) roads branch left from the main road to viewpoints for the lower Maligne Canyon.

5.5   **The Signal Mountain Fire Road** intersects from the right, a locked gate
3.4   across its entrance. The fire road climbs to Signal Mountain Fire Lookout in 9.0 kilometres (5.6 miles) and also serves as the gateway to the rolling alpine tundra of the Skyline Trail — a 44 kilometre (27.4 mile) hiking trail leading along the ridgetops of the Maligne Mountains to Maligne Lake.

6.0   **Athabasca Valley Viewpoint.** While this lofty viewpoint is situated
3.7   adjacent to the Maligne Canyon and provides a glimpse into that narrow chasm, it is better known for its fine panoramic view of the Athabasca Valley.

As one stands at the overlook just beyond the main parking area, a magnificent view opens up on the largest valley in the mountain parks. The Whistlers is the first prominent mountain visible on the extreme left of the panorama, identifiable by the Sky Tram which runs up its north face. The town of Jasper is nestled near the base of The Whistlers, and the low, forested Miette Valley runs westward from the townsite toward the historic Yellowhead Pass. The distinctive reddish-orange quartzite summit of Pyramid Mountain stands immediately north of the town, and the sheer, forest-topped limestone cliff of The Palisade lies directly beneath that valley landmark. Further north, beyond Pyramid Mountain and The Palisade, stand the sharp peaks of the Victoria Cross Ranges.

Maligne Canyon winds directly beneath the valley overlook and drops rapidly into the broad Athabasca Valley. As the nearby interpretive display indicates, the Maligne is a "hanging" valley which was left perched high on the side of the Athabasca following the passage of a large valley glacier during the Pleistocene ice epoch.

Maligne Canyon is one of only three nesting areas for black swifts on the Alberta side of the Rocky Mountains, and this viewpoint at dusk is the best spot to watch for these darting daredevils. Ravens and Townsend's solitaires also nest in the canyon environs and on the slopes above.

Maligne Canyon.

6.3 **Maligne Canyon** is one of the most spectacular gorges of its kind to be
3.9 found in the Canadian Rockies. Like its sister canyons of Marble in Kootenay Park and Mistaya in Banff, Maligne has been carved from limestone bedrock. The waters of the Maligne River, undoubtedly diverted to this area during the last ice age, have sought out joints and cracks in the rock, and over many centuries have widened and deepened them to form the canyon. Limestone is readily soluble in water, a factor which speeds the erosion process.

As you walk down along the canyon to the various bridges and viewpoints, you will see how the bedrock has been smoothed and rounded by the flow of water along its surface. Hollows and deep depressions called "potholes" have been worn into the canyon walls by boulders and rocks tumbling round and round in the current. The limestone through which the river cuts is from the massive, cliff-forming Palliser Formation: dating back some 350 million years, the formation is the same as that composing the cliffs near Banff townsite over 250 kilometres (160 miles) to the south.

From Maligne Canyon, the valley narrows as it passes between the Colin Range and Roche Bonhomme on the north, and the Maligne Mountains on the south.

14.8 **Picnic Area.** A pleasant roadside stop which will be of most interest to
9.2 those returning from the Medicine Lake area. Note how the flow of the Maligne River has increased from the dry outlet at Medicine Lake, just six kilometres (four miles) upstream.

18.6 **Watchtower Trail.** A short dirt road leads down off the Maligne Road to
11.6 the right to a parking area for the Watchtower trail — a steady, uphill hike which leads to a beautiful alpine valley on the side of the Maligne Mountains in nine kilometres (six miles).

21.1 **Medicine Lake** is probably the most intriguing feature of the Maligne
13.1 Lake drive, being a six kilometre (four mile)-long lake with no visible outlet stream. A rock strewn stream bed can be seen at the picnic area just west of the lake, but it lies barren and dry for most of the year. Judging from the large amount of broken rock which clogs the valley immediately below Medicine Lake, it seems probable the lake was at least partially formed by a massive rockslide which originated on the slopes of the Colin Range. The trapped waters of the Maligne River eventually found a route through the jumbled rocks of this natural dam, so that the water was able to escape via underground passages and resurface in the Maligne River just a few kilometres downstream. But like many lakes created by man-made dams, Medicine Lake's water level fluctuates dramatically over the course of the year. In early summer the basin is nearly filled with water, and the lake looks quite similar to any other mountain lake. In the

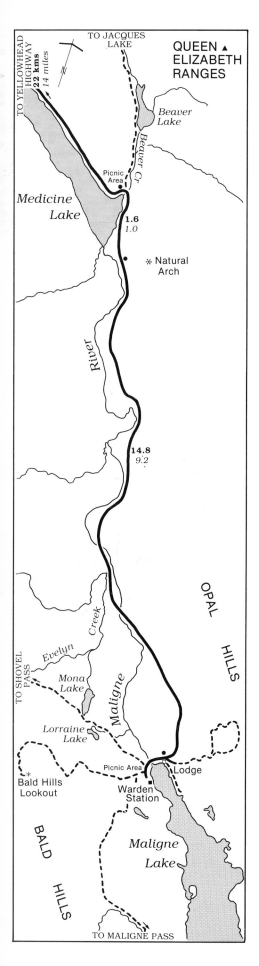

autumn and winter the lake betrays its "sink" structure with water drawn down, a wide band of gravel beach fringing its edges, and extensive mud flats at its southeastern end.

Standing above the northeast shore of the lake is a perfect example of a sawtooth mountain range. Great slabs of grey limestone were tilted nearly vertical during the uplift of the Rocky Mountains about 70 million years ago. Since that time, the slabs have eroded to form a distinctive range of serrated peaks.

The road skirts the northeast shore of Medicine Lake for the next six kilometres (four miles), with several pull-outs along the way to provide an overview of the lake's placid, blue waters and the rounded summits of the Maligne Mountains beyond.

28.0   **Beaver Creek** flows through a small, forested picnic area, beneath the
17.4   road, and into the east end of Medicine Lake. A trail leads out from the rear of the picnic area to Beaver Lake, 1.6 kilometres (1.0 mile), and Jacques Lake, 12.2 kilometres (7.6 miles). For those who cannot spare the time for the longer trek to Jacques Lake, the Beaver Lake option is well worth the hour or two it requires as it is set in a pleasant forest environment and is often inhabited by a family of common loons.

Looking up the Beaver Creek drainage to the north, more serrated slabs of limestone pierce the sky — the peaks of the Queen Elizabeth Ranges.

For the next sixteen kilometres (ten miles), the road follows along the Maligne River through a forest composed primarily of lodgepole pine. Along the valley floor are huge boulders which have been transported by a valley glacier and deposited here during the last advance of the ice age.

Many sections of the Maligne River are easily accessible from the road, and birdwatchers should stop and scan these areas of rushing water for dippers. Taking to the water with all the enthusiasm of ducks, these grey, robin-sized birds frequent the rocks and riffles of the Maligne River in search of insects and small fish.

29.6   **The Natural Arch.** On a high ridge above the road to the east is a natural
18.4   arch weathered from the limestone bedrock, its opening visible against the sky.

44.4   **Maligne Lake.** Maligne is a French word for something which is wicked
27.6   or malignant — a reference to the current of the river near its intersection with the Athabasca River probably made by an early fur trade voyageur. The earliest known visit to the lake was made by the railway surveyor Henry MacLeod in the summer of 1875. Searching for a possible route for the Canadian Pacific Railway, MacLeod and his party ascended the Maligne River from the Athabasca Valley, and named this picturesque jewel Sore-foot Lake (obviously, it wasn't an easy journey). MacLeod examined the lake for some distance along its shore, but decided the valley was a *cul de sac* and of no possible use to the railway.

The lake wasn't revisited until 1908, when a small party composed of two adventurous women and their two guides reached it via a long and gruelling horseback trek from Lake Louise. This unlikely party built a raft and poled the length of the lake, naming the peaks and other features encountered along the way.

Located at an elevation of 1673 metres (5,490 ft) above sea level, Maligne Lake stretches for nearly 22 kilometres (14 miles) through the mountains of the Front Ranges, but never exceeding a mile across at its widest point. Looking down the lake from near the Maligne River outlet, the two high, glacier and snow-covered summits on the right are Mount Charlton (3217 m/10,554 ft) and Mount Unwin (3270 m/10,728 ft); these peaks contrast with the bare, glacier-less mountains rising on the left-hand shore — Leah Peak (2801 m/9,191 ft) in the foreground and Samson Peak (3081 m/10,108 ft) beyond.

Medicine Lake.

As you stand on the shore at the northwest end of the lake, perhaps you can picture the scene near the end of the last ice age, over 11,000 years ago. A massive tongue of ice advanced down the valley from a large icefield nearly 32 kilometres (20 miles) distant to the southeast, slowly and inexorably year by year, carving out the broad U-shaped valley and gouging the deep basin which contains today's Maligne Lake. As the climate warmed near the end of the Pleistocene, the glacier began to retreat, but not before depositing a substantial amount of rock and gravel debris where you now stand — the dam which created Maligne Lake.

Though the lake looks quite extensive from this shore, there is much more hidden from view. About 15 kilometres (9 miles) up the lake, a brook flowing down from a glacier on Maligne Mountain has deposited an alluvial fan out into the lake, nearly cutting it in half. Called the Narrows, it serves as the ultimate beauty spot on the lake, providing the picture-postcard view of the rugged, glacier-studded peaks surrounding the true head of the valley.

There are two main parking areas at the northwest end of the lake, the first just above the tour boat office — a concession providing excursions down the lake to the Narrows throughout the summer months. Another parking and picnic area is across the Maligne River bridge and on the southwest shore of the lake.

The bridge which spans the Maligne River at the lake outlet is a good place to look for harlequin ducks, particularly in early summer. The male of this species is one of the most colourful and strikingly patterned of all ducks, and they are often spotted with the drab-coloured females near the rapids below the bridge. And a large colony of cliff swallows nests under the bridge; the adult birds are nearly always to be seen darting and diving for insects above the water's surface.

Harlequin duck.

A trail leads out from the rear of the boat dock parking lots, climbing steeply in 2.6 kilometres (1.6 miles) to the meadows beneath the Opal Hills and providing an outstanding overlook of the Maligne Valley. The parking area on the lake's southwest shore is adjacent to the trail head for the Bald Hills Lookout — a 5.1 kilometre (3.2 mile) hike to another timberline viewpoint for Maligne Lake. Immediately above the parking area, another trail sign indicates the southeast terminus of the 44 kilometre (27.4 mile) Skyline Trail, which climbs onto the alpine meadows of the Maligne Mountains and runs along the crest of the range to emerge near Maligne Canyon on the rim of the Athabasca Valley.

Index

Abbot, Philip, 32
Agnes, Lake, 79
Alberta, Princess Louise Caroline, 77
Alexandra River, 107
Alpine Club of Canada, 32
Alpine zone, 12, 110, 145
Altrude Creek, 39
Amery, Mount, 107
Amethyst Lakes, 120, 129
Androsace, sweet-flowered, 15, 18
Anemone, alpine, 15, 17; prairie, 16, 21
Angel Glacier, 122, 129
Anthracite, 35
Arnica, heart-leaved, 15, 19
Arnica Lake, 82
Ashlar Ridge, 134
Aspen (see Poplar, aspen)
Assiniboine, Mount, 31, 32, 84, 85
Aster, 16, 21
Astoria River, 129
Athabasca Falls, 117, 124, 131
Athabasca Glacier, 100, 111, 112, 113
Athabasca, Mount, 101, 103, 111
Athabasca Pass, 29, 30, 32, 130, 131, 143
Athabasca River, 115, 116, 117, 134, 135, 138
Athabasca Trail, 29, 30, 130, 131
Athabasca Valley, 104, 115, 136, 137, 138, 145, 146
Avalanches, 47, 48, 83, 84, 85, 92, 93, 113
Avens, white mountain, 15, 18
Avens, yellow mountain, 15, 19

Baker Creek, 73
Bald Hills, 149
Banff, 31, 51, 58
Banff formation, 65
Banff-Jasper Highway, 33
Banff Springs Golf Course Drive, 66, 67
Banff Springs Hotel, 31, 33, 51
Banff-Windermere Parkway, 81-88
Bankhead, 54
Barbette Glacier, 96
Bath Creek, 41
Bear, black, 24, 26; grizzly, 24, 27
Beauty Creek, 113
Beauvert, Lac, 32, 33, 143, 144, 145
Beaver, 26, 52, 53
Beaver Creek, 148
Beaver Lake, 148
Big Hill, The, 32, 43
Birch, white, 14, 47
Birds, 28, 29
Bluebell, common, 16, 21
Boating, 9
Bohren, Christian, 32
Boom Creek, 82
Boom Lake, 82

Bosche Range, 126, 135
Bourgeau Lake, 37
Bourgeau thrust fault, 68
Bow Falls, 67
Bow Glacier, 93
Bow Lake, 93, 98
Bow River, 56, 66, 67, 69
Bow Summit, 94
Bow Valley, 31, 68, 74
Bow Valley Parkway, 68-76
Brachiopod, 10, 136
Bridal Veil Falls, 109, 110
Brisco Range, 87
Brussels Peak, 104, 116
Bubbling Springs, 114
Buck Lake, 115
Buffalo, 36
Bunchberry, 15, 17
Burgess, Mount, 46
Burgess Pass, 45, 46
Buttercup, alpine, 15, 18

C Level Cirque, 55, 59
Calypso, 16, 19
Camas, white, 15, 18
Campion, moss, 16, 20
Canadian National Railway, 140, 143
Canadian Northern Railway, 33, 141, 143
Canadian Pacific Railway, 30, 31, 32, 41, 42, 43, 51, 75, 77, 148
Cardinal, Jacques, 135
Cardinal, Suzan, 137
Carnegie, James, 30
Carrot Creek, 35
Cascade Fire Road, 55
Cascade Mountain, 36, 65
Castelets, The, 108
Castle Fire Lookout, 73
Castle Junction, 39, 72, 81
Castle Mountain, 38, 60, 70, 72
Castle Mountain Syncline, 106, 108, 109
Cave and Basin, 51, 52
Cavell Lake, 129
Cedar, western red, 14, 88
Celestine Lake, 137
Chancellor Peak Campground, 48
Charlton, Mount, 149
Chateau Lake Louise, 31, 33, 77
Chephren Lake, 96
Chephren, Mount, 96
Chipmunk, least, 22, 25
Christie, Mount, 104, 115, 116
Christine Lake, 140
Cinquefoil Bluff, 136
Cinquefoil, shrubby, 16, 19
Cirque, 11, 41, 91, 92, 111, 116
Cirque Lake, 96
Cirrus Mountain, 108, 109
Clematis, blue, 16, 21
Climate, 11, 12
Coal, 35, 36, 54, 55, 133
Cobb Lake, 87
Cold Sulphur Spring, 136
Coleman, A. P., 32, 114, 115
Coleman, L. Q., 32
Colin, Mount, 137
Colin Range, 137, 139, 145
Columbia Icefield, 32, 110, 111, 112
Columbine, yellow, 15, 19
Committee's Punch Bowl, 29, 130

Consolation Lakes, 80
Copper, 39, 72
Copper Lake, 39
Copper Mountain, 72
Cory, Mount, 38, 69
Cory Pass, 53
Cotton Grass, 15, 17
Cottonwood, black, 14
Cottonwood Slough, 144
Coyote, 24, 26
Crowfoot Dike, 93
Crowfoot Glacier, 93
Crowfoot Mountain, 93

Daisy, ox-eye, 15, 17
David Thompson Highway, 106
Dawson, George M., 31, 71
Deer, mule, 24, 27, 53
Deerlodge Cabin, 48
DeSmet, Father Pierre, 134
DeSmet Range, 134
Devil's Lake (see Minnewanka, Lake)
Dipper, 28, 53, 71, 148
Disaster Point, 134
Dog Lake, 87
Dolomite Pass, 92, 93
Dolomite Peak, 92
Dome Glacier, 100, 101
Dorothy Lake, 140
Douglas, David, 30
Drummond, Thomas, 29
Duck, harlequin, 149

Eagle, bald, 28, 53, 136
Edith Cavell, Mount, 116, 117, 121, 129, 138, 139
Edith, Lake, 146
Edith Pass, 53
Egypt Lake, 37, 38
Eiffel Lake, 80
Eisenhower, Mount, 38
Eisenhower Peak, 38
Elephant head, 123
Elk, 23, 27, 67, 69, 86, 118
Emerald Lake, 45, 46

Fairholme Range, 37
Fairview Mountain, 79
Fiddle River, 132
Field, 31, 45
Field, Cyrus W., 45
Fir, alpine, 13, 74; Douglas, 14, 48, 54, 87, 144
Fireweed, 16, 20, 60
Fishing, 9
Fitzhugh (see Jasper)
Fleabane, golden, 15, 19
Fleming, Sandford, 30
Floe Lake, 84
Forbes, Mount, 106
Forest fire, 39, 42, 48, 54, 73, 81, 82, 106, 114, 118, 144
Forget-me-not, alpine, 16, 21
Front Ranges, 10, 38, 54, 138, 145
Fryatt, Mount, 116
Fryatt Valley, 131

Gaillardia, 15, 18
Geology, 9-11
Geraldine Lakes, 131
Glaciation, 73, 95, 112, 149
Glacier Lake, 106
Glacier striae, 47

Globe flower, 15, 17
Goat, mountain, 24, 27, 85, 102, 106, 116
Grand Trunk Pacific Railway, 32, 33, 133, 140, 143
Grass-of-Parnassus, fringed, 15, 17
Graveyard Flats, 107
Great Divide, The, 41, 75, 140
Green Spot, The, 54
Ground squirrel, columbian, 22, 25, 42, 71, 87, 138; golden-mantled, 22, 25, 58

Hamilton Lake, 46
Hanging valley, 11, 40, 41, 92, 116
Harkin, James B., 86
Harkin, Mount, 86
Hasler, Christian, 32
Hawes, Jasper, 135
Hawk Creek, 84
Healy Pass, 37
Heather, red mountain, 16, 20; white mountain, 15, 18
Hector, Dr. James, 30, 38, 41, 42, 70, 72, 73, 75, 86, 91, 135, 138
Hector Gorge, 85, 86
Hector Lake, 91, 92
Hector, Mount, 91, 92
Helen Creek, 92
Helen Lake, 92, 93
Henday, Anthony, 29
Henry, William, 143
Henry's House, 29, 139, 143
Herbert Lake, 91, 97
Hiking, 8
Hilda Creek, 111
Hilda Peak, 111
Hillsdale Meadows, 70
Hillsdale slide, 70
Hole-in-the-Wall, 38, 69
Honeymoon Lake, 115
Hoodoo Creek, 48
Hoodoos, 48, 56, 64
Horetzky, Charles, 30
Horn, 11, 111
Horseshoe Lake, 117
Hot springs, 51, 52, 65, 66, 89, 134
Howse, Joseph, 29, 105
Howse Pass, 29, 30, 105
Howse Peak, 96
Hudson's Bay Company, 29, 135, 137
Hunter, Edwin, 77

Icefield Chalet, 100, 111
Icefields Parkway, 90-119
Igneous rock, 93
Ink Pots, 71
Iron Gates, 88
Ishbel, Mount, 38, 70

Jacques Creek, 136
Jacques Lake, 136, 148
Jacques Pass, 136
Jacques Range, 135
Jasper, 32, 143-145
Jasper Lake, 126, 136
Jasper National Park, 32, 143
Jasper Park Collieries, 133
Jasper Park Lodge, 33, 143, 144, 145
Jasper's House, 29, 135, 143
Jay, gray, 28, 123
Jennings, Major P. J., 70
Johnson Lake, 56
Johnston Canyon, 71
Juniper, Rocky Mountain, 14

Kain, Conrad, 32
Kane, Paul, 30, 133, 135
Katherine Lake, 92, 93
Kaufmann, Christian, 105
Kaufmann Peaks, 105
Kerkeslin, Mount, 116, 139
Kicking Horse Mine, 44
Kicking Horse Pass, 30, 31, 41, 42, 75
Kicking Horse River, 44, 45, 47
Kimpton Creek, 88
Kitchener, Mount, 104, 113
Kootenay National Park, 33
Kootenay Pond, 86
Kootenay River, 86, 87
Krummholz, 12

Lady slipper, sparrow's egg, 15, 18
Lake Louise Campground, 40, 41, 74
Lake Louise Chalet (see Chateau Lake Louise)
Lake Louise service centre, 40, 41, 74
Lake Louise Ski Area, 40
Lake Minnewanka Drive, 35, 36, 54-56
Lake O'Hara Fire Road, 75, 76
Lakes in the Clouds, 79
Lamoreau, Alfred, 133
Landslides, 70, 80, 144, 147
Larch, alpine, 14, 66, 92; western, 14, 87
Larch Valley, 80
Leach Lake, 131
Lead, 44
Leah Peak, 149
Leather Pass (see Yellowhead Pass)
Life zones, 12, 13
Lily, avalanche, 15, 18; western wood, 16, 21
Lizard Lake (see Pilot Pond)
Loon, common, 56, 148
Lorne, Marquis of, 77
Louise, Lake, 31, 33, 62, 77-79
Lousewort, contorted, 15, 17

Maccarib Pass, 120
Macdonald, Lady Agnes, 75
McGillivray, Duncan, 29
MacLeod, Henry, 31, 148
McLeod Meadows, 86, 87
Magpie, black-billed, 28
Main Ranges, 38, 73, 80, 138, 145
Maligne Canyon, 47
Maligne Lake, 31, 125, 148, 149
Maligne Lake Road, 146-149
Maligne Mountains, 120, 146, 147, 148, 149
Maligne River, 148, 149
Mammals, 22-28
Marble Canyon, 61, 83
Marmot Basin Road, 120
Marmot, hoary, 22, 26, 130, 145
Marsh marigold, 15, 17
Massive Range, 69
Meadow Creek, 140
Medicine Lake, 147, 148
Meeting-of-the-Waters, 44
Merlin Pass, 136
Mesozoic era, 10
Miette Hot Springs, 134
Miette Hot Springs Road, 133, 134
Miette River, 119, 139, 140
Miette, Roche, 126, 127, 133
Minnewanka, Lake, 30, 55, 59
Minnewanka Landing, 55

Mirror Lake, 79
Mistaya Canyon, 105
Mistaya Valley, 95, 96, 105
Mistletoe, dwarf, 49
Mitchell Range, 86, 87
Moab Lake, 131
Moberly, Ewan, 137
Moberly Flats, 137
Moberly, Henry John, 137
Moberly, John, 137
Moberly, Walter, 30
Molar Pass, 92
Monarch Mine, 44
Montane zone, 12, 13, 53, 56, 69, 137
Moose, 23, 28, 107
Moose Meadows, 71
Moraine, 112, 130
Moraine Lake, 63, 80
Moraine Lake Road, 74, 80
Mosquito Creek, 92
Mount Edith Cavell Road, 129
Mount Hunter Fire Lookout, 49
Mount Norquay Drive, 53, 54
Mount Shanks Fire Lookout, 85
Mount Stephen House, 31, 45
Muleshoe Lake, 69
Murchison, Mount, 106
Mushroom Patch, The, 136
Muskrat, 26, 53, 56

National Parks Act, 33
Natural arch, 148
Natural Bridge, 46
Nigel Creek, 108, 110
Nigel Pass, 110
Nigel Peak, 110, 111
Nixon Creek, 87
North Saskatchewan River, 107, 109
North West Company, 29, 105, 135
No See Um Creek, 92
Numa Creek, 84
Num-ti-jah Lodge, 93
Nutcracker, Clark's, 28, 65, 95

O'Hara, Lake, 76
Old Fort Point, 139, 144, 145
Olive Lake, 88
Onion, nodding, 16, 20
Opal Hills, 149
Osprey, 53
Ottertail River, 47
Outram, Rev. James, 32

Paget Lookout, 43
Paintbrush, Indian, 16, 20, 123
Paint Pots, 84
Paleozoic era, 10
Palisade, The, 138, 144, 146
Palisade Fire Lookout, 144
Palliser Expedition, 30, 38, 41, 70, 72, 75, 91
Palliser formation, 65, 147
Panther Falls, 109, 110
Paradise Valley, 80
Parker's Ridge, 110
Park Interpretive Service, 9
Patricia Lake, 144
Patterson, Mount, 96
Perdix, Roche à, 132
Peyto, Bill, 95
Peyto Glacier, 94, 95

Peyto Lake, 94, 95, 98
Phacelia, 16, 21
Pika, 22, 25, 130
Pilot Mountain, 70, 71
Pilot Pond, 70, 71
Pine, limber, 14, 56; lodgepole, 13, 39, 73, 82, 114, 118, 144; whitebark, 14, 66, 95
Pinto Lake, 107
Plain of the Six Glaciers, 79
Poboktan Creek, 114
Pocahontas, 133
Pocahontas Ponds, 133
Poplar, aspen, 14, 35, 59; balsam, 14
Poplars, cottonwood, 14
Porcupine, 26
Portal Creek, 120
Potholing, 71, 83, 105, 115, 117, 147
Prairie de la Vache, 118
Precambrian era, 9, 10
President Range, 46
Protection Mountain, 73
Ptarmigan, white-tailed, 95, 99
Pulpit Peak, 92
Punchbowl Falls, 128, 133, 134
Pussy-toes, pink, 16, 20
Pyramid Lake, 144
Pyramid Lake Drive, 143, 144
Pyramid Mountain, 138, 139, 144, 145, 146

Queen Elizabeth Ranges, 148

Radium Hot Springs, 89
Rampart Creek, 107
Raven, 28
Red burn, 117
Redearth Creek, 38
Red snow, 110, 111
Redstreak Creek, 88
Redwall fault, 88
Robson, Mount, 32, 145
Rockbound Lake, 72
Rockwall, The, 84
Rocky Mountains National Park, 31, 51
Rogers, Major A. B., 31, 41
Rose, wild, 16, 21
Ross Lake, 75
Rundle formation, 65
Rundle, Mount, 35, 37, 54, 56, 57, 65, 67
Rundle, Rev. Robert, 30

Saddleback, 79
Salamander, long-toed, 71
Samson Peak, 149
Saskatchewan Glacier, 109, 110
Saskatchewan, Mount, 107
Saskatchewan River Crossing, 105, 106
Sawback Range, 37, 38, 70
Sawtooth mountains, 37, 38, 70, 134, 137, 148
Saxifrage, spotted, 15, 18
Sentinel Pass, 80
Settler's Road, 87
Shadow Lake, 38
Sheep, bighorn, 24, 27, 53, 89, 102, 112, 134
Sherbrooke Creek, 43
Sherbrooke Lake, 43
Sherbrooke Lake, 43
Shooting star, 16, 20
Sibbald, Frank, 32
Signal Mountain, 138, 146
Signal Mountain Fire Road, 146

Silver, 72
Silver City, 72
Silverton Falls, 72
Simpson, George, 29, 30, 55, 85, 130
Simpson, Jimmy, 93
Simpson River, 85
Sinclair Canyon, 30, 88, 89
Sinclair Creek, 88
Sinclair, James, 30, 88
Sinclair Pass, 88
Sink Lake, 42, 75
Sink lakes, 42, 75, 86, 131, 147, 148
Skyline Trail, The, 146, 149
Smith, Joe, 72
Snake Indian Falls, 137
Snake Indian Valley, 135, 137
Snaring River, 137
Snowbird Glacier, 96
Sorrel, mountain, 16, 20
Southesk, Earl of, 30
Spiral tunnels, 32, 43, 44
Spruce, black, 14; Engelmann, 13; western white, 13
Squirrel, red, 22, 25
Stanley Falls, 113
Stanley Glacier, 83
Stephen, George, 45, 51
Stephen, Mount, 44, 45
Stewart Canyon, 55
Stewart, L. G., 32
Stonecrop, 16, 19
Storm Mountain, 81, 82
Storm Mountain Lodge, 82
Stromatoporoids, 136
Stutfield Glacier, 113
Subalpine zone, 12, 13, 74, 79, 95
Sulphur Mountain, 58, 65, 66
Sulphur Mountain Gondola Lift, 66
Sulphur Mountain Road, 65, 66
Sundance Canyon Road, 52
Sunset Pass, 107
Sunshine Village Road, 37
Sunwapta Falls, 114, 115
Sunwapta Lake, 111
Sunwapta Pass, 111
Sunwapta Peak, 114
Sunwapta River, 112, 113
Sunwapta Valley, 104
Survey Peak, 106, 107
Swift, black, 71, 147

Takakkaw Falls, 44, 64
Talbot Lake, 126, 135, 136
Tamarack, 14
Tangle Falls, 113
Taylor Creek, 39
Taylor Lake, 39
Tekarra, Mount, 138
Temple, Mount, 32, 39, 40, 73
Thompson, David, 29, 105, 118
Tocher Cabin (see Deerlodge Cabin)
Tocher, Jack, 48
Tokuum Creek, 83
Tonquin Valley, 129
Tower Lake, 72
Trans-Canada Highway, 34-39
Tree-in-the-Road, 70
Trees, 13, 14
Trilobite, 10
Tunnel Mountain, 65, 67

Tunnel Mountain Campground, 35, 65
Tunnel Mountain Road, 35, 56, 65
Twin flower, 16, 20
Twin Lakes, 82
Two Jack Lake, 55

Unwin, Mount, 149
Upper Hot Spring, 65, 66

Valley of the Five Lakes, 118
Valley of the Ten Peaks, 80
Vavasour, Mervin, 30
Vavasour, Nigel, 110
Verendrye, Mount, 84
Vermilion Lakes, 36, 37, 52, 53
Vermilion Lakes Drive, 52, 53
Vermilion Pass, 30, 72, 73, 82, 83
Vermilion Pass burn, 60, 81, 82, 83
Vermilion Range, 84
Vermilion River, 85, 86
Vermilion River Crossing, 84
Victoria Cross Ranges, 140, 146
Victoria Glacier, 77, 79
Victoria, Mount, 62, 77
Villeneuve, Frank, 133
Violet, yellow, 15, 19
Virl Lake, 140
Vista Lake, 82

Wabasso Lake, 117
Wapta Falls, 49
Wapta Lake, 42
Waputik Range, 91
Warre, Henry James, 30
Watchtower, The, 147
Waterfowl Lakes, 96
Weeping Wall, 108
Whirlpool Fire Road, 131
Whistlers, The, 139, 145, 146
Whistlers Sky Tram, 139, 145, 146
Whitehorn Sedan Lift, 40
White Man Pass, 30
Whymper, Edward, 46
Wildflowers, 15-21
Willow herb, broad-leaved, 16, 19
Wilson, Mount, 106, 107
Wilson, Tom, 31, 46, 77
Wind flower, 16, 21
Wintergreen, one-flowered, 15, 17
Wolverine Creek, 37
Woodpecker, pileated, 70

Yale-Lake Louise Club, 32
Yellowhead Highway, 132-141
Yellowhead Pass, 30, 32, 33, 119, 140, 141, 143
Yoho Park Reserve, 32
Yoho Pass, 46
Yoho River, 44
Yoho Valley Road, 43-45

Zinc, 44